KT-547-366

ANGLO-AMERICAN LANDSCAPES

ANGLO-AMERICAN LANDSCAPES

A STUDY OF NINETEENTH-CENTURY ANGLO-AMERICAN TRAVEL LITERATURE

Christopher Mulvey
SENIOR LECTURER IN ENGLISH
AND AMERICAN STUDIES,
KING ALFRED'S COLLEGE, WINCHESTER

CAMBRIDGE UNIVERSITY PRESS
CAMBRIDGE
LONDON NEW YORK NEW ROCHELLE
MELBOURNE SYDNEY

Published by the Press Syndicate of the University of Cambridge
The Pitt Building, Trumpington Street, Cambridge CB2 1RP
32 East 57th Street, New York, NY 10022, USA
296 Beaconsfield Parade, Middle Park, Melbourne 3206, Australia

First published 1983

Printed in the United States of America

Library of Congress catalogue card number: 82–4380

British Library cataloguing in publication data

Mulvey, Christopher
Anglo-American landscapes: a study of 19th century Anglo-American travel literature.
1. England–Description and travel–19th century
2. United States–Description and travel–19th century
I. Title
914.2′0481 DA625

ISBN 0 521 23755 6

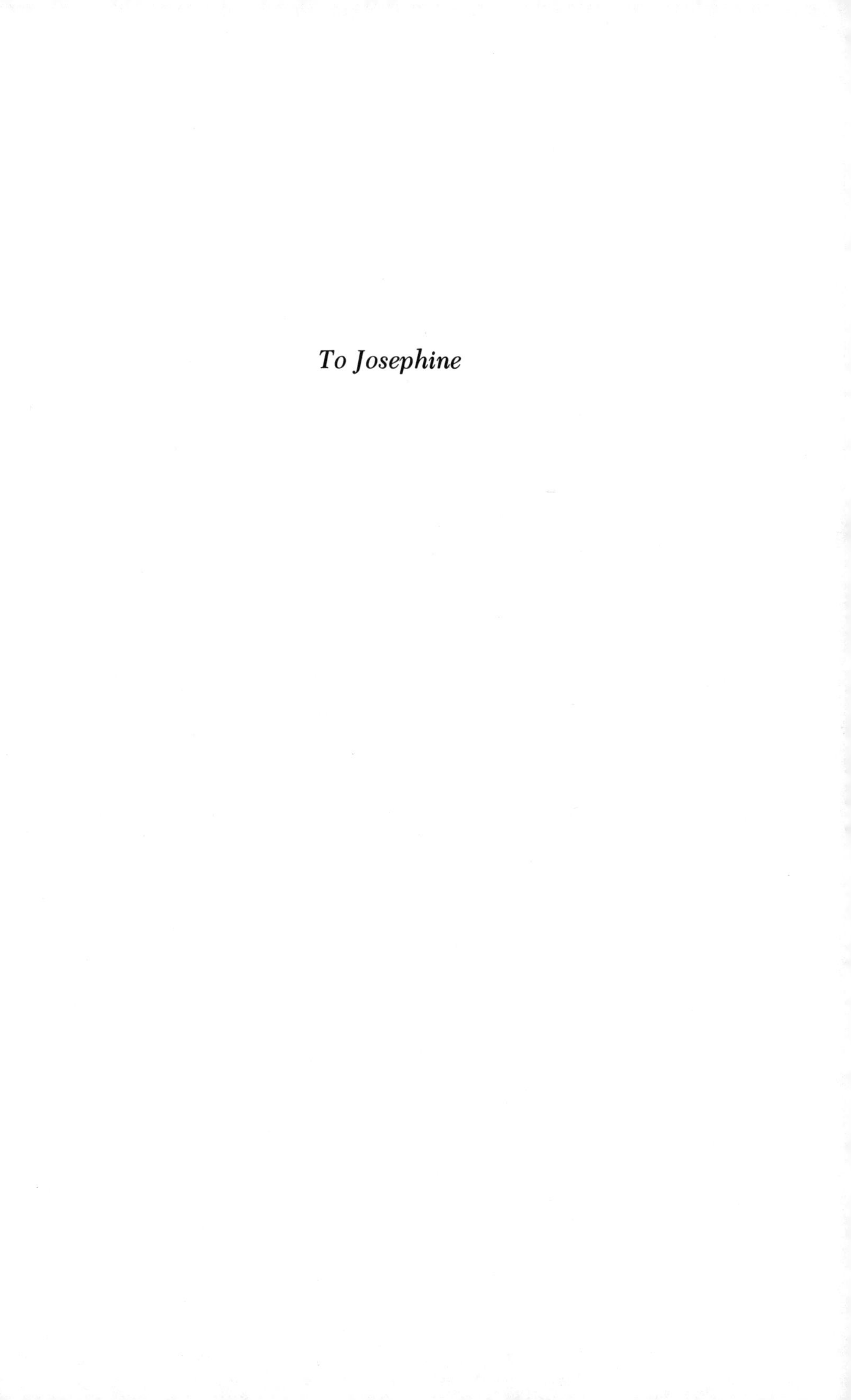

To Josephine

CONTENTS

ILLUSTRATIONS

SOURCES

No. 31: John Graham Brooks, *As Others See Us*; no. 50: G. M. Bungay, *Off-Hand Takings*; no. 47: Richard Burton, *The City of the Saints*; nos. 6, 46, 51: Thompson Cooper, *Men of Mark*; nos. 2, 29, 32–5: Eyre Crowe, *With Thackeray in America*; nos. 44, 45: Charles Dickens, *Martin Chuzzlewit*; nos. 16, 20, 36: E. A. Duyckinck, *Portrait Gallery of Eminent*

Men and Women; no. 28: G. W. Featherstonhaugh, *Excursion Through the Slave States*; nos. 22, 24: Henry James, *English Hours*; nos. 38, 39: Charles Lyell, *Travels in North America*; nos. 21, 23, 26: Robert B. Mowat, *Americans in England*; nos. 5, 49: *The New Monthly Magazine*, 1831; no. 4: *The New Monthly Magazine*, 1839; nos. 42, 43, 48: Laurence Oliphant, *Minnesota and the Far West*; nos. 7, 11–13: Frederick Law Olmsted, *Walks and Talks of an American Farmer in England*; no. 15: William Stevens Perry, *The Episcopate in America*; no. 14: *Scribner's Monthly Magazine*, 1873; no. 10: Benjamin Silliman, *A Visit to Eurpe in 1851*; no. 3: Robert E. Spiller, *The American in England*; nos. 8, 9, 17–19, 25: Harriet Beecher Stowe, *Sunny Memories of Foreign Lands*; nos. 1, 40, 41: Frances Trollope, *Domestic Manners of the Americans*; nos. 27, 30, 37: sections of wallpaper made in France in the 1830s and 1840s for the American market. Reproduced by kind permission of the manufacturers, Zuber et Cie, Rixheim, France. All photographs: University Library, Cambridge except nos. 14, 15, 16, 20, 36, 50: By Permission of the British Library.

PREFACE

The idea for this book came in America; it was written in England. It is a book which attempts to present some elements in the history of the cultural relationship of the two countries, America and England, by examining two kinds of nineteenth-century travel literature. Books about England written by Americans are read along with books about America written by Britons. It is my hope that the parallels of contrast and complement that are so established provide some understanding of the images that these travellers carried to and from the country visited. From the great range of things and thoughts that the travellers discussed, I have focused on what they had to say about their first impressions of the new land, about their reactions to old city and country places or to boom town and wilderness, about their experience of the land they travelled through, and about their response to landscape. The figures in the landscape are treated as part of the composition so that this book does not have a great deal to say about society, about social order and social justice except as these influenced the perspective of the traveller. *Anglo-American Landscapes* is about the visual impressions of two countries and consequently about the personalities of those recording their impressions.

The travel writings that I have selected are of a literary kind. I have not used the emigrant guide nor the tourist itinerary. The travel books that I have used are valuable more as imaginative statement than as documentary evidence. This kind of travel literature is a version of autobiography and I have supplemented my reading by turning to diaries and letters to provide the description of travel that might never have been transformed into the travel book proper, or that might provide a more intimate account of a journey already known by way of an author's published record. In telling their tales, both private and public, these men and women of the nineteenth century talk a great deal about themselves. What they do not make explicit is very often made implicit by what they choose to describe and by what they choose not to describe, by what they conceal as well as by what they reveal.

This was a genre that relied almost exclusively upon the word. In the original editions, usually of two or three octavo or sixteenmo volumes, the travellers provided their readers with few if any illustrations. Many were without even a frontispiece. If they had one, it was as likely to be a portrait of the author as anything else. Maps were more often provided than pictures but even these were scarce. Only half the books about America carried maps – usually elaborately folded into the first papers. Americans seldom provided maps of England. This might reflect a conviction on the part of the American author that the American reader was already familiar with the geography of England. It is evident on the other hand that many homes in the nineteenth century had an atlas and authors may have relied on their readers to make use of it. I discovered for myself that maps folded into a book that I was reading were most inconvenient. A good atlas, open on the table, proved an indispensable aid for following the long journeys through the United States but I felt no need of an atlas for reading the more intense travel literature of the Americans describing England. Men and women in America emphasised their sense of the distances covered as central to the experience of the land. The Americans' experience was not in this sense geographical. What was sought "was the human, the English picture itself," said Henry James in *The Wings of the Dove*, "as they might see it in their own way – the concrete world inferred so fondly from what one had read and dreamed." Maps may be dispensed with in these circumstances.

Towards the end of the nineteenth century, illustrations became more numerous in travel books and they brought some problems. Forty years after being with Thackeray in America, Eyre Crowe produced an elegant green-and-gold bound volume of reminiscences filled with vignettes and sketches – some made in America in 1853 and some drawn from memory in 1893. The etchings are very good but the prose that accompanies them is pallid, lifeless. In 1905, *English Hours* appeared: "By Henry James. With Ninety-Two Illustrations by Joseph Pennell." James was distressed by these same illustrations – rightly so because they create a pattern of sensations quite different from those suggested by his prose. Travellers did best sticking to their word.

Although I have already made reference to a work of fiction and have spoken of travel literature as as much imaginative as documentary, I have mainly resisted the impulse to include fictional accounts of England and America in *Anglo-American Landscapes*. Travel books may aspire to the condition of the novel; some do in fact become a species of novel, and the novel often contains a higher truth, but the lesser truth of the travel book has its own light to shed – one which is likely to be lost in the greater illumination of fiction. Sometimes the impulse to turn to the fiction of men like Charles Dickens and Henry James has proved irresistible but the autonomy of the genre of travel literature demands recognition and it is the subject of another book to explore the relationship between this travel literature and what might be called Anglo-American fiction.

Some of these generic questions I have taken up in more detail in my introduction but I should like to say something here about the special pleasures of reading travel literature, for they arise in part from the chronic insecurity of the form. Nathaniel Hawthorne might be speaking for hundreds of his fellow writers when he said in *Our Old Home*: "While writing these reminiscences, I am continually impressed with the futility of the effort to give any creative truth to my sketch." He went on to this pointed disclaimer: "In truth, I believe that the chief delight and advantage of this kind of literature is not for any real information that it supplies to untravelled people, but for reviving the recollections and reawakening the emotions of persons already acquainted with the scenes described."

At the same time, Hawthorne made a narrow but important claim for the genre. This goes beyond the simple pleasures of revived recollection and reawakened emotion: "Give the emotions that cluster about it (the actual scene), and, without being able to analyze the spell by which it is summoned up, you get something like a simulacre of the object in the midst of them." This emotional holography is the joy of travel literature. It is this that is promised by the leather-bound little volumes that contain the journeys.

Having access to so many of these travel books in very often their original editions has been a special privilege, and I would like to begin my acknowledgements by thanking two great libraries that have helped in every way my reading of nineteenth-century materials. The Syndics of the University Library, Cambridge gave me use and borrowing rights from 1978 to 1980 during which time I spent whole months in the Reading Room. The Trustees of Columbia University gave me use and borrowing rights in the Butler Library which houses the collection of travel literature brought together by the late Allan Nevins. My thanks are due to the Librarians and staff of both libraries for their help and patience.

I am grateful to the Board of Higher Education of the City of New York and the President of the City College of New York for granting me a Fellowship leave for 1978 and 1979.

I am also grateful to the Master and Fellows of St John's College, Cambridge for making me a sponsored scholar for the year 1978 to 1979 and for renewing this privilege for 1979 to 1980; and I should like to thank the Master and Fellows of Magdalene College, Cambridge for permitting me the use of their Library and Hall while I was working in Cambridge.

I would like to express my gratitude to the Department of English of the City College of New York for granting me travel funds in 1974 and 1975 to begin work on this book.

I must begin my personal acknowledgements by paying thanks to two editor friends who have helped me write this book. First, John F. Thornton, then of Schocken Books, now of the Washington Square Press who, in 1974 in Manhattan, suggested that I write this book. With a true editor's insight for author and topic, he focused my attention on what I have now made my subject. Secondly, Dr Andrew Brown of the Cambridge University Press who, in 1979, told me that what I was writing was exactly what he wanted. Andrew Brown has been all that an editor should be – responsive, encouraging, decisive. His own great knowledge of the nineteenth century has been the firm foundation on which he has judged my typescript.

I should like to thank the following friends in both England and America, some for discussions of the subject and some for readings of portions of the manuscript: Clare Gaustad, Professor Joan Grumman, Professor Norman Kelvin, Professor Karl Malkoff, Professor Samuel I. Mintz, Jeremy Mulvey, Dr Henry Pelling, Dr Michael Smith, and Ruth Smith. I should like to thank Dr Peter Linehan of St John's College, Cambridge for sponsoring me before the Master and Fellows of his College. He and his wife Christine welcomed me and mine to Cambridge and smoothed the way. So too did Dr Roderick Mulvey and his wife Christabel. They made their friends our friends.

Finally, I should like to thank my son and daughter, Julian and Antonia, for remaining unchangingly wonderful through ever-changing climates, schools, and accents.

To my wife, Josephine Mulvey, the book is dedicated with love and thanks. She heard through the ideas; she typed through the manuscript; she helped through the crises. These are important debts but she did more: through a year of a leave-of-absence, she supported me and the children by her intelligent business mind and her remarkable courage.

King Alfred's College,
Winchester

CHRISTOPHER MULVEY

INTRODUCTION

It began at first to dawn upon me slowly, and was then forced upon me in a thunderclap, that I had myself become one of those uncivil travellers whom I so heartily condemned...

Robert Louis Stevenson, *The Amateur Emigrant*

1

TRANSATLANTIC EYES

In the nineteenth century, some hundreds of Britons and Americans travelled to each other's country and then published accounts of their journeys in the form of travel books. There are hundreds of English titles and almost as many American. There are more travel accounts in the form of journals and diaries that remained unpublished during the writers' lifetimes but which have been published by descendants and scholars, and there are further accounts to be found in the letters sent home by travellers. These often formed the basis of a travel book; sometimes they are a source of information additional to a travel book; sometimes they are the only record of any kind that the traveller left of his journey. Among the most interesting and complex of these records, it is not surprising that the most prominent are those by men and women otherwise famous as leading literary figures of the day, both English and American. It may well be surprising, however, to discover quite how many famous literary figures did in fact write travel books or leave journals, diaries, or letters as a record of a transatlantic journey.

The traveller, especially the American traveller, might make a deliberate artefact out of the record of his journey. This sometimes involved the consciousness of the writer that he was himself an artist, and the most obvious and interesting instances arose with those travellers who were professional authors. Some presented their material under pseudonyms – Geoffrey Crayon (a name invented for the occasion), Artemus Ward, Petroleum V. Nasby, Mark Twain – but these were not necessarily indications of any greater distance between narrator and author than was the case with writers like Nathaniel Hawthorne and Henry James who did not conceal their identity. The work might in special instances become more of a novel than a travel book, as did Washington Irving's *Bracebridge Hall*, and the peculiar example of *Notions of the*

Americans, which purported to be an Englishman's view of America, but it was in fact a creation of James Fenimore Cooper. Similarly, in authors like Dickens, Marryat, Anthony Trollope, Stevenson, and Kipling, the reader encountered a highly organised individuality that might speak intimately or publicly but was at all points recognisable, conveying in the tones of its voice a strong impression of the man that saw, heard, and experienced.

This kind of distinctiveness was in contrast to an unindividualised *persona* cultivated by less imaginatively capable writers. They adopted a voice that was insistent in its self-assurance, unawed by any society that it encountered (whether in Boston or in London), only to be surprised by gross violations of taste, expecting the same standards of its auditors that it set for itself. Despite a wide variety in the social backgrounds of authors, the voice was adopted with great uniformity and by many writers. At its best it reverberated with an almost Augustan wit, taking the traditional stance of the satirist whose moral fervour raised him above those he criticised. This tone of condescension was particularly re-enforced by the Englishman's automatic assumption of superiority to the social values and cultural life of America. The hierarchical attitude, however, could be perceived in American writers also, for America preserved class as a social and cultural formulation long after it had abandoned it as a political and commercial structure. A special modification of the voice was made by those writers, British and American, who saw themselves as men of learning, political scientists, or professional observers. Here some form of scholarly, scientific, or reportorial standard re-enforced, even replaced, the judgement based on taste, gentlemanly instinct, or good breeding.

Travellers are said to be great liars. The prefaces of nineteenth-century travel books abound with noble reasons for crossing the Atlantic though in fact their authors were often motivated by rather meaner considerations. Such discrepancies, however, were not necessarily the result of lies. Washington Irving came to the mouth of the Mersey in 1815 to lend a hand with the Liverpool end of his brothers' hardware business. Fanny Trollope came to the mouth of the Mississippi in 1827 to find a way of supporting husband, self, and children. Both ventures ended in bankruptcy. But *The Sketch-Book of Geoffrey Crayon, Gent.* and *Domestic Manners of the Americans* breathed not a word that might betray the gentility of their authors.

1. "Box at the Theatre," Cincinnati

The theatre was really not a bad one, though the very poor receipts rendered it impossible to keep it in high order; but an annoyance infinitely greater than decorations indifferently clean, was the style and manner of the audience. Men came into the lower tier of boxes without their coats; and I have seen shirt sleeves tucked up to the shoulder; the spitting was incessant, and the mixed smell of onions and whiskey was enough to make one feel even the Drakes' acting dearly bought by the obligation of enduring its accompaniments. The bearing and attitudes of the men are perfectly indescribable; the heels thrown higher than the head, the entire rear of the person presented to the audience, the whole length supported on the benches, are among the varieties that these exquisite posture-masters exhibit. The noises, too, were perpetual, and of the most unpleasant kind; the applause is expressed by cries and thumping with the feet, instead of clapping.

(Frances Trollope)

Both writers presented a picture of men, manners, and society as they would have them to be and a picture of themselves as they would have others believe them to be. To do so, they both adopted a social voice that presumed equality with a gentlemanly reader. And why not?

Travellers who wrote travel books crossed the Atlantic for all manner of reasons. They were going to do business, they were accompanying other more wealthy travellers, appearing on stage and taking exhibitions on tour, writing for newspapers, outmanoeuvring copyright pirates, even emigrating. Travellers went simply for holidays (though few admit to no higher purpose), to visit friends and relatives, to recuperate from illnesses. Richard Burton, having just discovered the source of the Nile, took six months off from travelling in Africa to visit the holy city of the Great Salt Lake. J. Bayard Taylor took two years off from the printing trade to go abroad, "*at the cost of only $500, and this sum earned on the road*", to show that the poor as well as the rich man could travel to Europe.[1] All he needed was a knapsack (and strong feet). Higher and lower motives merged.

Men who wrote travel books crossed the Atlantic to teach, to improve, to proselytise, and to reform one another. Frederick Douglass fled America to escape slave takers and to speak out for abolition. William Cobbett fled England to escape the "tyrants" of his native country (and to teach Long Island farmers how to cultivate the rutabaga). Travellers came to England to establish international peace and travellers came to America to fight civil war. In a class all his own, Robert Louis Stevenson travelled as cheap as he dared – second cabin and emigrant train – from London to Monterey to marry another man's wife. He waited out her divorce on the Californian beaches and took her to honeymoon in the Californian hills. (Beyond a sly pun in its title – *The Amateur Emigrant* – Stevenson's account of his journey made no mention of the woman; *The Silverado Squatters*, his account of the honeymoon, made no mention of the divorce.)

English lecturers went to America for fame and for money. In the letters sent home by Thackeray during his tours of 1852 and 1855 the only topic more frequent than dollars was Dickens. Boz's lecture tour of 1842 set the standard by which not only Thackeray but Charles Kingsley, Oscar Wilde, Matthew Arnold and Edmund

2. Thackeray lecturing at New York

Gosse judged themselves. When he was asked by the ladies of Plymouth, Massachusetts for a lock of his hair, Dickens had had to refuse on the grounds that if he were to grant all such requests it were "likely to terminate before long in [his] total baldness." Arnold had no such problems but in return for his lecture fees undertook no less than the civilisation of America. He acknowledged that "our dissenting ministers think themselves in paradise when they visit America," but thought it a very different place himself.[2]

American clergymen went to Europe for rest and recuperation. Should they be so worthy, ministers would find themselves offered a passage to England by a congregation grateful for their labours and eager to reinvigorate their preaching. Duty and pleasure combined nicely here. A published account of the journey seemed only a proper return. Henry Ward Beecher's first tour of Europe in 1850 was made by way of recreation after three energetic years on the platform of the Plymouth Congregational Church in Brooklyn. The English essays in his *Star Papers* were evidence of his renewed spirits. A. Cleveland Coxe, one day to be a bishop, and like Beecher a recuperative clergyman, found his tonic in 1851 by taking possession of England in the name of his Anglican faith, his Saxon race, and his English tongue. Some years before he set sail, he had brought himself nearer to his motherland by abandoning Presbyterianism and changing the spelling of his name, allegedly believing that the addition of an "e" gave it an earlier, more English, form.[3]

Americans of all dispositions made reference to their childhood as they approached and as they first explored England. The sense of impending excitement as a ship closed on the Mersey estuary was always intense, sometimes painful. For Coxe in 1851, the realisation that he would have to exchange the England of fancy for the England of fact was too much and he had had to retire to his stateroom. Even for Henry James, who had, by 1869, been to England many times, the excitement of re-arrival was "almost intolerably strong." The Englishman's arrival at Halifax, Boston, or New York was by no means unexciting. Dickens spoke of his indescribable interest as the "first patches of American soil peeped like molehills from the green sea," but there is no record of an Englishman's being overcome. The Englishman was more likely to speak of his or his reader's ignorance of America than to indulge childhood reminiscence. When Fanny Trollope's eldest sons had finished their schooling at Harrow and joined her to help run the bazaar she had set up in Cincinnati, she found them as knowledgeable about America as they were about Fairyland.[4] To dispel this kind of ignorance and to make the two peoples better known to each other were the declared aims of many English travel books.

The Englishman, imaginative or otherwise, was turned into something of a fact-finder when he landed in America. Whether what he found were facts or fictions, polemics took hold of him and put a curb on the romantic impulse. The Englishman's preconceptions about America were strong but they were not deep. They were not usually positive nor were they usually precise. Henry James said that the American mind had a "latent preparedness" for English life. The reverse held true for the English mind and American life. There were no rooted childhood ties. Few had been fed tales of America by their mothers though some may have heard adventure stories from their fathers. John Lambert, Charles Kingsley, and Robert Louis Stevenson had had boyhood romances with the excitements of pioneer danger and the glories of Indian war. Arthur Hugh Clough had actually spent part of his childhood in Charleston but this seemed to have left no sentimental ties whatsoever. Because of England's imperial power, because of the actual wars of 1776 and 1812, and because of the recurrent threats of war until as late as 1865 (indeed, rumours of war occured as late as 1898), attitudes could be distinctly hostile. War and the rumour of war made the American traveller unhappy; war and the rumour of war made the English traveller indignant. The American may have had all kinds of artificial and fanciful notions about England before he arrived, but as often as not England proved to be what he expected it to be. With all the information available to the American about England and Europe and the cultural and social value attached to this knowledge by other Americans, it was likely that the American had a more lively and more accurate perception of England than the Englishman had of America. The Englishman had usually read little about the United States and came from a society that prided itself, if anything, on its ignorance of its ex-colony. When the American arrived in England, his emotional needs conspired to make him feel an identity with what he saw. The American's preconceptions became accurate because he wanted them to have been accurate.

The Englishman was, then, more bewildered by America than the American by England. The Englishman's latent unpreparedness began to show itself as soon as he landed. He had known it was a rude country but his body felt the affront of hard roads, benches, and beds with a force that intellectual anticipation did little to mollify. The Englishman knew he had come to and had known he was going to a democracy but his dignity felt the affront of bold coachmen, landlords, and steamship captains with a misery that intellectual anticipation did little to assuage. All these men addressed him as "Sir", but it was a democratic "Sir" from men who believed themselves to be his equal, not a reverential "Sir" from men who knew themselves to be his inferior. (Caught between admiration for self-improvement and anger at bad manners, Anthony Trollope had wanted to weep.) So it was with spitting, and smoking, and sprawling. It was much harder to go from a country that did not spit to one that did than *vice versa*.

3. Washington Irving

The Englishman in America was on the look out for England. When he found a deferential servant, he recorded it as a sign of improvement; when he found a rude one, he recorded it as a sign of progressive decay. This attitude led to stress. An American did not look for America in England; he (like the Englishman) was looking for England, and was more likely to find it. With his ill-conceived images of America, the Englishman did not know what he was

4. Frances Trollope

looking for and this led from stress to boredom, to Matthew Arnold's complaint that America was not "interesting," that American life lacked "savour." With no perceptual scheme ready to receive and to organise impressions, the English suffered from a kind of perceptual impoverishment that was quite the reverse of the enriched, imaginatively organised vision that the American brought to his looking at England.

Those who came to the American landscape with a professional purpose – the army officer, the botanist, the geologist, the hunter, the illustrator – did not complain of that landscape's lack of interest. But the American wilderness filled most other travellers with a sense of threat and oppression. It contrasted so absolutely with the garden-like appearance of England that so impressed American travellers. A repeated source of complaint from the English traveller was the condition of American farms and the absence of any garden around the American home. The ragged fences, tree-stumped fields, and unkempt property made the Englishman miserable.

The most positive emotional response of the English traveller faced with the American landscape was awe in the presence of the sublime – an element for which the American looked in vain in the English landscape. The Hudson River and its great glacial valley

5. James Fenimore Cooper

through the Catskills never failed to excite an interested response. It became an occasion for a set piece in landscape description and always evoked comparison with the Rhine Valley or the Scottish Highlands. A European model was available as an aid and response was immediate. A greater challenge was set by Niagara Falls. Here the travellers found no European equivalent. But this did not make them turn from the sight. Niagara Falls was a great stimulant to the Romantic imagination; it provided an example of divine sublimity found elsewhere only in the sea. It became a crucial test of the sensibility of writer and reader. Both felt relief when this portion of the journal or travel book had been written up. But the trial of sensibility set by the Mississippi River proved too much. With the Hudson, the travellers felt comfortable; with Niagara, they felt tested; with the Mississippi, they felt overcome. Many more turned from it with disgust and anxiety than turned to it with reverence and awe. The river, still more the valley, was too huge for Romantic reverie. Only in its upper reaches where the river is more "European" did the Mississippi excite the pleasant responses

6. Captain Richard Francis Burton

triggered so readily by the Hudson. The Mississippi, like the forest at the beginning of the century and the prairie in the middle, overwhelmed most travellers, leaving them depressed and exhausted by what they could *not* see as much as by what they could see. Wordsworth had set no pattern for response to Nature on this scale.

But the Americans had found a way and some Englishmen could follow them. Puritan iconography had provided a pattern for response to natural phenomena too great to be seen, too great for sensual apprehension.[5] A universal, cosmological scheme focused upon America, represented by the Great Forest, the Great Valley, or the Great Prairie, could generate a religious and millennial awe as it excited a personal and patriotic identity. The corresponding outflow of emotion could give an energising value to the very boundlessness of the landscape and at the same time aggrandise the viewer with a daemonic activity. The landscape did not, then, diminish the viewer into a depressive passivity.

The English obviously had real difficulties adapting to this millennial and patriotic pattern. It was not their religion and it was not their country. The resistance to all the elements in this emotional mix was especially marked in the English reaction to 4 July rhetoric. Most agreed with William Russell of *The Times.* He described the holiday as an occasion when the nation became as drunk on words as on liquor. This annual, national, and colossal bacchanalia gave pyrotechnic release to emotions that the English found difficult enough to tolerate in the modest, quotidian form of the American's boast that his was a great country. Englishmen found 4 July celebrations ludicrously disproportionate. They could allow themselves no part in the emotions released and judged those emotions to be an over-reaction, a typical manifestation of the superficial excitability of the Americans, to which many English travellers objected.

But the English worshipped the same God and were members of the same race, and a diffused version of the American topological emotion was possible. It grew increasingly more so as the two peoples admitted and permitted closer identity towards the end of the century. The more that the English were able to acknowledge the Americans as partners, or at least potential partners, in the business of world shaping and world power, the more the English could begin to rejoice in the notion of the resources and prospects of the Mississippi Valley. Some English travellers fastened on to the numerical expression of the American religious and patriotic vision. Romantic nature took on a statistical appearance. With this statistical Romanticism, the willing Englishman was able to project himself across the void between the Alleghenies and the Rockies and join in the hymn of praise to Numbers, the number of acres to be filled and the number of people that would be called forth and was being called forth to fill them.

But numbers and boundlessness continued to appal the Englishman and he often gave the impression that he had crossed the Atlantic to confront his fears; the American often gave the impression that he had crossed the Atlantic to take possession of things long dreamt about. It was the strong conviction of the American who loved England to believe that he loved it more than did Englishmen. "To enjoy England one must be an American and a hearty and earnest member of the Anglican Church."[6] And if, like the Reverend Coxe, you were so lucky, you need ask permission of no

7. “On Salisbury Plain”

Charming vales of rich meadows and clusters of farm-houses and shepherds' cottages, darkly bowered about with the concentrated foliage of the whole country. (Frederick Law Olmsted)

Englishman to walk the land, enjoying all that was best while the Englishman filled his head with details of trade and taxes. Coxe could put the land of his forefathers to better use than that. He had not gone to England to watch a people engaged in a political process but to gaze at a land that was the stuff of history. The English could be wished elsewhere and the imagination could be allowed to take flight. America without people would be a wilderness; England without people might be a paradise.

The American landing in nineteenth-century England was invariably impressed by the tame quality of the landscape. He began to see England as a series of gardens revealing a perfection of domesticity from the small plots of the cottager to the great grounds of Blenheim Palace. For Hawthorne and for James, the cathedral close added a spiritual to a vegetative peace to make paradisal spots. In London itself, the gardens of the Inns of Court, the Royal Parks, and of individual homes became oases, repose in pandemonium. They spoke to the American like Richard Rush, Washington Irving, James Russell Lowell, of an English life that had its roots in the country and not in the city. In this gentle landscape there was no wilderness and no sublimity. The American found neither in the Lake District or in Wales. Some few found both in Scotland, but only the sea itself could remind them of the immense wilderness they had left at home. The great wealth of England (though anticipated) took traveller after traveller by surprise, but a world of desolation – in itself a wilderness – was found by these same travellers in the blasted industrial landscape and the desperate populations of the great cities.

The English landscape was for all Americans interesting because of its variety and associations. Two great views, that from Richmond Hill and that from Warwick Castle, contained every kind of association, and called upon each traveller to test to the limits his expressive power. Above all other kinds, literary memories enhanced a view for the American traveller and the prospect of Richmond and the view from Warwick looked upon the valleys of two rivers, the Thames and the Avon, that contained more literary reference for the speaker of English than all other rivers in the world. Their literary relationship to the landscape of England was the source of the most frequent and deep-felt satisfactions for these American men and women.

This kind of response might be expected from a group of travellers among whom were so many professional writers. This, of course, accounted for the fact that among these particular travellers nearly half met and talked with professional English writers. They made acquaintance with Scott, Wordsworth, Coleridge, Southey, Byron, Hazlitt, Lamb, Landor, Campbell, Moore, Hunt and De Quincey; with Sydney Smith, Francis Jeffrey, Lockhart, Brougham, Macaulay, and Harriet Martineau; with Tennyson, the Brownings, and Matthew Arnold; with Newman, Mill, Ruskin, and Carlyle; with Dickens, Disraeli, Bulwer Lytton, Thackeray, Trollope, George Eliot, Meredith, Stevenson, and Hardy; with Swinburne,

8. Shakespeare's birthplace

The prints of this room, which are generally sold, allow themselves considerable poetic license, representing it in fact as quite an elegant apartment, whereas, though it is kept scrupulously neat and clean, the air of it is ancient and rude. This is a somewhat flattered likeness. The roughly-plastered walls are so covered with names that it seemed impossible to add another. The name of almost every modern genius, names of kings, princes, dukes, are shown here. (Harriet Beecher Stowe)

Rossetti, Morris, Patmore, Wilde, and Yeats. Meeting these writers in their homes and at meals, going for walks and taking holidays with them, the American traveller experienced a special instance of the ideal becoming real – the results were sometimes amusing, sometimes moving, always intense.

But meeting the living poets and writers of England in England was only one way of establishing the relationship of literature and landscape. More important, and a way open to all travellers, obscure as well as distinguished, was to visit those houses and towns made sacred as the birthplaces and homes of dead writers. The journey that Hawthorne said all Americans had to make was to Stratford, and he, like others, made it. The journey to Stratford became for many

Americans a matter not simply of personal pleasure but of cultural pilgrimage and something more than that yet, an occasion of patriotic duty, an insistence that this poet was as much America's as he was England's. Shakespeare and Stratford were the most potent combination of place and writer, but it was a formula that was repeated in journey after journey throughout England. A third way of realising the relationship of literature and landscape was achieved by visitation to those places and buildings that figured in poem, play, and novel and were the scenes of great moments in literature themselves. The journey to Kenilworth was undertaken not to see a place where the acts of history had really happened long ago but to see a place where the deeds of fancy were fictionally recurring forever.

The experience of the literature that he counted his own shaped the search of the American traveller for the spot "most sacred" in his ancestral soil. The time-and-space journey became a mythological and psychic one in which the traveller might reconstruct his childhood of tales, books, pictures, legends, and dreams. A passionate moment when England might most be England was continuously sought. The travellers anticipated what Henry James called the "rare emotion" when they might "feel England." They expected it at landfall, at landing, at the first sight of an ancient city. Two places above all others inspired a sense that the traveller had finally reached his goal – Poets' Corner in Westminster Abbey and a narrow triangle of Warwickshire bounded by Kenilworth, Warwick, and Stratford. This might be midmost England.

In their moments of enriched perception, the travellers saw far more than was presented to the senses; what they saw was shaped by their deepest needs and values. It was the repeated experience of American travellers to feel that all they were now seeing for the first time they had already seen before. Travellers most susceptible to the "rare emotion" were those who felt a strong religious identity with England, those who felt a strong racial identity with England, those whose parents or grandparents had been born in England, those who were willing to admit the social superiority of the English and were eager to gain acceptance among them. The travellers predisposed to appreciate what they saw intensified experience by selective perception. The American in England in his moment of excitation simply did not see what would destroy his preconceived image, and cause him distress. The visual ugliness of industrialisation, urban squalor, and rural degeneration were not permitted to impose upon the "rare emotion," though the traveller might be very distressed by these things in more sober moments. The perceptual defence gave no meaning to what was offensive and the traveller took only limited notice of it.

The picture of England created by the sentimental American traveller was the reverse of Matthew Arnold's description of America. For Arnold, America was England minus its castles, churches, cathedrals, and palaces. America, that is, was a place of industry, railroads, new towns, and huge populations. For the sentimental traveller, England was exclusively the England of castles, churches, cathedrals, and palaces. He filtered out of his vision industry, railways, new towns, and did his best to overlook the population. Perceived England was England minus America. The image of England that the traveller had brought from America was little modified by any contradictions that experience presented, whereas every castle or cathedral reinforced preconception. From the sketchiest outline of his image of England, the traveller could make up his reality. His consciousness was poised to seize upon and to enjoy the prize and so could make all it needed out of a ruin or a cottage garden. The more highly susceptible, like Washington Irving, Harriet Beecher Stowe, or A. Cleveland Coxe, actually peopled their scenes with visionary figures from history and literature. Henry James spoke of the landscapes as compositions and undertook to rearrange them with strokes of his pen.

Travellers who had good reason to be hostile to the United States but had diminished racial ties with England – escaped slaves like Frederick Douglass and William Wells Brown – were quite capable of the sentimental impulse that was usually found in those who identified strongly with England. This suggested that the emotional openness to "England" involved some rejection of "America." Correspondingly those American travellers who had identified themselves very closely with America or who had special cause to dislike England vigorously resisted the sentimental impulse. (The same traveller, however, might be capable of both sets of emotions at different times and in different moods.) The classically republican figures of the early nineteenth century, men like William Austin and James Fenimore Cooper, countered any impulse to the sentimental by their stern disapproval of monarchical rule and aristocratic luxury (plus their unremitting anxiety that the English might show them condescension). These postures hardly outlived the Jacksonian Republic but another source of resistance to sentimentality was found in the disposition of the intellectuals of the mid and later nineteenth century. The historian John Motley was quite unsentimental about historical evidence; Henry Adams, the writer of *The Education*, was severe on Henry Adams, the subject of *The Education*, for his lapses into the softer mood; Charles Eliot Norton showed tense caution in the face of temptation, and William James showed disdain for his brother's enthusiasm. Any American like Horace Greeley, David Locke, or Henry James's sister, Alice, who felt sympathy for the Irish was more likely to be made angry than to be seduced by the "English effects." This did not, however, preclude fascination by them.

The sentimental American could and did dream about an England that he had all to himself, or at least one that he shared with the men and women of history and literature only; the Englishmen did not indulge dreams of solitary possession of America. (With the exception of a few like Richard Burton or Laurence Oliphant, most English travellers were not explorers, and were there no whitemen in America, they would not have gone there.) Moreover, the English spent a good deal of their time justifying to their readers the fact that they were burdening them with an account of a journey that they were not always certain themselves had a purpose beyond curiosity. The American seldom questioned why he had gone to Europe, did not expect his readers to do so, and could, when he needed to, give simple, lofty, and convincing arguments in his own support. The American did however apologise to the reader for doing once again what so many had done before. The great number of travel accounts of Europe that had already been published were at once an inducement and a deterrent.

All travel writers who thought of themselves as such suffered from a kind of generic insecurity. This made them turn on their craft, on themselves, or on their readers at the least provocation. Richard Burton protested that he had no less right to go into the details of "his bed, his meat, and his drink" than had the novelist "to elaborate, in the 'domestic epic,' the most trivial scenes of household routine." To strengthen his case, Burton reminded his readers that Dr Johnson himself had written a travel book. The Lady Emmeline Stuart Wortley explained that she had only resorted to publication at the earnest entreaties of friends to whose "better judgement" she felt bound to defer. Isabella Bird apparently found herself in the same dilemma, and Mrs Sarah Maury published only because of a promise impulsively given to Mr (later President) Buchanan of Washington. Thomas Hamilton, officer and gentleman, published a travel book only because the political exigence of the times – the Reformed Parliament – demanded that the English be made aware of the outcome of popular government.[7] Protestations of this kind were so frequent that they became conventional, like those of novelists in the previous century. (In Sarah Maury's case though, there was a reason to take her literally. *An Englishwoman in America* was so misshapen and chaotic that some apology to the reader was in order.)

Though American authors were more confident about the overall justification of their journeys, they could become as diffident as the English about the business of publication. Professor Benjamin Silliman, like Lady Emmeline and Miss Bird, explained himself by appeal to the importunities of friends. Washington Irving told the readers of the revised edition of *The Sketch-Book* that his reluctance to publish had extended only to Great Britain; he had believed his subject one of interest to Americans alone. He had at the same time been "distressed by the severity with which American productions had been treated by the British press." (He wept when he learnt that his was the first to be treated kindly.) The Reverend John Freeman Clarke justified his contribution to a glutted market by the excuse that "every new pair of eyes sees something new" and he liked to think that his friends and acquaintances would be glad to know how Europe affected his mind. Since his congregation paid for his trip, he might well have been right. It was refreshing to learn that one travel book at least was "not issued in compliance with any demand for it . . . The volume is a purely mercantile speculation, which may or may not be successful." Its author, David Locke, obviously felt that by 1881 some debunking of the reluctant travel writer was in order.[8]

In a highly competitive market and with an insecure literary identity, it was not surprising that the most frequent object of attack was other authors. William Austin, an American resident in London at the beginning of the nineteenth century, cursed the whole tribe indiscriminately: "Of two men," he said, "in all respects equal, one of whom is not an author, I prefer the company of him who has not written a book." This may have been a paradoxical way of establishing Austin's own social standing. Other travellers were more selective and singled out their own kind for special insult. Near the end of her lively, lengthy, and highly unreliable book, *The Englishwoman in America* (1854), Isabella Bird wrote that "it has been truly observed that a reliable book on the United States yet remains to be written."[9] Her contribution did not alter the situation, but writing it seemed to have made her alive to the requirements of one who would do the job properly. He must not, she said, be a tourist or a temporary resident; he must examine every state for years; he must be a discriminating student of republican politics and racial groups; not least, he must be able to distinguish the real from the false.

Isabella Bird's specification of such demanding qualifications reflected her own apprehensions that her readers would see that she fell very short of fulfilling them. Like others, she anticipated criticism of her craft by making the criticism herself. Travel writers feared that travel writing was socially inferior to other occupations. It was too close to a trade, too easily identified with commercialised forms of writing like journalism – and indeed many travel writers, both English and American, were journalists. Travel writers feared that travel writing was artistically inferior to other genres. It was not given serious consideration by literary critics. Travel writers feared that travel writing was academically inferior to other sciences. It was not clearly an art or a science. It could be either, which was suspicious; it was frequently neither, which was shameful. The self-defensive postures adopted in prefaces and introductions, in first and last chapters, tried to counter charges that were anticipated on all these grounds. Like the novelists of a previous age, the travel writers needed to justify themselves to a silent but possibly accusing readership.

The hostility of travel writers to their craft and to each other was an expression of self-contempt, and this dislike of their own reflection was pronounced in the travellers' reactions to other travellers whom they found touring the country innocent of the ambition of writing a travel book perhaps, but otherwise not unlike the travel writers themselves. Richard Burton, English gentleman, traveller, and sportsman took special exception to other English gentlemen-traveller-sportsmen that he ran into in America. In New York, Burton was disgusted to find, there were so many that the Americans had "learned to look upon this Albionic eccentricity as 'the thing.'" Rudyard Kipling had similar reactions. In Montana, he met up with "a young English idiot . . . knocking about inside his high collars, attended by his valet." When the idiot Englishman began to criticise America and Americans, Kipling rushed to their defence: "Now that man was a barbarian (I took occasion to tell him so.)" Up to this point in his narrative, *From Sea to Sea*, Kipling had been cheerfully slanging everything from Boss Buckley in San Francisco to Old Faithful in Yellowstone.[10]

The response of American travel writers to Americans in England was very similar to that of their English counterparts. Henry James was one of the few travel writers who had the self-confidence to identify himself with the sorry being, the tourist. Occasionally in *English Hours*, James spoke of the "American tourist" as if both he and the reader might be such a one. The device had curious effects of irony. Applied to others the term "tourist" could be nasty, and it was used by most travel writers in the nineteenth century to separate the serious traveller from the frivolous and the serious writer from the superficial. Democratic manners did not allow the American to criticise his fellow countrymen with the condescension that came so easily to Englishmen, and American writers who were living in England became sensitive not only to the behaviour of tourists but to their own reaction to that behaviour.

James subtly insulted and slyly appeased his American readership by saying in one of his *Transatlantic Sketches* (later to be republished as one of the *English Hours*) that "Haddon Hall lies among the Derbyshire Hills, in a region infested, I was about to write, by Americans." Bret Harte wrote to an English friend that he found Henry James, "nervous, in a nice, ladylike way, at the spectacle" of the unconventional behaviour of Americans abroad, but Harte had not been in Europe long himself then. Three years later, in 1882, he had had enough. He wrote sorrowfully to his wife that "every American who comes to England helps to swell the inordinate conceit of the English." A few years earlier, a junior member of the American Legation in London, had published an essay entitled,

"Americans Abroad." He pointed to those things that Americans might and might not do to avoid ridicule when they were in Europe.[11] It was painfully clear that the American-in-residence suffered more than the American-on-vacation from this ridicule.

A painful sense of self-identity marked these encounters with compatriots in foreign lands. The hostility of the traveller to his own kind was to some extent an expression of a curiously displaced sense of territoriality that overtook men outside their own country. This arose in large part from the traveller's conviction that he *understood*. The tourist was, by contrast, an "idiot." The traveller saw into things. He could distinguish between the real and the false. He might criticise, or praise; others might not. If the traveller could establish the worthlessness of the tourist's response, he could confirm the value of his own; if that traveller wrote a book about his journey, he could by the same show of contempt for the tourist increase his, the writer's, stature in his readers' eyes.

There was a correspondence here between authenticity of statement and authenticity of feeling. The English travel writer was preoccupied with the first; the American with the second. English travel literature was primarily directed at the intellect and the political imagination. American travel literature was primarily concerned with the sensibility and the cultural memory. The American travel book was likely to be, at its best, intense where the English was, at its best, comprehensive. Periodically the English produced a work of great scale and reach, minute in its description and lofty in its conception, attempting to match its continental subject. The grand ambition of this literature was "the aim of portraying the whole political system of the country in its practice as well as its theory" – the aim that James Bryce set himself in *The American Commonwealth*.[12] The result was a book that created widespread admiration and debate on both sides of the Atlantic. Paradoxically, the paradigm was the work of a foreigner to both lands, Alexis de Tocqueville. The great studies of the American people made by Harriet Martineau, Alexander Mackay, and James Bryce must be judged against the achievement of *Democracy in America*.

The British went to America as to a laboratory in which democracy was under investigation; the Americans went to England in a different frame of mind. The greatest studies of England were done not by men of theory but by men of feeling, by men like Ralph Waldo Emerson, Nathaniel Hawthorne, and Henry James. At an intellectual and spiritual level, two great and complementary drives impelled one group of writers east and one group west. Travellers repeatedly made the point that to go to America was to look at a Europe of the future. It is, wrote Anthony Trollope, "the best means of prophesying, if I may say so, what the world will next be, and what we will next do." Travellers repeatedly made the point that to go to Europe was to look at a world of the past. "My ancestors left England in 1635," wrote Nathaniel Hawthorne, "I return in 1853. I feel sometimes as if I myself had been absent these two hundred and eighteen years."[13] Even if he did get the date wrong (his ancestors left in 1630), the point was made. There was a time dimension to these space journeys.

PART 1

ENGLAND

Say what we will, an American, particularly a New Englander, can never approach the old country without a kind of thrill and pulsation of kindred . . . Our very life-blood is English life-blood. It is Anglo-Saxon vigor that is spreading our country from Atlantic to Pacific.

Harriet Beecher Stowe, *Sunny Memories of Foreign Lands*

2

LANDFALL AND LANDING

It was a fine sunny morning when the thrilling cry of "land"! was given from the mast-head. None but those who have experienced it can form an idea of the delicious throng of sensations which rush into an American's bosom, when he first comes in sight of Europe.

Washington Irving, *The Sketch-Book*[1]

After the long, empty days of the Atlantic wastes, it needed little enough in truth to stimulate the hungry imagination, and here a lifetime's stimulation compressed itself into a moment. The Reverend Charles Stewart discovered in 1832 that, "every view, indeed, of the shore tells us that we are in the Old World. And at this distance it surely appears a beautiful and happy world, and would lead no one to suppose it to share so largely as we know to be the fact, in the poverty, wretchedness, and vice entailed upon our race." How delightfully this clerical traveller allowed his mind to play with the theological fancy of an unfallen world, suggested by the very continent that was the antithesis of the innocent landmass of his own New World. Others might satisfy themselves with less complacent speculations. Ralph Waldo Emerson, on the deck of the *Washington Irving* in 1847, saw "the green shore of Ireland like some coast of plenty. We could see towns, towers, churches, harvests; but the curse of eight hundred years we could not discern." For a fugitive slave in 1849, the first sighting of Ireland made his escape from the old land of bondage real to him and made him aware at the same time of a new land of bondage when he saw "the gray hills of old Ireland. Yes; we were in sight of the land of Curran, Emmet and O'Connell."[2]

Irving's "throng of sensations" was a throng of ideas, of associations, as much as it was a throng of feelings. The "idea" of England, Ireland, France, Europe excited men in a way that the traveller discovered to be an experience simultaneously intellectual and emotional. Emerson felt this as a kind of psychic phenomenon; it became an experience that transcended the normal modes of perception: "As we neared the land, its genius was felt. This was inevitably the British side. In every man's thoughts arises now a new system, English sentiments, English loves and fears, English history and social modes."[3] Emerson hit on just that moment when the balance of sensation tilted from the American to the European; the adjustment in moral and personal values that mastered all but the most obdurate seemed to take place in the biological as well as the intellectual order of things.

Europe had been so much a part of the ideal life of the American thinking man that its transition from the world of speculation to that of fact could never be experienced with equanimity: "And am I actually on my way to Europe?" John Freeman Clarke asked himself, "Am I to change into a part of my real life, that which has so long been floating before me, a part of my ideal life?" There was a delicious relish in this moment; it was a consummation so certain of satisfaction that the sentimental traveller could afford to delay possession. He might even become afraid of so rich, even if so refined, a pleasure. When A. Cleveland Coxe approached England in 1851 and caught a first glimpse of Welsh mountains, his impulse was to hold back: "To exchange, forever, the England of my fancy for the matter-of-fact England of the nineteenth-century, was something to which I was now almost afraid to consent."[4] He offered his readers a trembling on the brink of experience, a holding back, a lingering for a last moment in the ancient state of innocence, a self-indulgence in turning from so much delight, and a taking, if ever so briefly, to the stateroom bed.

Others, like Harriet Beecher Stowe, sated their appetites more robustly. Landfall in 1853 made her "ravenous for old towers." Her ship's journey up the St George's Channel excited her to a racial ecstasy: "Say what we will, an American, particularly a New Englander, can never approach the old country without a kind of thrill and pulsation of kindred . . . ," she wrote in *Sunny Memories of Foreign Lands*, "Our very life-blood is English life-blood. It is Anglo-Saxon vigor that is spreading our country from Atlantic to Pacific."[5] Hereditary identification with England invariably gave a special intensity to the moment of landfall.

The sensitive American was he or she who could demonstrate a proper degree of this excitement and there were some nineteenth-

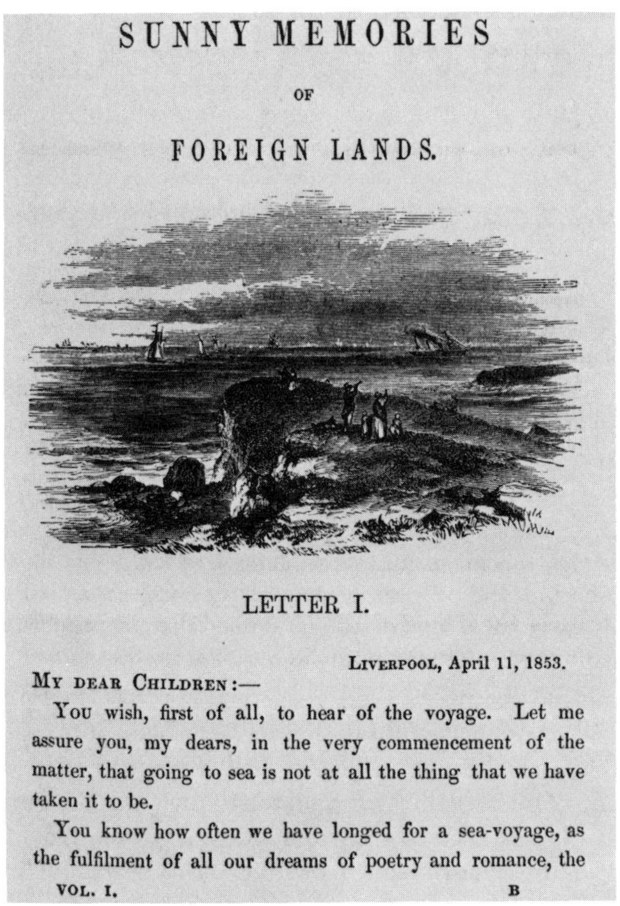

SUNNY MEMORIES

OF

FOREIGN LANDS.

LETTER I.

LIVERPOOL, April 11, 1853.

MY DEAR CHILDREN:—

YOU wish, first of all, to hear of the voyage. Let me assure you, my dears, in the very commencement of the matter, that going to sea is not at all the thing that we have taken it to be.

You know how often we have longed for a sea-voyage, as the fulfilment of all our dreams of poetry and romance, the

VOL. I. B

9. Harriet Beecher Stowe's first letter "from the Old Country," with a view of the Mersey.

century travellers who made the European landfall equal to the meaning of life itself. In the March of 1877, Oliver Wendell Holmes wrote from Massachusetts to London that it would be worth a year of his life "to walk once more under the high-groined arches of Westminster Abbey. I never expect to see England or Europe again," he added in his letter to his old friend John Lathrop Motley. In 1886, at the age of 77, Holmes granted his own wish and fifty years after his first visit to Europe, he returned. "I had," he then said, "a certain longing for one more sight of the place." England was no one place to an old man who had grown up on tales about English bishops crushed by falling chimneys and of English ladies struck dead while lying; it was no one place to an old man whose nights had been spent reading the English poets, essayists, and novelists, and whose days had been spent dreaming of the haunts of Gilbert White, Robert Burns, Sir Walter Scott, and William Wordsworth: "There are twenty different Englands, every one of which it would be a delight to visit, and I should hardly know with which of them to begin."[6]

This combination of sensations, theological and political, biological and emotional, literary and intellectual, reminiscent and anticipatory, racial and personal, induced pleasures so strong (and sometimes so painful) that travel writers delighted, in the tranquillity of after years, to recollect what once had been their emotions as they had approached England. In 1888, Henry James recalled how it had been almost twenty years before as his ship had pulled up the Mersey:

> The sense of approach was already almost intolerably strong at Liverpool, where, as I remember, the perception of the English character of everything was as acute as a surprise, though it could only be a surprise without a shock. It was expectation exquisitely gratified, superabundantly confirmed. There was a kind of wonder indeed that England should be as English as, for my entertainment, she took the trouble to be.[7]

In the England that the traveller saw making itself every moment more actual, there was nothing that had not been anticipated. The fantasy that thus became a reality had a magical hold over the imagination of the traveller and dictated its own mode of perception. The Henry James of 1888 slyly alluded to a certain naivety in the response of the Henry James of 1869. There was an untoward ordering of priorities in the comment that England had been constituted English in order to entertain its young visitor.

The moment of landing turned the sense of approach into the act of arrival and the transition brought a new kind of emotional experience of England. In 1833, Emerson landed at the steps of the Tower of London having crossed the Channel from France. He had already been in Europe six months, having made his landfall off Gibraltar and his landing at Malta. Despite the historical suggestiveness of his London landing site, Emerson did not make much of the occasion. The heightened sensibility generated by his approach to Liverpool in 1847 was not matched by any similar apprehensions in 1833. Then he was more struck by the fact that he and his travelling companion could no longer criticise out loud the country in which they found themselves.[8] A familiar enough experience, it served to show that Emerson had become immune to traveller's fever by way of his exposure to Italy, the Alps, Switzerland and France. But coming to England by way of the Continent or returning to England from the Continent did not always produce this indifference.

In 1828, James Fenimore Cooper brought his family from Calais to Dover, "a magnificent gateway to á great nation." Though Cooper had once been filled with reverence, admiration, and love for England – at least, he said he had – this simple, boyish faith had, Cooper felt, been badly served by the English themselves in subsequent years. By 1828, he had come to believe that no Englishman liked him because he was an American, though he did not deny that he had made friends of individual Englishmen. Everywhere he went people were hostile, unfriendly, anti-American. For this Cooper himself must bear a deal of responsibility. With mixed feelings then, Fenimore Cooper took his family to the top of Dover Cliffs to see the land where they were to stay for the next two months. "We looked at this view of England with very conflicting sensations. It was the land of our fathers, and it contained, with a thousand things to induce us to love it, a thousand to chill the affections." (Chilling things were, in the event, more numerous than warming things. His final comment on England was that it was "a country that all respect but few love.") The ambiguity of Cooper's response to the land of his fathers was to be explained in part by his thinking of it as a land of fathers, powerful aggressive figures who demanded respect and were slow to love. Cooper was filled with anxiety throughout the months of his stay in England. He feared that he would be dealt a social snub, direct or oblique. And he feared this not because he believed that he was not a gentlemen – he believed in his own gentility with passion. Cooper feared that the English would not give him a chance because he was an American. He feared they would not realise that he was an unusually excellent kind of gentleman – an American gentleman. He feared that they would not admit this because they were not gentlemen themselves. To Cooper's alarm (as his editor points out), he was well received and well liked by London society.[9]

Rank, class, and gentlemanliness were obsessions with James Fenimore Cooper. But he was not the only American who approached the "fatherland" with apprehension. England had a threatening as well as a friendly aspect and many travellers were wary of the personal, social, and emotional testing that they were likely to undergo when they landed. Possibly a great deal of fear went unrecorded. Travellers may not have wished to expose themselves to the ridicule of armchaired readers but it was also true that private journals and letters did not dwell very much on nervous fears of this kind though they were often frank about homesickness and loneliness. But certain kinds of fears were openly acknowledged; they were indeed morally commendable. When Cooper expressed his personal anxieties in terms of apprehension of insults to his person as an American citizen, then the homebased audience might well forgive the writer's admission. Fears that the moral integrity of the traveller would be impugned by the immoral contagion of Europe were well appreciated by the American readership. In this, a simple provincial timidity combined with a more complicated republican self-righteousness. Together these contrasted the good and well-known life of the New World with the evil and unknown life of the Old.

The first page of what has been claimed to be the first book by an American to present the English as a nation different from the Americans as a nation made this point in earnest:

London, June 19th, 1802. Dear Sir, I have just arrived in the land of our ancestors, a land not much less strange to me, than were the shores of New England to Standish, Carver, Winslow, and the other adventurers. They were awfully impressed with the grandeur of nature, before she yielded to cultivation: I am apprehensive I shall not be less affected with the excesses to which pride, vanity, and ambition carry those, who endeavouring to rise above, sink far below the standard of nature.

The writer of this letter was a Mr William Austin, a Bostonian who ate his dinners at Lincoln's Inn for the year 1802 to 1803. Austin approached England with diffidence and disdain. He asserted in every letter home the superiority of the republican simplicity of American life and society. In manners, dress, conduct, even in some respects in culture, Austin thought Europe inferior to Boston. A young man, the citizen of a country that had declared its independence only two years before he was born, William Austin put on a bold face when he landed in London. His ancestors had thought three thousand miles and a desert better than a kingdom; he was not going to regret their decision. The moral and political principles of Europe had indeed followed those same ancestors across the Atlantic but these were maxims "which, distance, in some degree, served to cleanse of their leprosy."[10]

The imagery of illness and infection used to describe Anglo-American relations was a standard trope of republican rhetoric. Jefferson, himself a model of the eighteenth-century rationalist, was especially fond of it. It reflected a robust attitude among all those who had helped to shape the revolution, its armies, its declarations, and its constitutions. It remained strong into the first quarter of the nineteenth century. Lord Melbourne was well aware of this strain in Anglo-American diplomacy. He told an American fellow guest at a reception at Holland House in 1835,

> that as we get further from the period of the Revolution and the feelings that accompanied it, we get along easier together; that Jefferson and Madison disliked England so much that they took every opportunity to make difficulty; that Monroe was a more quiet sort of person, but that J. Quincy Adams "hated England"; and that they much preferred the present administration, which seemed sincerely disposed to have all things easy and right.[11]

The "present administration" was General Jackson's. It was less a paradox of politics than an effect of indifference that a populist democrat like Andrew Jackson should have made easier terms with the Court of St James than a punctilious federalist like John Quincy Adams. (The old-style dislike and mistrust of England were to reappear everywhere in the letters and *The Education* of his grandson. It was an attitude that was almost always linked with a suppressed wish for approval.) The hero of New Orleans never troubled himself to cross the Atlantic.

The attitudes of those who did concern themselves with England and Europe in the nineteenth century underwent a change according to an American *habitué* of London diplomatic and social circles of the 1870s. "Our early attitude towards Europe was one of separation. We admired Europe far more than we do at present, yet at the same time we were much further away than now. We looked on with wonder and sympathy, and yet all the while prayed to be delivered from temptation." It was this mixture of attraction and repulsion that gave Fenimore Cooper his censorial energy. He could rage at the English reviews and newspapers (widely circulating in the United States in the 1830s) and denounce them as "the very putrality of foreign corruption."[12] And at the same time he could be setting out on what were eventually thirteen separate court actions against American newspapers because they were defaming him and because his opinion of American journalism was even lower than his opinion of English journalism.

The censorial, Roman strain in early nineteenth-century American letters has been identified as essentially eighteenth-century in sentiment and as such to be contrasted with the romantic sentimentalism that became fashionable with the publication of Washington Irving's *The Sketch-Book of Geoffrey Crayon* in 1820. But that rationalist sensibility was not necessarily antithetical to England. Philip Rahv points out, in his book *The Discovery of Europe*, that Americans visiting England in the first half of the eighteenth century did not appear to regard themselves as foreigners or outsiders of any kind. If they did, their travel literature provided no evidence of the fact. After the Declaration of Independence, there was no simple switching of sentimental ties, any more than there was a simple switching of political allegiances. William Austin may have looked upon the shore of the Thames as a foreign land, as alien to him as the American strand had been to Edward Winslow, but other Americans, who as much as Austin were children of the Enlightenment, might still be capable of seeing nineteenth-century England as a homeland and a motherland. The scholar George Ticknor was a man whom Rahv rightly describes as a writer of eighteenth-century sensibility.[13] But Ticknor felt a strong surge of filial emotion when, in 1818, he returned to England from his years as a student at the University of Göttingen: "and as I once more put my foot upon kindred ground, I could have fallen down and embraced it, like Julius Caesar." With three thousand miles of his journey still to go, he felt that he was more than half-way home.

England after Germany and Portugal was a very different place from England after America. George Ticknor's repressed gesture of homage to the soil was undeniably classical and not a little theatrical but William Austin himself might have been seduced from his posture of republican righteousness had he been arriving at the Port of London by way of Lisbon and not by way of Boston. Washington

Irving, the very prototype of the romantic American in England, felt an intense alienation when he landed at Liverpool directly from New York: "I stepped upon the land of my forefathers – but felt I was a stranger in the land."[14] Homesickness could overtake a man at any point. The "throng of sensations" that had been so delicious at landfall could leave the traveller empty and depressed at landing.

The most florid expressions of homage to the English soil came from the clerical travellers who set out to delight their homebound congregations with just that succession of emotional sensations that Washington Irving had made fashionable. In this class of traveller came the Reverend Wilbur Fisk with *Travels on the Continent of Europe*, the Reverend James Freeman Clarke with *Eleven Weeks in Europe, and What May Be Seen in That Time*, the Reverend Henry Ward Beecher with *Star Papers; or Experiences of Art and Nature*, and the Reverend A. Cleveland Coxe with *Impressions of England; or, Sketches of English Scenery and Society*. Wilbur Fisk and Mrs Fisk returned from Rotterdam to London in 1837 "with feelings of joy and gratitude, second only to those we expect to experience, if Providence permit us again to reach our native land." A. Cleveland Coxe could only reiterate the same sentiments that had been his when first he had seen England: "In touching once more, the free and happy soil of England, if I could not say – 'This is my own, my native land,' I could yet feel that it was the sacred land of my religion, of my parentage, and of my mother tongue."[15] Coxe was untiringly capable of this kind of reverence.

LIVERPOOL AND THE MERSEY

Liverpool was the port of arrival for the majority of American travellers coming direct from the United States, and Liverpool could be a severe trial to the romantic sensibility. The introduction to the land of religion, race, and language was something of a let down: "Before us lies the great city of Liverpool. No old Cathedral, no castles, a real New Yorkish place." Harriet Beecher Stowe was ravenous for old towers but she had to wait some time before she got to grips with what was, for her, the real England. Real England was a fantasy place and the particular species of reality represented by the nineteenth-century industrial city was not part of this fantasy. The squalor and destitution of the city's inhabitants were merely a factor in the general disillusionment. It was only a few like Nathaniel Hawthorne, American consul at Liverpool from 1853 to 1857, who got some solid idea of the squalor of this Liverpool and its brand of reality. The majority of travellers simply got out of Liverpool as quickly as they could; just as Horace Greeley did in 1851: "Liverpool impressed me unfavorably, but I scarcely saw it. The working class seemed exceedingly ill dressed, stolid, abject, and hopeless. Extortion and beggary appeared prevalent. I must look over that city again if I have the time." But he did not and although Greeley was in no way a sentimental traveller, his response was typical of a majority of those arriving at Liverpool. Hawthorne's main recommendation of the city on "the abominable Mersey" was that it had a rail service so excellent that he could get out of it whenever he wished.[16] The main objection to Liverpool as far as most Americans were concerned was that it looked so much like what they had left behind and that a transatlantic crossing was a hard journey to make for so little return. In this experience the traveller of the nineteenth century was not unlike the airline passenger of the twentieth century for whom one terminal is much like another. In the disorientation of landing, there is not much at Heathrow to reassure the jet-lagger that he has not been returned to Kennedy.

The identity of New York and Liverpool was established at the very beginning of the nineteenth century. The great and continuous trade between the two made them eventually the leading ports in their lands. And as they grew together so they grew alike. When Benjamin Silliman arrived in Liverpool in 1805, to begin a year's work purchasing books and scientific instruments for Yale College, he found Liverpool harbour filled with vessels, and everywhere he could see the American flag. American trade to this port, he thought, was probably greater than that to all other ports of Britain together. Hardly a week went by without communication with New York and the result was that not only was the harbour filled with American ships but Liverpool's streets were filled with American citizens. Liverpool was "in a sense identified with America." Silliman discovered an inn that called itself the "American Hotel" and it came complete with eagle and national motto, *e pluribus unum.* The food was plentiful and cheap; the crowd gregarious but not genteel. Silliman decided to dine at the "American" but not to board there. Not only were there a lot of Americans about, the

10. Benjamin Silliman

Liverpudlians themselves looked like Americans. "The general appearance of the population of Liverpool, is extremely like that of our own countrymen in our large cities. Every body here talks, dresses, and acts, and every thing looks, so much like America, that I can hardly believe I have actually crossed the ocean."[17] It was rare for an American to say that Englishmen looked like Americans. It was a demonstration of the American influence upon Liverpool and of the similarity of social and economic forces that were shaping alike Liverpool and the seaboard cities of America.

The key fact was that Liverpool was a new city – it was this that made it "American." Indeed it was younger as a commercial port than its American counterparts, the seventeenth-century cities of Boston, New York, and Philadelphia. In 1805, Benjamin Silliman criticised it on just those grounds that Englishmen in the nineteenth century criticised American towns. The rude, yellow brick of Liverpool's private houses was cheap in construction and raw in appearance. "We look in vain for the highly finished surface which is presented by the finest houses of New-York, Philadelphia, and

Boston."[18] Within another forty years, Liverpool was to present a very solid appearance to the American visitor, but the bustling and the business, the expansion and the excitement, the growth of docks, warehouses, streets, and public buildings, all going on at once and emerging from a wilderness of mud flat, gave Liverpool the character of a New England boom town. This did not upset Silliman though it did disorient him a little; as he said, he could hardly believe he had crossed the ocean.

The similarity of New York and Liverpool to which Silliman gave so decided expression was sufficiently well established by the 1830s for some travellers to start disagreeing with the received opinion. "Many American travellers have recognised a resemblance, between this port and New York, which I do not perceive," wrote one passenger in 1832. Charles Stewart was willing to admit that Liverpool was "as modern in its rise and history as any of the principal American ports" but he found it smoky and black, with none of the airiness of American ports. New York was brighter, gayer, more attractive even if Liverpool showed more good taste and magnificence. (The unfinished quality that Silliman had complained of in 1805 was already passing; it was a temporary phase of an English city not the permanent condition of an American one.) No, the main objection to Liverpool was that it was new: "All is modern; and thus to a transatlantic visitor destitute of the peculiar charm which draws him, from the new world to the old." The traveller felt cheated; he was disappointed and disbelieving. In the powerful preconceptions of England that had induced these travellers to cross the Atlantic, there was no place for the new, the industrial, the urban, the modern, the efficient, the up-to-date. "So, then, we were really in England"; wrote John Freeman Clarke, "but, as yet, there was nothing to make us realize it, for Liverpool looks very like New York or Philadelphia."[19]

Realisation of England could not take place until the real England corresponded more closely with the ideal England – the England that had been apprehended so powerfully at landfall. Few American travellers had a good word for the "detestable Mersey." For none of them was it the England they had come to see. For only the most susceptible did Liverpool contain a special kind of hope. For Henry James, the greyness of the Mersey, "shading away into black at every pretext, appeared in itself a promise."[20] But James was already an experienced traveller, was already practised in the emotions of the Mersey when he landed once again at Liverpool in 1869. The city was a dark and gloomy gateway to a golden land; its New-Yorkish appearance and American crowds were a rite-of-passage that the initiated gladly repeated.

3

CHESTER: THE REAL ENGLAND

The Atlantic – The Mersey – The Adelphi – Chester

Millions of Americans have felt this succession of emotions. Possibly very young and ingenuous tourists feel them still, but in the days before tourists, when the romance was a reality, not a picture, they were overwhelming.

Henry Adams, *The Education of Henry Adams*[1]

The antidote to the modern city of Liverpool was the ancient city of Chester. The American traveller who found Liverpool so like New York that he felt cheated had only to go to Chester by rail, one hour away – a time still quoted by British Rail – to find a reality that exactly matched his romance. "Were Chester the first place on which an American should cast his eyes, after arriving in England, he would at once feel himself to be in an old and foreign land," said the Reverend Charles Stewart in 1832.[2] The travellers knew the sensation they were after – a trandscendency of time that could be achieved by movement in space. Three thousand miles, Franklin had said, are as three thousand years. And though Chester had less than two thousand years of history, it had nonetheless a lot of it. Its Roman foundation was Deva, base camp for the 20th Legion; its walls, its gates, its streets, its rows, its castle, and its cathedral carried the willing traveller back through time in a sensational fashion.

Chester presented, said Margaret Fuller,

a *tout ensemble* highly romantic in itself, and charming, indeed, to Transatlantic eyes. Yet not to all eyes would it have had charms, for one American traveller, our companion on the voyage, gravely assured us that we should find "the castle and that sort of thing all humbug," and that if we wished to enjoy them, it would "be best to sit at home and read some *handsome* work on the subject."

The Proustian advice that lands of the imagination were best visited by way of the imagination pointed to the fact that travel literature was as much a substitute for travel as a record of it, and that the real England that the Americans were looking for by rushing out of Liverpool could itself be a humbug. Henry James began his essay, "Chester," by emphasising just how well the little city could serve the purpose of escape: "If the Atlantic voyage be counted, as it certainly may, even with the ocean in fairly good humour, an emphatic zero in the sum of one's better experience, the American traveller arriving at this venerable town finds himself transported, without a sensible gradation, from the edge of the new world to the very heart of the old." The Mersey and the Liverpool of the Adelphi Hotel were an edge of the new world – they did not add to the zero sum of the Atlantic. Valuable, accountable experience began with Chester. Nonetheless, the self-aware, self-assured prose of James's little essay made gentle fun of its subject and the "good Cestrians" who inhabited its "brave little walls." More to the point, the prose made gentle fun of the time-travelling tourist. When Henry James had arrived in Liverpool in 1872, he had not been alone. He had been chosen by a solicitous family in Boston to escort his sister Alice and his aunt Kate to Europe. His sketch of Chester filtered the naive enthusiasm of his companions through his own less ingenuous response. James did not call Chester "humbug"; but reporting to his father on the progress of the tour, he wrote, "We feel as if we have been seeing the cream of common England."[3]

In an earlier, less elegant, less handsome work than James's essay, Frederick Law Olmsted described without irony or reservations the attractions of the city of Chester. The robustly naive sentiment of *Walks and Talks of an American Farmer in England* showed how the travel book could be a powerful vehicle of nineteenth-century Romantic historicism. Olmsted, a Staten Island farmer, visited England in 1850 with two good fellows of stout boots and stouter hearts. They were as ready as Olmsted himself to trudge the English hedgerows and to rejoice in the English rain and to welcome the English sun. Olmsted is well known, at least he would be well known if there were any justice in things, to the inhabitants of many of America's greatest cities because he designed their parks. First he designed Central Park in New York; then he made parks in Brooklyn, Boston, Philadelphia, Washington, Rochester, Buffalo, Chicago, Detroit, Louisville. He created parks in California and he created parks in Canada. The inspiration and the design for these

WALKS AND TALKS

OF AN

AMERICAN FARMER IN ENGLAND

NEW YORK:

GEORGE P. PUTNAM, 155 BROADWAY.

M.DCCC.LII.

11. Title-page of Frederick Law Olmsted's *Walks and Talks*

parks, he conceived on his tour of England in 1850. He had gone as a scientific farmer intending to study English agricultural methods; he returned believing that the park was the highest artistic form:

Probably there is no object of art that Americans of cultivated taste generally more long to see in Europe, than an English park. What artist, so noble, has often been my thought, as he, who with far-reaching conception of beauty and designing power, sketches the outline, writes the colours, and directs the shadows of a picture so great that Nature shall be employed upon it for generations, before the work he has arranged for her shall realize his intentions.[4]

Frederick Law Olmsted with his brother John and their friend Charles Loring Brace began his walking tour of England by making a route due south from Liverpool docks towards the city of Chester. They took the ferry to Birkenhead and here they came on a ruined abbey and a public park. Both deeply impressed Olmsted. In the middle of the growing suburb on the south bank of the Mersey, he stumbled upon two of the most important elements that went to make up sentimental England – monuments and landscape. Olmsted was most impressed by the fact that he had never heard of either Birkenhead Abbey or Birkenhead Park and did not expect that his readers had either. This town was not like the renowned Chester to which every traveller made pilgrimage; abbey and park were simply part of the largesse of a land that could take them for granted – "but coming upon it so fresh from the land of youth, as we did, so unexpecting of anything of the kind – though I have since seen older ruins, and more renowned – I have never found any so impressively aged." Birkenhead Park impressed Olmsted as much as the ruined abbey, not only because it displayed gardening of a perfection of which he had never dreamed, but because "all this magnificent pleasure-ground is entirely, unreservedly, and for ever the people's own. The poorest British peasant is as free to enjoy it in all its parts as the British queen." This democratic ejaculation came from deep springs in Olmsted's emotional being. "The park at Birkenhead across the river from Liverpool," says a biographer, "was the first he had ever seen, and it broke on him like a revelation."[5]

Olmsted and his friends pressed on until, after lunch, they reached the open country of Cheshire for the first time. They were now really on their way to Chester:

> There we were right in the midst of it! The country – and such country! – green, dripping, glistening, gorgeous! We stood dumb-stricken by its loveliness . . . English May –sunny, leafy, blooming May – in an English lane . . . A cart meets us – a real heavy, big-wheeled English cart; and English horses – real big, shaggy-hoofed, sleek, heavy English cart-horses; and a carter – a real apple-faced, smock-frocked, red-headed, wool-hatted carter – breeches, stockings, hob-nailed shoes, and '*Gee-up* Dobbin' English carter.

Olmsted savoured the words *English* and *real*, playing with them, turning them round, exploring them, sucking on them, probing them in his bursts of verbal energy. The word *real* was driven by this prose to mean its opposite – to mean *unreal.* (And in vernacular American, *unreal* now means something of such heightened reality that normal emphasis will not bear the weight of expression.) The word *English* was diminished by this prose to mean something narrow and specific. The word did not have its more general reference; it did not include any associations of the present or the new. A mile further on Olmsted saw a Cheshire village church. The church was made of good things only: "Old weather-beaten stone and mortar, glass, lead, iron and matted ivy, but not a splinter of wood or a daub of paint. Old England for ever! Amen."[6] No "Amen" could be given to painted wood even if it had appeared in Cheshire. Olmsted was aware that wood was used extensively by medieval builders; he may not have been aware that they daubed bright paint over every thing. But that was not the point. Painted wood was New England's architectural medium. It was American. Therefore no "Amen." "Old England" meant an England perceived in the here-and-now; it had (Moebius-like) one surface with modern England. It was not the historical England that might actually have been perceived by a man living in the year 1350; "Old England" was the historical England conceived by the man living in 1850 and looking through the distorting lens, the rosy-coloured spectacle, the Claude-glass of Romantic vision. Both more and less was seen in these exciting, passionate moments of travelling ecstasy than presented itself to the accustomed or to the sober eye.

Olmsted was particularly adept at this Romantically reconstructed history and he took for his elements the materials stylised by fashion and literature. The influences of Washington Irving and Charles Dickens were strong, but picturesque England had its own inner determinants and there is no reason to suppose that Olmsted was deliberately aping anyone as he acted out so emphatically, so theatrically, the sensations of the sentimental American. Some miles beyond his old English church, Olmsted found his old English inn, "The Red Lion," with a kitchen as warm and as snug and as bright as the kitchen at Dingley Dell. To welcome the travellers was a landlady with whom no fault could be found (at least, no fault was found). The distinctions between autobiography and novel, between fact and fiction, between reality and romance blurred:

We turn into a dark hall, and opening a door to the left, enter – the kitchen. Such a kitchen! You would not believe me if I could describe how bright everything is . . .

The landlady rises and begs to take our hats – a model landlady, too. What a fine eye! – a kind and welcoming black eye. Fair and stout; elderly . . . We hesitate to cross the clean-scoured, buff, tile floor with our muddy shoes; but she draws armchairs about the grate, and lays slippers before them, stirs up the fire, though it is far from needing it, and turns to take our knapsacks.[7]

A mundane past tense was abandoned for the timeless historic present to represent for writer and reader alike the dateless reality of this intensely domesticated scene. Tired, hungry, wet men are welcomed to fire, chair, and slippers by a supernally womanly woman. The sudden reversal of physical fortune from the outcast condition of the road to the welcome security of the inn is one of the perennial pleasures of travel. Olmsted made his finding of the Red Lion a fairy story, and at the same time he no doubt felt that his luck in finding it was princely indeed. Curiously Olmsted had not suggested that he had been any less happy in the Cheshire countryside though he had been soaking wet and walking all day.

The following morning Olmsted woke up to look out of his bedroom window at a view of thatched cottages, ivy hedges, clover fields, grazing sheep, grouped trees, low hills; he saw the dawn coming up. The depth of his emotion took him by surprise (though his reader might be forgiven if it surprised him less). Olmsted wondered that he could be so deeply moved by a scene that was so ordinary. The source of his joy, he decided, was in the familiarity of something that he had never seen before: "Such a scene I had never looked upon before, and yet it was in all its parts as familiar to me as my native valley." Familiarity was here exhilarating; familiarity in Liverpool was depressing. (Not, it must be admitted, for Olmsted particularly. His gusto was not much dampened by the Mersey.) If Liverpool were familiar, it was because it was like New York. If the Cheshire landscape were familiar, it was because it had been seen so often in imagination: "Land of our poets! Home of our Fathers! Dear old Mother England! It would be strange if I were not affected at meeting thee at last face to face."[8] Olmsted's rhetoric borrowed a great deal from the taste of the nineteenth-century novel for a highly melodramatic, soliloquising direct speech, and it owed something to

12. "Sunday night at the inn"

There is a continual and universal beer-drinking in Chester. Mrs. Jones tells us that the quality of the beer made here has long been a matter of town pride, though now there is very little brewed in families, every one almost being supplied, at a great saving of trouble, from the large breweries. She says there used to be a town law that whoever brewed poor beer should be publicly ducked. Sunday night, young men with their sweethearts and sisters, of very reputable appearance, and quiet, decent behaviour, came into our back-parlour, and sitting by the round-table ordered and drank each their glass or two of beer, as in an American town they would take ice-cream. Now and then a few remarks would be made about the sermon and who had been at church, or about those who had been, or were soon going to be, married, or other town gossip; but for the most, they would sit and drink their beer in silence, perhaps embarrassed by our presence.

(Frederick Law Olmsted)

the nineteenth-century custom of the toast. Rhodomontane pledges were a special feature of the American public dinner. Magnums of champagne might be thrown back to punctuate Olmsted's more exuberant paragraphs. But his rhetoric had a religious origin as well. His "Amen" to "Old England" did not jar; his reference to meeting her "face to face" only suggested the creative confusion of his patriotic, literary, and religious emotions. One excitation followed upon another in a prose driven on by exclamation marks.

The centre point to which Olmsted was threading his way through lanes and villages was Chester itself. For many travellers who preferred to use the fast coach or railway, the ancient city was only one hour from Liverpool – "being," as Hawthorne said, "the one only place, within easy reach of Liverpool, which possesses any old English interest." But Olmsted was going by foot and Chester was two days from Liverpool. Ever since he had broken into the countryside beyond Birkenhead, he had been in "Old England." Chester, "the very heart of the old" world, was in danger of becoming an anticlimax. Fear that this might be the case did not allow for the indefatigable energy of these tourists; nor for Olmsted's special capacity for enthusiasm. He faced the problem boldly when he at last (on page 117) took his readers round the walls of Chester: "Are you tired of ruins? Here is one that may rouse your Puritan blood: a heavy tower built into the wall." And he provided a description to set coursing the blood in the New England vein. He drew himself and his readers close to the stones of the building to marvel at something that only going there could make him (and, by a strange contradiction, his readers) realise: "How old they look! No painting and no descriptions had ever conveyed to me the effect of age upon the stone itself of these very old structures. How venerable! how stern! how silent – !"[9]

Walks and Talks is an exhausting but a delightful book; its unflagging enthusiasm and appetite for "dear old England" disarm criticism. Like children in toyland, the three boisterous Americans hunted up and down Chester to find the very oldest English building in which they could be accommodated – but accommo-

13. "God's Providence is mine Inheritance – 1652": the inn at Chester.

Another house has these words cut in the principal horizontal beam: *God's Providence is mine Inheritance* – 1652. It is said the family residing in it was the only one in the city that entirely escaped the great plague of that year.

You may imagine how intensely interesting all this is. We cannot keep still, but run about with a real boyish excitement. We feel indeed like children that have come back to visit the paternal house, and who are rummaging about in the garret among their father's playthings, ever and anon shouting, "See what I've found! see what I've found!" If we had been brought here blindfolded from America, and were now, after two days' visit, sent back again, we should feel well repaid for the long sea-passage. If we were to stay here a month, we should scarcely enjoy less than we now do, rambling about among these relics of our old England.

(Frederick Law Olmsted)

dated comfortably. When they had found the right place, Frederick Law Olmsted sat himself down at an old oak table, in an old oak chair, in an old oak tavern, and there he wrote his journal. Outside he could hear the local militia at its drill. He fancied they were musters for the Civil War –

when shall I again get as near as this to *Prince Charlie* and the Ironsides? and shall I not make the most of it? At least, there is no prompter's bell, no carpenters in shirt-sleeves rushing and sliding off the scenery. That 1539 over the way is TRUE; I can see the sun shine into the figures. Away, then, with your 1850! I will drink only old wine – or better – *What ho! a cup of sack!* Shall I not take it easy "in mine inn?"[10]

Olmsted was hungry for the old. And he wanted to know that his chair, his table, his tavern, and his town were old in order to confirm historical fancy not to guarantee historical fact. The date carved across the way was TRUE, he said with a typographical thump. Because it was, so was his fantasy. Olmsted had to convince himself as well as his readers. He feared that his experience of the past was a fabrication and that at any minute a bell would ring and scene-shifters would rush into his room and the whole of Chester would be dismantled before his eyes. The image is very amusing. The old table, chair, and tavern would be pulled away from around him and he would find himself back with a bump – where? In England in 1850 or in America? But the sunshine in the date gave a three-dimensional proof of the reality of his fantasy. With a still more amusing irony, Olmsted proved to himself that he was not in a theatre by acting out a role from *Henry IV*. If he did call out to his Victorian waiter, "*What ho! a cup of sack!*" it is to be hoped that the servant played along in the right spirit.

Chester did not fail Olmsted and his friends; they were, he said, like children come home. "If we had been brought here blindfolded from America, and were now, after two days' visit, sent back again, we should feel well repaid for the long sea-passage." An important image. Olmsted was like a man whose sight had been restored. Washington Irving said of the long voyage that "the temporary absence of worldy scenes and employments produces a state of mind peculiarly fitted to receive new and vivid impressions." In Chester, Olmsted saw with the heightened reality of childhood, of theatre, of dream. And like a dream was the final experience of the first day in Chester. At night, in the pitch dark near the cathedral, a watchman told Olmsted that the bell that could be heard was the curfew: "as the long waving boom of the bell pulsed through us, [we] looked wonderingly at each other, as if America and the nineteenth century were a fading dream, slowly repeating, 'The curfew; the curfew.'"[11] It was the here-and-now – America and the nineteenth century, Olmsted's reality as a scientific farmer on Staten Island – that was the fading dream. The there-and-then – England and the thirteenth century, Olmsted's endless fantasy of being a country man of "Robin Hood and Richard the Lion-hearted" – was becoming the tangible reality. That was TRUE; the other was merely true. Through a kind of historical mysticism, Olmsted was transcending, in a comfortable fashion, time and space.

Having slept well through the night following the curfew bell, Olmsted set out the next day to see Eaton Park – a great estate hard by the city of Chester – the country seat of the dukes of Westminster:

> Ah! here is the real park at last.
>
> A gracefully, irregular, gently undulating surface of close cropped pasture land, reaching way off illimitably; dark green in colour; very old, but not very large trees scattered singly and in groups – so far apart as to throw long unbroken shadows across broad openings of light, and leave the view in several directions unobstructed for a long distance. Herds of fallow-deer, fawns, cattle, sheep and lambs quietly feeding near us, and moving slowly in masses at a distance; a warm atmosphere, descending sun, and sublime shadows from fleecy clouds transiently darkening in succession, sunny surface, cool woodside, flocks and herds, and foliage.

This passage might have come direct from the writings of the Reverend William Gilpin. *Observations on the River Wye ... Relative Chiefly to Picturesque Beauty; Made in the Summer of the Year 1770* anticipated all the aesthetic theories of the American farmer's *Walks and Talks* in England. And the novel idea that the Reverend Gilpin proposed for himself in his tour of 1770 – his "new object of pursuit; that of not barely examining the face of the country; but of examining it by the rules of picturesque beauty"[12] – might have served to describe what Olmsted was actually doing in England in 1850, if not why he had gone there.

Olmsted had an innate sense of the picturesque although he had made no special study of it. He had begun life as a ship's "green-boy," sailing before the mast to Canton, before he went into farming (though he had had a good education, including a year at Yale). A sure feeling for the principles of the gentlemanly art of landscape gardening combined with a farmer's knowledge of ditching and draining to make a winning formula when Olmsted submitted his plan for New York's Central Park on 1 April 1858. Called "Greensward," it was one of thirty-three entered in the competition set by the Board of Commissioners for a design for the new park. By that time Olmsted had already secured for himself the job of superintending the levelling and clearing of the section of the city set aside for the project, and he had taken as a partner the English-born and English-trained architect, Calvert Vaux. But it was only because Washington Irving had been a member of the committee consultant to the Commission that opposition to Olmsted's appointment on the grounds that he was "too literary to be practical" had been overcome. Olmsted remained an amateur; it is an architect's opinion that, "Much of the technical success of Central Park was owing to Olmsted's ability to attract workers of very high technical competence."[13]

"Greensward" proposed to put an aristocratic estate right in what was to become the middle of Manhattan – "'at the precise centre of [a] city of two millions'" – and Manhattan wanted him to do it, even though in 1858 it was a city of less than one million. For the Americans of "cultivated taste" who formed the selection committees, it did not count against the plan that a park intended for a mass population in one of the world's largest and most modern cities was inspired by the setting for that symbol of aristocratic exclusion and rural elegance, the English country house. The idealism of Congregationalist theology and Fourierian Socialism combined in New York's determination to have a great park. William Cullen Bryant and Horace Greeley demanded that it should be laid out. When Olmsted and Vaux presented New York with "Greensward," there was not a city in the United States that had such a park. Their design was intended to suggest "'to the imagination a great range of rural conditions. This style was dictated as much by the nature of the ground as by the popularity of the English school of landscape gardening.'"[14]

But the English school of landscape gardening was apparent in

"Olmsted's early insistence on a small-scaled, flexible design of land . . . [and] his adaptation of a picturesque, rather than a formal and perfectly symmetrical arrangement." The English school had shaped the aesthetic theory that led Olmsted to believe the landscape gardener the most noble kind of artist; and it provided a prominent member of the committee that advised the Central Park Commission to award the first prize of $2,000 to "Greensward." Edward Kemp who had worked on the making of the park at Birkenhead had been invited to New York to take part in the judging. Birkenhead Park had been Olmsted's revelation and it had been designed by the leading figure of the English school of landscape gardening, Joseph Paxton. Starting in 1844 with 120 acres of flat farmland, Paxton had, by 1847, completed a park with lake and prospect, hill and promenade.[15] Before Joseph Paxton had undertaken his commission for the Birkenhead Corporation, he had been head gardener at Chatsworth House, the country seat of the dukes of Devonshire. A year before the greatest triumph of Paxton's art – the Crystal Palace – was to make him known to the world, Frederick Law Olmsted found in Birkenhead a mode by which the aristocratic ideal represented by Chatsworth and Eaton Park could be rendered in popular form.

That the city fathers of Birkenhead should have wished to offer to the people of their municipality the upper-class amusements of the prospect and promenade was not surprising. The upper classes were known as the betters of the lower, and the notion that it should be morally and culturally improving for the lower classes to imitate the upper in these ways would have found few opponents on the city council. The traditional uses that the lower classes had made of open green space – whether royal hunting forest, common land, or country estate – were disapproved of in the new nineteenth-century towns. City parks were not to be places for wood gathering, cattle grazing, poaching, fairs, country games, prize fighting, or love making. Nor were the parks that Olmsted was to design for the new cities of America. These offered the gentlemanly pleasures to the inhabitants of those new cities. In this Olmsted gave expression to a principle implicit in nineteenth-century American democracy: all men were created equal in order that they might become gentlemen. Within eight years of Olmsted's idyllic ramble through Cheshire, Central Park was being laid out at a cost (for land purchase and landscaping) of over ten million dollars. Richard Cobden saw the park in 1859 and thought that when planted and completed, it would be "one of the largest and most beautiful parks in the world." A dyspeptic Scotsman who frequented the planted and completed park during the Civil War years complained that its main fault was the regulations that confined visitors to the walks and roads so that they could not wander at their leisure as they could in any of London's five parks. "I have heard it asserted that the people cannot be trusted with unrestricted liberty, lest they should injure the plants and young trees."[16]

The rules restricting free wandering in the Park have now been relaxed or abolished; they are certainly ignored, though there is still a formidable number of things that the visitor is not free to do and these are listed at every entrance. Even with free wandering, Central Park is not exactly like an English park. In the nature of things the translation, from one side of the Atlantic to the other, of so noble a concept was no simple matter and was not to be done without seachange. Whatever criticisms transatlantic visitors might have made, or still make, about Central Park, it remains a splendid democratic statement of an aristocratic ideal. It and the other parks that Olmsted designed for New York – Riverside, Morningside, St Nicholas, and Prospect (then in the separate city of Brooklyn) – are the loveliest ornaments of the five boroughs. Even though vandals destroy the daffodils every spring, New Yorkers live in the hope that one day their Parks Commission will be given enough funds to refurbish these lovely places, to rescue them for those who like to wander *rus in urbe*, to restore them to something like the plan for a park that began to shape itself in Olmsted's imagination as he wandered through Cheshire in 1850.

When, like a succession of Americans before and since, Olmsted had made the English country house real for himself by seeing Eaton Hall, he returned to Chester for the sabbath and the cathedral. This was to be the high point of his face-to-face encounter with his Mother England. Now for the first time since Olmsted had landed at Liverpool, did he admit to disappointment and depression of spirits. It was a dark morning of his soul because he found himself painfully cheated by what he had fondly promised would be the most profound moment of communion – worship with Englishmen at the common table of the Eucharist. Instead, he found himself dismayed by the clergy, distressed by the chanting, and distracted by the levity of the graven caricatures that stared at him from every pillar, boss, and angle. He tried hard to become solemn but he could not. Perhaps more than anything the peculiar intonation of the English clergy caused the most acute distress. Olmsted kneeling expectantly in the cathedral of Chester on the morning of his sabbath in Mother England found the reading of the lesson by the dean, "*sing-song* of the *worst* kind."[17]

At this point Olmsted might have profited from the example of Henry James. James claimed to have saved himself the disappointment that many American travellers gave themselves by attending divine service in England by the simple expedient of not going to church: "The outside of an old English country church in service time is a very pleasant place: and this is as near as I often dare approach the celebration of the Anglican mysteries." James contrived to make his non-attendance at church, non-attendance inside at least, an occasion of religious merit. Actually when James had been in Chester in 1872, it had been one of those occasions when he had gone inside. He had attended a cathedral service, escorting his sister and his aunt. Though he had been pleased with the play of light on ancient stone and very pleased with the music, he had, like other Americans, been disappointed by the clergy. In that instance, he had had to listen to a sermon delivered by the Reverend Charles Kingsley.[18] It had failed to be what it should have been.

Olmsted's attendance at church was neither so purely aesthetic nor so ironically respectful as James's attendance or non-attendance. Olmsted might have saved himself some disappointment had he remained in the cathedral yard but such a thing was not to be thought of. He went inside and endured the vexatious rituals. He tried to overcome the gothic levities of medieval stone carvers. He struggled to achieve the crowning reward of his meeting old Mother England face to face, but transcendency does not come to the self-conscious and he failed. But when the service moved forward to the organ voluntary, Frederick Olmsted found, as Henry James did twenty years later, that the music of the Anglican church was all he could have wished it to be. He lost himself in its cadence, harmony, and majesty. And with the loss of self, transcendence came:

I was of a sudden brought back and awakened again in the dim old cathedral with such emotion, as if from eternity and infinity, I was remanded to mysterious identity and sense of time, that I choked and throbbed; and then, as the richest deepest melody I must ever have heard passed away . . . I kneeled and bowed my head with the worshippers around me, acknowledging in all my heart the beauty and sublimity of the place and the service.[19]

Olmsted was redeemed by an act of humility; he bowed his head not only to Him he called his God, but to the men who had designed the cathedral and who had made part of that design the caricatures and the grotesqueries. He bowed his head to the deviations of the service from his Puritan, Congregationalist expectation. Building and ritual were acknowledged to be beautiful and sublime. Olmsted had passed through one of the most demanding tests set by the Old World for the inhabitants of the New. He had chosen to identify with forms of the culture that were unexpected by him, that were not as he had told himself they would be, that were not as he had promised himself to enjoy just as he had imagined them to be.

The majority of American travellers admitted without hesitation that Europe was the superior of America in its literature and in its history. In the case of England, that admission was made easier, made more welcome, by the conviction that the literature and the history of England belonged as much to the visiting American as to the native Englishman. In a Chester tavern one night, a friendly Englishman had apologised to Olmsted and his companions for the fact that the men in the bar had been singing national songs only. Olmsted had answered:

"Excuse me, sir, . . . those are our national songs as much as yours. You forget that we are also countrymen of Will Shakespeare, and Robin Hood, and Richard the Lion-hearted. Our mothers danced with your fathers under the same 'greenwood' and around the 'May-pole.' Our fathers fought for their rights in this land against the Turk, Frenchman, Spaniard, and Pretender. We have as much pride in Old England, gentlemen, as any of you. We claim the right to make ourselves *at home* on that ground with you. You must not treat us as strangers."

Whether or not the Englishmen were surprised by this outburst Olmsted did not say, but the reply by one of them must have pleased him: "'You are right; you are welcome. Give us your hand. The old blood will tell!'"[20] For a man like Olmsted, racial and linguistic identity with the English was easily established. And in these

14. Frederick Law Olmsted

matters he did not require exact likeness – he was delighted by the differences between the English he spoke and that of the Cheshire folk. But in spiritual and political matters, identity with these Englishmen was not so easily established, and spirituality concerned Olmsted in a way that could not be disregarded. The differences between English and American rituals could not be embraced with an enthusiasm like that appropriate for dialect variants. The issues were too close to the sources of a man's own vital force.

The landscape of England had been exactly what Olmsted had wanted it to be; the city of Chester had been exactly what he had wanted it to be; the fabric and the service of the cathedral had been more than he had wanted them to be. More had seemed to be less. The emotional distress of this was common to transatlantic visitors; not all responded with the joyous humility of Olmsted. When England did not exactly match expectation, many decided that the country was not coming up to expectation; fewer realised that on some occasions it may have gone beyond. The tourist then got more than he bargained for. The medieval energy and the monumental creativity of the cathedrals could stun. Nineteenth-century North

America had nothing like them at all. (In 1850, Quebec alone had a stone-built cathedral and few of these travellers had seen it.) By a leap, as it were of faith, the void could be crossed. And so it was that Frederick Law Olmsted found himself reaching *O Altitudo* in the cathedral of Chester on that sabbath morning. He added a footnote to his experience: the emotion of that moment, he said, forced a belief in "immortality and eternity."[21] Little wonder that Henry James called these men passionate pilgrims.

4

THE SENTIMENT AND POETRY OF ENGLAND

A year after Frederick Law Olmsted had made his walking tour of the land of his forefathers, Arthur Cleveland Coxe landed at Liverpool. Coxe was a preoccupied man and he spoke with a priest's boldness about his preoccupation. When he finds emotions about which he may legitimately and venerably speak, a priest brings to the occasion an energy that has not been wasted elsewhere, and what Coxe had to say about himself and England in 1851 makes for an interesting excursion into the hinterland of the nineteenth-century mind. *Impressions of England* presented a single view of England though it did not present an entirely simple view. A. Cleveland Coxe, Rector of Grace Church, Baltimore, believed that the possession of material England disqualified Englishmen from possession of spiritual England. Coxe believed that he was able "to claim 'a richer use of his,' than [the Englishman] himself enjoys." To the Englishman, ignobly concerned with malt liquor taxes and manufactories, England presented a workaday face, but England presented herself to a man like Coxe "only in her higher and nobler character." Only an American could feel "the entire and unmixed sentiment and poetry of England."[1]

The Englishman had made his kingdom of this world, but, Coxe made plain to the readers of the New York *Church Journal* (where the *Impressions* first appeared), "To enjoy England one must be an American and a hearty and earnest member of the Anglican Church." A. Cleveland Coxe, like Frederick Law Olmsted, fused religious and aesthetic emotions. It was difficult to say where one began and the other ended. The difference between the England of the spirit and the England of the flesh (a difference that Olmsted had experienced in the previous year as a difference between the TRUE England and the true England), the difference between the higher and the lower uses of England was also a difference between the England of fact and the England of fancy. Coxe had been reluctant to exchange the one for the other as his ship had approached Liverpool, and as soon as he had landed he had been anxious to re-establish his possession of the England of fancy in face of the England of fact. Apprehensions that his landing in material England might cause him to lose forever his possession of imaginary England were not realised. He found himself seeing in the world of fact the names and destinations of a lifetime's fanciful journeys. He saw a cart marked "Ashby-de-la-Zouche," a stage marked "Oxford," a sign-post marked, "Stratford." He was overwhelmed.[2]

Coxe told his readers that his book was "a record of the memorable year 1851" but he had not gone to England to see the Crystal Palace. He snorted at the thought: "The idea of going to England to look at anything short of England itself! Besides, I supposed it a mere toy of Prince Albert's." And against Prince Albert, Coxe was sorely prejudiced. Albert was a German. He should have been an Englishman. Coxe made a point of avoiding the Crystal Palace altogether when he was first in London but he could not resist the promise of pomp and ceremony offered by the 1 May opening of the Great Exhibition by the Queen herself. He actually hastened from Oxford where he had been attending the May Morning Celebrations in a euphoric state. He was somewhat ashamed to discover that the Great Exhibition had in no way merited his earlier contempt.[3]

This was in large part owing to the ceremonial nature of the opening day. Industry and Commerce were not prominent. There were many Americans in the crowd. Some took a different view of the proceedings from the Reverend Coxe. Mr Horace Greeley had come to England expressly to report on what the Americans were already calling the World Fair.

> The ludicrous, the dissonant, the incongruous, are not excluded from the Exhibition: they cannot be excluded from any complete picture of its opening . . . The Queen, we will say, was here by Right Divine, by right of Womanhood, by Universal Suffrage – anyhow you please . . . But in inaugurating the first grand cosmopolitan Olympiad of Industry, ought not Industry to have some representation?

In place of the Gentleman Usher of the Sword and State, Lords in Waiting, Master of the Horse, Groom of the Stole, Master of the Buckhounds, "and such uncouth fossils," Greeley wanted to see real representatives of the "children of Watt, of Arkwright and their compeers (Napoleon's real conquerors)." He thought that it was no way to honour Industry to pass over the Ironmasters and "summon instead the descendants of some lucky dozen Norman robbers." But those were exactly the people that Cleveland Coxe did want summoned, and them he saw in great number. A day that had begun for him with the celebration of a May Morning festival, that had its origins in England's ancient past, was in no way disrupted by attendance at the first World Fair. Coxe had been spared contact with the kind of England that he did not want to know about. The excursion from Oxford to London was in the event as pleasing as the excursion that he made from Oxford to Burford, of which obscure place he wrote: "Here, now, was England – the England we read of. None of your Manchesters and Liverpools, but an innocent, sleepy old village that was of vast repute when those snobbish places were unknown. Here met a Church Synod, A.D. 685."[4]

Coxe was very capable of a certain kind of introspection and especially able to focus his attentions on the meaning of his being an *American in England*, but nowhere in his book did he try to enter into the consciousness of the English or attempt analysis of the context of his experience. A very little would have told him that a great deal of English energy was devoted to keeping England, "the England we read of." That the English were in large part bewitched by the spell of their own history – even in this period of industrial development and colonial expansion – escaped Coxe's attention. He was only conscious of modern English behaviour where reformers, modernisers, up-daters had undone the work of time. Like most sentimental travellers, he did not recognise in the apparently phlegmatic response of the English to their heritage a cast of mind that concealed a deep tie with history and concealed it partly because the euphoric condition of the tourist in the presence of old towers was not a state in which a man could pass his life. It was not chance that made feudal ritual the order of the day at the opening of the Great Exhibition, but it took the antagonistic perspective of Horace Greeley to see that England was doing on a grand scale what the Reverend A. Cleveland Coxe did for a holiday.

Coxe's visits to the House of Commons a week after the opening of the Great Exhibition thoroughly confirmed him in his belief that the English had no feeling at all for their occasions of history and legend. On the first night, Coxe heard a debate about the Malt Liquor Tax

Act (a subject of intense backbench interest); discussion was confined to the issues of financial necessity and political advisability. It seemed a sorry topic to preoccupy lawmakers in so venerable a chamber. (Coxe had already referred to this tax in his lyrical exposition of the superior capacity of the American to enjoy the sentiment and the poetry of England.) On the night of Coxe's second visit to the House of Commons, he was even more surprised. He discovered the members debating what should be the House's response to the episcopal titles that the Pope of Rome had instituted for use by a Catholic hierarchy in England. That the matter should be under discussion at all dismayed Coxe; that it should be debated with circumspect regard for international political opinion disgusted him. The Rector of the Grace Church, Baltimore, felt that there was only one appropriate reply for true-born Englishmen to make – gun boats should be sent at once to the Civita Vecchia.[5] That gun boats were not sent suggested that the members were not true-born.

Hostility to the Church of Rome and a violent antipathy to the person of the Pope himself were manifestations for Coxe of his ancestral ties with England and the Church of England. He had not been raised in the Anglican faith – in the Protestant Episcopal Church, as the Church of England had become in post-Revolutionary America – but he had, says a biographer, "early displayed a liking for the Episcopal Church," and in 1842 he had been ordained a minister in its practice. He was to decline the episcopate of Texas in 1856 and to accept that of Western New York in 1865. He was strongly opposed to any revisions of ritual that might separate yet further the sister churches of America and England and "he opposed revisions of the Bible on the ground that the authorized version was a bond that united the churches."[6] His ancestors had indeed been Quakers; his father had become a Presbyterian; Coxe in turn had become Episcopalian. This movement towards religious orthodoxy, often matched by a parallel improvement of family fortunes, was a familiar pattern of American conversion. Having adopted his new faith, Cleveland Coxe held to his middle ground with a passion. His identification with England combined with his Presbyterian childhood to make him regard with a special loathing the steps that had led a man like John Henry Newman beyond Canterbury to Rome. For Coxe, Canterbury was no staging post.

In Birmingham, on his route south from Liverpool, Coxe had deliberately gone out of his way to find Newman as though to treat himself to something of specially bitter taste. Newman was, in 1851, accommodated in a temporary chapel, or "oratory." Coxe described this as a "low and dirty-looking place of worship," and he told the readers of the New York *Church Journal* that it was dominated by "an immense doll representing the Virgin." "There was no denying the craft of no common artist" in Newman's sermon but his behaviour in the sanctuary was "violent and excessive." Coxe described Newman's entry in theatrical terms: "When the singing was going on a lank and spectral figure appeared at the door of the chancel – stalked in, and prostrated himself before the altar." In a detail which elicits more sympathy for Newman than for himself, Coxe reported that he laughed when the apostate Anglican accidentally quoted from the King James Version instead of from the Douai Bible. Oratorianism was, said Coxe bitterly, "The Methodism of the Trent religion." Its Italian Baroque ritual and its devotional fervour were not what Coxe wanted to believe were "English," and he was pleased to hear that the local people had taken to jeering at the robed and tonsured Oratorians as they went about the streets of Birmingham. "There is after all, much sturdy commonsense in John Bull's hatred of the absurd."[7]

A. Cleveland Coxe had a hand in the founding of the Anglo-Continental Society which had as one of its objectives, "the promulgation on the Continent [of Europe] the principles of the English Reformation." This was a mission exactly opposite to that of John Henry Newman. Newman was doing the work of the sixteenth-century Counter-Reformation in nineteenth-century England. Coxe's ambition was to do the work of the sixteenth-century Reformation in nineteenth-century Europe, and his enthusiasm for the Anglican Church led him to endorse some unlikely spiritual activities. One such was the "most primitive visit to the Pope" of Canon Townsend, who had gone to Rome in an abortive attempt to convert the Bishop of that ancient city to Protestantism. "In my opinion," said Coxe, "Canon Townsend need not be ashamed of having preached the Gospel at Rome."[8] Coxe was ready to give Townsend comfort when the Canon returned home to Durham Cathedral amidst a certain amount of ridicule, because Coxe was himself open to ridicule as one whose identification with

England and the Church of England represented a similar kind of excess. His anger and ridicule were reserved for those who had gone to Rome as John Henry Newman had gone to Rome, as pilgrim and religious supplicant. That a true-born Englishman should deliberately abandon the faith and allegiance that Coxe had so deliberately adopted seemed a mockery. By leaving Canterbury for Rome, Newman belittled the three-thousand mile pilgrimage of him who had left America for England. The convert abhorred the apostate.

Coxe eagerly embraced the religion, the history, and the language of England, but there remained something less easily embraced – the government of England. It was not in the American make-up to admit the superiority of Europe in political matters, even less perhaps than in religious matters. A lifetime of political education taught him that in her Constitution was the source of America's greatness. To call the political achievement of the Founding Fathers into question by admitting the merits of other political systems would be to question the basis of America's greatness in the present, to question the demonstration of her greatness in the past, and to question the promise of her greatness in the future. Few Americans cared to do so.

Before the Civil War, in 1851, when A. Cleveland Coxe was visiting the Houses of Parliament in England, it was certainly the fact that the Constitution of the United States was still the uncontested, if not still the single, great achievement of American genius. The allegiance of the American was to this Constitution. It might have seemed odd to feudal eyes, as James Bryce was to point out, that "allegiance" should be given to a legal instrument,[9] but it was the undeniable reality of American political life that the Constitution embodied that element of mystery which Walter Bagehot said was essential for the proper functioning of a body politic. The Constitution of the United States shared in the divinity of kings no matter how rough shapen it might become in the process of amendment, interpretation, and usage through the years. Cleveland Coxe did not directly question the political truths enshrined in America's Constitution and yet those same truths were keeping him from the things he loved. In *Impressions of England* the fledgling bishop made moves to reconcile the notion of monarchy with the principles of the Founding Fathers.

The presence of Queen Victoria and her noblemen had reconciled Coxe to the industrial actualities of the Great Exhibition, and the same elements began his reconciliation with the Houses of Parliament with which, in the form of the House of Commons, he had been disgusted. Enthusiasm for monarchy and aristocracy were to carry beyond the historical perspective into an idealised vision of political reality. In the House of Lords, Coxe did not have to struggle to match romance with reality and fancy with fact. And one of the most impressive features of the House, and the most potent vehicle for imaginative speculation, was the great throne from which the monarchs addressed the gathering of nobles and the press of commoners on those days that solemnly inaugurated Parliaments. Here was a potent image of the mystery of monarchy, and Coxe challenged his readers not to respond to so majestical a sight: "I defy anyone to look at the Throne of England without veneration."[10]

Nineteenth-century Americans, in general, objected to monarchy, but not, usually, to monarchs. English kings and queens were usually liked, even enjoyed. William IV, it was true, came in for a good deal of mockery. Oliver Wendell Holmes wrote home in 1834 that the royal brow, in view at the Opera, was "probably the largest uncivilized spot in England," and that the King himself looked like a butcher and his Queen like a milkman's wife. But this republican high-spiritedness (which only served to point out that kings and queens were men and women) did not arise from any potent hostility. A more representative judgement on William IV was that of the Reverend Charles Stewart, who believed that the King was "no doubt, as generally reported, a plain-hearted and generous-spirited sailor." (Stewart wrote a whole chapter on the "Levee of the King, and the Queen's Drawing Room" and in it showed a keen interest in every detail of procedure, custom, dress, and etiquette.) Nobody had much good to say about George IV, whose treatment of his wife distressed Americans, but his father, George III, was all but an object of affection for the American travelling in England in the first quarter of the nineteenth century. Even the fierce republican, William Austin, could not but say, "If the countenance be allowed to indicate the disposition, his Majesty has a very good heart; and he has more intellect than you could judge from his countenance on the coin." When it came time for the old King to die, on 29 January 1820, Richard Rush, the American

Minister at the Court of St James, found himself deeply moved. George had reigned for sixty years, and all men had grown up with him as their monarch. The early years of his reign and his part in the American War of Independence had by 1820 become "historical." Rush did not think that recrimination was in any way appropriate.[11]

These friendly, sometimes sentimental, tributes to monarchs were even more the pattern of American travellers' feelings towards Queen Victoria and her family. Affection and respect for her flowed from the transatlantic pen. In 1851, Professor Benjamin Silliman of Yale (the same that had visited England in 1805) on a pleasure cruise around the Isle of Wight, drew his readers' attention to the simple but royal residence of Osborne House, the principal attraction of which was that "it contains a happy family, the wise and blameless lives of whose heads is exerting an excellent influence upon the nation." The moral capital invested in the person of Victoria did much to reconcile the American traveller to the notion of English monarchy. She set a good example. In an evangelical age, this meant a great deal. The politically corrupt fact of monarchy was scrupulously separated from the morally pure monarch. Horace Greeley may have been angered by the feudal anachronisms of the opening ceremonial of the Great Exhibition but he exempted the royal couple from his criticisms: monarchy was fated, but Queen Victoria was not personally to be blamed for that.[12]

Coxe would not have been unusual had he limited himself to praising the reigning monarch; he was unusual among American travellers to the extent that he displayed a reverence for monarchy itself. And symptomatic of this were his expressed reservations about the royal couple. He did not like and did not approve of Prince Albert. The German consort was an object of curiosity for other Americans; for Coxe, he represented a threat to an idealised notion of monarchy. Though, by 1851, the English themselves were reconciled to a foreigner next to the throne, Coxe was not: "He is an alien to true British feeling, and an enemy to the Anglican Church."[13] "True British feeling" was not the same as the feelings of Englishmen, and the inhabitant of Maryland believed it his duty to instruct the readership of New York in the difference.

Just as Coxe liked monarchy as well as monarchs, so he liked aristocracy as well as aristocrats – more than aristocrats perhaps,

15. Arthur Cleveland Coxe

since he does not seem to have met any of them. This also reversed the common American reaction. Usually Americans liked lords but not lordship. Cleveland Coxe dwelt with pleasure upon the idea of that body of men who filled the House of Lords when the throne itself was occupied. "The British aristocracy may be said, even now, to be a genuine one," Coxe declared. He believed that the British aristocracy on the whole presented a "wholesome example to other classes in the State," and that the British aristocracy was probably the most "virtuous" in history. Coxe thought that the English nobility offered that same kind of model family life that other Americans readily acknowledged was offered by Victoria and Albert. Elsewhere in his book, Coxe presented a picture of an English country estate as a model of domestic virtue precisely because the relationship between master and servant was not premised upon equality. Coxe visited the tenants of a Kent family in the company of the local squire's wife and discovered that "they treated her as they would have done a descended angel, while she, in the prettiest tone, inquired whether they 'had seen their Master thereabout,' and so, thanking them departed." This ideal master-and-servant relationship was possible because deference could exist at the same time as affection. The hierarchy of place and the sense of belonging that this permitted provided, in Coxe's opinion, a structure that confirmed all parties and rested, like that of the family, on a joyous identity of all in the whole. The virtue of the estate lay "chiefly in the entire ease and nature with which everybody, from the squire to his humblest menial, nay, even to the housedog, fitted his place, and seemed to enjoy it."[14] The dog overdoes it.

In American society, Coxe said, there was no deference: there, "all white complexioned people scorn to obey. Hence the misery and stiffness of housekeeping, and the deplorable multiplication of those vulgar establishments called fashionable hotels." Young couples in seaboard cities often preferred to take apartments in hotels rather than set up homes on their own. Moralists believed this destroyed the bases of family life by inducing idleness in the wife, disaffection in the husband, and precocity in the child. The excuse was the perennial difficulty in getting "help" in America. The hotel provided an easy, cheap solution. For Coxe this subordination of the family into an economic element of a larger whole – the hotel – was an antithesis to the ideal solution provided by the extension of the family into a larger whole – the English estate. And though the estate that he visited in Kent was not one owned by a nobleman, it was nonetheless a good example of that system of estates that culminated in the great holdings of those families whose leaders filled the seats in the House of Lords. When Coxe criticised England, he did so only because she failed to be venerable, solemn, archaic. He criticised Englishmen who failed to be his kind of Englishmen; he criticised Newman and he criticised Mr Benjamin Disraeli whom he heard speaking in the House of Commons. He detested oratorical manners and rhetorical gestures that, he believed, owed their origins abroad. In the House of Lords, he found a peculiar and amateur delivery among the speakers. He was immediately aware in this of some obscure, aristocratic distinction, setting these men apart from and beyond the professional excellence of a Catholic priest or a Jewish politician: "A hesitating, stuttering, and very awkward utterance would even seem to be the fashion in this noble House."[15]

Coxe was no New Englander. Though he had been born in the indeterminate state of New Jersey, his ancestors had been Quakers from Maryland. And at the time of his visit to England, Coxe was himself a resident of Maryland, a slave state. Much of his sympathy with the aristocratic philosophy and his dislike of democratic relationships reflected the attitudes of the South. These found a much less frequent expression in travel literature than those of the North because the overwhelming number of writers of travel books came from the northern states. No more than many Englishmen who insisted upon the happiness of slaves on Virginian plantations, was Coxe going to question the smiling faces of the tenants on the Kent estate. He accepted patrician rule as he acknowledged episcopal title. His monarchist instincts flowed from the same source, so that religious and political sentiment alike led him to champion the cause of Charles I, and led him to call that king, Charles the Martyr. But in his urgency to accept what was English and at the same time to limit so narrowly what he could acknowledge to be "true" English, Coxe was driven into logical peculiarities more and more tortuous. Coxe needed to remain true to those principles that were enshrined in America's Constitution while at the same time canonising Charles Stuart, the last king of England to insist that kings ruled by right divine. It was not easy. The idea that Charles was a libertarian in the great tradition of Anglo-Saxon freedom required paradoxes so extreme that they could be resolved only by the kind of logic which redefined all the terms of the argument. British liberty was liberty to be British and not a liberty to be anything else. Being "British" did not include behaving like Pym, Hampden, or Cromwell. Coxe would not (could not) leave the subject of Charles I until he had established (at least to his own satisfaction) that Charles was a defender of British liberty and constitutional freedoms.[16]

This constitutional paradox was of a kind with the hereditary paradox that had led Coxe to claim for the American a higher use of England than the Englishman himself enjoyed. It was a short step from this combination of contradictions, fabrications, and imaginative reconstructions to arrive at the conviction that the "real" Englishman was an American. A. Cleveland Coxe reached this conclusion when he arrived in Cambridge. And he got to Cambridge on 4 July 1851. The day and the place coincided painfully. The constitutional fact of American Independence was not easily forgotten on 4 July, though in Cambridge itself Coxe found very little to remind him that back home in Baltimore the speech makers would be hard at it and the fireworks about to rise in force. In Cambridge, there was the age-old peace, quiet, beauty. 4 July was a day in the Long Vacation like any other day – serenely lovely without intimation of political rebellion. This disparity of feeling in English and American breasts made Coxe uneasy. Racial, linguistic, and religious identity with Englishmen was threatened by political differences again. In Cambridge, 4 July was not a day for celebration but Coxe was too much of an American to switch sides – besides that was not the point. What he did do was to decide that the day celebrated not a rebellion but a defection – a defection by the British from their own best tradition. It was the English and not the Americans who had revolted: "Our fathers ceased to be Englishmen, because a corrupt and incompetent Ministry were resolved that they should no longer be freemen." The two peoples who should have been one had been separated by the evil practice of politicians. Coxe worked upon his theme until he had recast himself in the role of the child denied his birthright, the child denied his true patrimony, the child who must stand outside and watch his house and his treasure be enjoyed by those who have no more title than himself to their possession, by those whose possession is a debased stewardship, by those who are too sensual to appreciate the heritage that has fallen to them. In self-pity, Coxe passed his day in "venerable Cambridge, where," as he said, "some of my forefathers were educated, and where I felt it a sort of wrong to be disinherited of a filial right to feel at home." Coxe laboured by every shift of logic and every contrivance of emotion to make himself at home in England and succeeded so far that he might say, "I ask no Englishman's leave to walk the soil of England with filial pride."[17]

The personality of the Rector of the Grace Church, Baltimore, was not an attractive one. His constant sectarian jibes, his fulsome self-projection, his fatuous romanticism, all compounded to make his *Impressions of England* a book that can become very irritating, but he had a perfection and a beauty of type. The intensity of his feeling towards England was articulated in great and self-regarding fullness. He lingered about his emotions with a solemnity and a blandness that have helped to preserve them in their rich, florid development, so that what many others may have felt, he was able to say.

Coxe's admiration of things English was unusual among American travel writers only in its outspoken frankness, and even so it would not have been a cause for unusual notice among the Episcopalian readership of the New York *Church Journal.* It should not perhaps be too great a surprise that there lingered in the country that was proud to be known as the "Model Republic" an affection for monarchy. This affection was a temperate one and belonged more to the reflective and historical than to the active and present mood. The majority of American travellers had no quarrel with the monarchs of England, or those of Europe for that matter. They were part of the scene and the American wanted his scene to be as authentic as possible, and authenticity in England included kings and queens, lords and ladies.

The Southerner might have been expected to admire monarchical rule because he was himself a product of patrician society but it was by no means a simple formula of pro and con between South and North on this issue. Many Southerners were passionate republicans and bitter opponents of monarchy – the most radical of early Presidents was the Virginian Jefferson and the most conservative, the New Englander John Adams. Owning slaves did not necessarily imply that a man wanted to acknowledge an authority above his own; owning slaves meant giving orders not taking them. The planter was a petty king not a great courtier.

The New Englander, on the other hand, took a great deal of pride in the fact that he was an offshoot of Old England – and England was unthinkable without kings and queens. At least, no traveller ever thought of England without them. A staunch New Englander like Nathaniel Hawthorne who felt his Puritan blood strong in him as he went about England had no time at all for British Liberals. A real liberal was a genuine Massachusetts Brook Farm liberal; a British Liberal was neither a real Britisher nor a real liberal. John Bull was Hawthorne's Englishman. In 1886, when Oliver Wendell Holmes (another New Englander) had become a distinguished man of letters and a figure of some reputation, he returned to London and was adopted by fashionable society. He was introduced to members of the royal family so that he did not have to stare at them across an opera house as he had had to do in 1834. He received an invitation to spend Derby Day in the company of the Prince of Wales and he enjoyed it very much. He discovered, he said, that "it is really easier to feel at home with the highest people in the land than with the awkward commoner who was knighted yesterday."[18] Nineteenth-century republicans inclined to royal company by a kind of natural right that was not unlike snobbery. The embrace of the duke was as irresistible to the Yankee as to the Englishman, and that of a prince more so. The Yankee gal when she came to London lined up to be presented to the Queen as eagerly as the Southern belle. There was a convention that the father mutter a great deal about its all being a humbug, but American Ministers to London had their work cut out throughout the century taking Yankee families to the Court of St James.

Coming as he did from the mid-Atlantic states, A. Cleveland Coxe was neither wholly Yankee nor wholly Planter. His adoption of the Episcopalian religion did indeed represent a very positive identification with his English heritage, but it did not for that reason represent a break with his countrymen. Membership of the Protestant Episcopal Church was not then, any more than now, an un-American activity. For all England's powerful hold on him, Coxe remained in possession of an American perspective. Cambridge was beautiful, and as far as he was able, he repossessed it. Oxford, too, was beautiful but he did not think that his fellow countrymen should regret there was no Oxford in America: "God forbid! I love to think that is [for the English] to enjoy and mine only to remember." At the end of his journey, it came time to say goodbye to England, "a land, where, for centuries, everything has been steadily advancing towards a high realization of human capabilities, alike in the physical, and mental, and moral of man's nature."[19] But he said goodbye and returned refreshed to his pastoral duties. Once England had become a place to remember, it had been restored to the realm of fancy. Coxe could enjoy an image that had been enriched by personal encounter and mild adventure, but it was once again an image: identity and abstraction had been re-established. Remembering England was an experience quite as rich as imagining England. Memory and imagination were excellent ways to travel.

5

STRATFORD-UPON-AVON: BLESSED BEYOND ALL OTHER VILLAGES

In no place in England has the tourist's imagination, both American and English, so indulged itself as at Stratford-upon-Avon. In the nineteenth century (as in the twentieth), it was the lure of all tourists, and no literary shrine of English-speaking peoples has been more described and no town or village more deeply buried under accumulated literary and tourist sentiment. The simple outlines of an English market town have been endlessly embellished and all but lost in the monstrous development. A visit to Stratford was, as Hawthorne said, "one of the things that an American proposes to himself as necessarily and chiefly to be done, on coming to England." As the American approached the core and the centre of Warwickshire, "Shakespeare's county," the attraction of Stratford became irresistible. "I cannot linger in the beautiful groves of Warwick," wrote Bayard Taylor, "while further down the Avon, girdled by green meadows and embosomed in heavy-foliaged elms and limes, lies happy Stratford, blessed beyond all other villages in all lands of the Saxon race." The pulse quickened as the traveller neared a goal that promised to make real the dream and to consummate the labour – "I had possessed for years," wrote A. Cleveland Coxe, "a Stratford of my own; a pet village of my soul, such as Shakespeare should have lived in; and now – in a few hours, all this was to be deposed forever . . . Would the realization pay me for the downfall of the vision?" As ever Coxe acted out the grand situation and he had his wonted fulfilment as he reached the outskirts of the village: "At last . . . the spire of Stratford. The gentle tumult of feelings with which it ruffled my inmost nature, for a moment, and the calm enjoyment that succeeded, were enough to pay me for crossing the Atlantic." Coxe spent an hour in the churchyard trying to take in the "full idea of the spot," and when he left he plucked a branch of ivy to take back to the land where Shakespeare had more readers than anywhere else in the world. The impulse to repossess was strong in Stratford. The American tourist went to Stratford, as Washington Irving had said, "on a poetical pilgrimage" but he went with something more in mind as well. He went on a national mission to establish for himself and for the world that Shakespeare belonged to America, that Shakespeare was America's national bard, as much as he was England's. "The whole Anglo-Saxon race," thought Coxe in the yard of Trinity Church, "must ever recognize in him the original master of many of its forms of thought, a rich contributor to its idiom and language, and the constructor of some of its strongest sentiments of civilization, of morals, and of religion."[1]

"Of religion" might be questionable, but the pilgrimage to Stratford was for the American paid to the genius of the language, that is to the language itself, to that part, and the greatest part, of the English heritage which was indisputably his. The nineteenth-century American was immensely proud of his command of the English language; he was sensible of it as his birthright and highly sensitive even to being praised on the point. "By the way," wrote James Russell Lowell in a letter from London, "a Scotsman had the ill-manners one day to compliment me on my English. 'Why, I shouldn't know you weren't an Englishman. Where did you get it?' I couldn't resist, and answered with a couple of verses from a Scottish ballad –

'I got it in my mither's wame
Whaur ye'll get never the like!'

He will never compliment me again, I fear." On the death of Lowell, Henry James wrote of him that "the thing he loved most in the world after his country was the English tongue, of which he was an infallible master, and his devotion to which was, in fact, a sort of agent of his patriotism." This was no paradox to the American for in the matter of language more than in any other, he set himself forward as more English than the English. Lowell, said James, "was zealous to show that the speech of New England was most largely that of an England older and more vernacular than the England that to-day finds it queer." The myth that the New Englander spoke the language of Queen Elizabeth, William Shakespeare, and the Bible was passionately espoused by Lowell. Defending Emerson's use of English against Matthew Arnold's attack, Lowell wrote: "I greatly doubt whether Matthew Arnold is quite capable (in the habit of addressing a jury as he always is) of estimating the style of one who conversed with none but the masters of his mother tongue . . . Sir T. Browne is the only man I know worthy to be named with [him]." Henry James had himself the very same reverence for the tongue inherited by the two nations; in 1888, he called it "our consecrated English speech . . . the medium of Shakespeare and Milton, of Hawthorne and Emerson." On his return to America in 1904 his most painful shock was a linguistic one. The English language, he discovered, had been handed over "to the American common school, to the American newspaper, and to the American Dutchman and Dago." These were influences, he told an audience of young women at Bryn Mawr, lecturing them "on the Question of Our Speech," "that make for the confused, the ugly, the fat, the thin, the mean, the helpless, that reduce articulation to an easy and ignoble minimum, and so keep it as little distinct as possible from the grunting, the squealing, the barking or the roaring of animals." James voiced here a classical, a Tennysonian terror of civilisation's reeling back into the beast; it was the purist's perennial anxiety that the latest round of linguistic change presaged universal anarchy. But it spoke of something else, less important perhaps, but more immediately painful for Henry James, the dissociation of the two nations whose association had created his own complex fate. He voiced his fears about the loss of this linguistic heritage more directly in *The American Scene*. The language spoken in America (James did not call it the American language) "may be destined to become the most beautiful on the globe and the very music of humanity (here the 'ethnic' synthesis shrouds itself thicker than ever); but whatever we shall know it for, certainly, we shall not know it for English – in any sense for which there is an existing literary measure."[2]

Difficult as it might seem that a language that was degenerating into the barking and roaring of animals could evolve to be the most beautiful in the world, James's point was that whatever the ultimate state of the language in America, it would cease to be the language of Shakespeare and Milton, and presumably of Hawthorne and Emerson. And when this tie was broken, the most vital and the most real link with England and with Europe, with a consecrated past and a sacred tradition, would be broken. The spirit in which Washington Irving had undertaken his pilgrimage to the birthplace of the genius of the language could then no longer inspire Americans; the sentiment would no longer belong to their range of feeling. Irving undertook his pilgrimage in full consciousness of coming to the well-spring of his living language. The American was not a German visiting the birthplace of a great and universal mind; the American liked to believe that he visited Stratford as did the Englishman: to pay honour to the man who had made the English language honoured through the world, to see the schoolroom of the man whose plays recalled his own schoolhouse, to see the town (or village as most Americans called it) where that man had lived who had appropriated the title of all poets and was known simply as the Bard.

The Americans delighted in referring to Shakespeare as the Bard, and did so as frequently, perhaps more frequently, than the English themselves. It caught a familiar as well as a reverential note. The Gothic and Romantic flavour of this title had already by the beginning of the nineteenth century acquired some of those comic-ironic overtones that seem so provincial to the twentieth-century commentator. And this comic-ironic quality was exactly what Washington Irving exploited in his essay "Stratford-On-Avon": his narrator was at his most whimsical, benevolent, and fusty. Geoffrey Crayon was not in Stratford merely to describe what he saw; what he attempted to do for his readers here as elsewhere was to recreate the reveries inspired by scene. Everything including the weather was pleasant, and mildly amusing. He did all the things that a visitor was meant to do – Stratford's routines were already well-established – but Geoffrey Crayon did them in a spirit of gentle resignation as though questioning the folly of human nature that brought men to do such trivial things in the pursuit of such great ideals. He searched among the names of the mob who had scribbled their signatures all over the whitewashed walls of Shakespeare's birth-room for the names of the great. He sat, as all visitors to Shakespeare's childhood home sat, on Shakespeare's chair but commented "whether this be done with the hope of imbibing any of the inspiration of the bard I am at a loss to say."[3]

Irving's mixture of wry amusement and picturesque reverie combined two sets of reactions that shaped the response of American travellers to Stratford. (His essay was the earliest of its kind to receive widespread publication – the adoption of *The Sketch-Book* by the fashionable London public in 1820 ensured its being read throughout America.) His essay was important first because it was read by all American travellers who planned a literary pilgrimage to Stratford. It was also important because it so ably captured the two ways in which Stratford might affect the tourist. His wry amusement at the folly of his fellow tourists presaged the outrage and disgust of those who were to find the place an abomination; his picturesque reveries provided the pattern for those determined travellers who refused to allow the cockneyfication of the town to rob them of an occasion for exquisite indulgence in literary evocation.

For travellers in this class, Irving's pilgrimage became the model for their own. A. Cleveland Coxe told the readers of the New York *Church Journal* that he followed the path of Geoffrey Crayon, going to the Red Horse Inn exactly as Crayon had done and taking his seat in "Crayon's chair." It was Washington Irving who had made this inn famous (it was named after him for a brief period in the twentieth century) and Coxe felt that Shakespeare's own fame was rivalled in the very town of his birth by that of the American. And Coxe introduced into his descriptions of Stratford elements that were more characteristic in detail and tone of Irving than of himself. He found Anne Hathaway's Cottage "thatched in the picturesque style so dear to Crayon artists and sketchers; its little windows peeping out of the straw, like sharp eyes under the shaggy brows of an old pensioner, sunning himself in front of an ale-house." In the same year, Bayard Taylor on a return trip to Europe, and this time able to afford transport when previously he had been content and compelled to walk, took a coach so that he should show up at the Red Horse "well known to Geoffrey Crayon" as a preliminary to a visit to the haunts of Shakespeare. A few years earlier Margaret Fuller had entered Stratford with the same dual purpose. She saw the Shakespearean relics but, "At Stratford I handled, too, the poker used to such good purpose by Geoffrey Crayon. The muse had fled, the fire was out, and the poker rusty, yet a pleasant influence lingered . . ."[4]

The high minded had their work cut out nonetheless. Henry James forbore to speak of Shakespeare directly but in his essays on Warwickshire, he was led to the rueful comment that "with regard to most romantic sites in England, there is a constant Cockneyfication with which you must make your account. There are always people on the field before you, and there is generally something being drunk on the premises." If a man were determined enough he could block the cockney out and Bayard Taylor was rugged enough to do so. "Thank God," he prayed at Shakespeare's grave, "that in this irreverent age, there are still some spots too holy to profane, some memories too grand and glorious to neglect! I could have knelt and kissed the dusty slab, had I been alone. The profound sadness ith which the spot oppressed me, was one of those emotions against which the world soon hardens us."[5] But even in this pious expression, there was an admission that Taylor was not alone. No one ever seemed to be alone at Stratford.

And not every tourist had the sensibility of a Bayard Taylor or a Margaret Fuller. America sent her coarse as well as her fine spirits. The comic writer Charles Browne introduced such a one in the figure of his dialect character and *alter-ego*, Artemus Ward, whom he sent on the track of Washington Irving in 1867. The fourth letter that Artemus sent home to his eager readers, he called, "At the Tomb of Shakspeare." Like the sensitive American, Artemus had planned ahead: "I told my wife Betsy when I left home that I should go to the birthplace of the orthur of Otheller and other Plays." His account of his trip combined hyperbolic ignorance, mawkish sentiment and cynical cunning. The satire consistently struck in two directions, at the low cheating of the exploitive Briton who ran the town and the fatuous posturing of the American tourist who did not know why he was there or what he should feel. Part of the humour was based on the fact that the famous poet required some kind of identification for the hometown readership – "William Shakspeare was born in Stratford in 1564 . . . . [He] attended the Grammer School, because, as he said, the Grammer School would not attend him . . . He subsequently wrote *Hamlet* and *George Barnwell*." This facetious conflation of dramatic talents demonstrated both the ignorant confusion of the likes of Artemus Ward and pointed at the same time to the generic-mythic role of Shakespeare the Bard, representative of all playwrights, responsible for all plays. Charles Browne may have been exaggerating hometown ignorance, and then again perhaps not. Ellen Kean, on tour with her husband Charles in the United States, wrote indignantly home following a Shakespeare production in Oregon in 1864 – "Imagine the editor of the Portland paper in his critique upon us remarking that reverence for Shakespeare was so great among the English that they made pilgrimages to 'Abbotsford' to gaze on his residence."[6]

The grave of Shakespeare was especially the place for the literary meditation, where the writer gently contemplated the Bard's (and his own) mortality. Artemus Ward stood like Washington Irving, A. Cleveland Coxe, like Bayard Taylor and reflected on the mortal remains of the man he called "William W. Shakspeare." But when he took leave of the churchyard, he discovered that he had been standing in front of the wrong grave – his pious sentiments had, as it were, been addressed to the wrong body. Artemus Ward pursued the boy who had misdirected him, but the young rascal merely "larfed and put the shillin I'd given him into his left eye in a inglorious manner." The boy's trick was typical of the base commercialism of the local inhabitants making every penny out of the poet's memory. But the scene, evoked by Charles Browne, directed its satire more painfully at the American citizen, shiftless and ignorant and acting out a ritual of national appropriation of the Bard that he little understood. Browne's satire did not exclude the sentimental American whose *Sketch-Book* had sent so many compatriots to spend their time and money in pursuit of emotional and literary sensations they were ill-equipped to experience. After his frustrating time in the graveyard, Artemus Ward decided to give up the literary business for the day:

I returned to the hotel. Meetin a young married couple, they asked me if I could direct them to the hotel which Washington Irving used to keep?

"I've understood that he was onsuccessful as a lan'lord," said the lady.

"We've understood," said the young man, "that he busted up."

I told 'em I was a stranger, and hurried away. They were from my country, and ondoubtedly represented a thrifty Ile well somewhere in Pennsylvany.

Stratford could be disgusting and it got worse as the century got older. In 1902, William James wrote from his brother's house in Rye to his friend Charles Eliot Norton in Boston:

The absolute extermination and obliteration of every record of Shakespeare save a few sordid material details, and the general suggestion of narrowness and niggardliness which ancient Stratford makes, taken in comparison with the way in which the spiritual quantity "Shakespeare" has mingled into the soul of the world, was most uncanny, and I feel ready to believe in almost any mystical story of authorship. In fact a visit to Stratford now seems to me the strongest appeal a Baconian can make.[7]

The Stratford mixture could become so gelatinous that it is tempting to end with William James's dyspeptic dismissal of the whole phenomenon and retire quietly to the Strand to meditate on the birthplace of Francis Bacon. But the disgust of the intellectual and the fastidious was not the typical Stratford note. That was struck by the middle-century, middle-class, middle-aged American traveller of religious disposition. In 1850 the Reverend Henry Ward Beecher and in 1853 his sister, Harriet Beecher Stowe, rose to the occasion of Stratford effortlessly, fulfilling their own and their readers' expectations as if by prescription. The brother and sister provided model literary and sentimental responses to Stratford. Washington Irving's mixture of wry amusement and bachelor reverie was simplified to an attitude of pious reverence, interrupted only by brief outbursts of indignation at the enormities of commercial exploitation. These were treated as simonious, as if they were not merely vulgar but actually blasphemous.

"No more Puritan mind than Mrs. Stowe's ever contributed to the literature of New England," says Vernon Parrington, "Daughter of a minister and wife of a minister with brothers and sons ministers, she lived all her life in an atmosphere of religion." William Shakespeare's birthplace was in Oliver Wendell Holmes's phrase "the Santa Casa of England" and it required a holy child to inhabit it. To the fanciful creation of such a being many bent their imaginations and Harriet Beecher Stowe's efforts to this end deserve some kind of commendation. In *Sunny Memories of Foreign Lands* she faced her problem with determination. She was troubled by William Shakespeare's will. The business of the second-best bed seemed unfeeling and unseemly. More to the point, Harriet Beecher Stowe was made uneasy by the report of Shakespeare's character which the inhabitants of Stratford seemed proud to promote as that of a profligate and a poacher. The anomaly of presenting Shakespeare the Stratford-man as a model of Christian behaviour troubled her because she could find little of an explicitly religious nature in either his conduct or his writing. When she had visited the home of her beloved Sir Walter Scott, she had been faced with a similar dilemma. She resolved her problem in Stratford as she had resolved her problem at Abbotsford. She decided that Shakespeare, like Scott, was a man of religious temperament at bottom, despite the secular surface. "No man," she declared, "could have a clearer perception of God's authority and man's duty."[8] Shakespeare the man raised serious

16. Harriet Beecher Stowe

problems nonetheless. Shakespeare the boy was more susceptible to pious suggestion.

Harriet Beecher Stowe filled the Santa Casa with a Holy Family, of which William was the divine child. Her lively imagination excited, Mrs Stowe found herself beset with images of Shakespeare's childhood wherever she went in Stratford: "All these things I seemed to perceive as if a sort of vision had radiated from the old walls." And what the visions revealed to her was remarkable. She saw a curly headed boy and with him a gentle and lovely woman. In a crude age in which Queen Elizabeth herself enjoyed the impurities of *The Merry Wives of Windsor*, Harriet Beecher Stowe had to ask herself where the curly headed little boy found that image of feminine purity such as he modelled in Desdemona. It could only have been his mother – "I saw a vision of a lovely face which was the first beauty that dawned in those childish eyes." Her brother did not look to Shakespeare's mother for the image of feminine beauty but went in more sprightly fashion to Shottery and the features of Anne Hathaway for his model. He ventured to picture her for himself, "Well, I imagine that Anne was a little below the medium hight, delicately formed and shaped . . . This is my Anne Hathaway."Mrs Stowe held fast to her mother image and complemented it by one of a father to match – "I seem, too," she wrote, "to have a kind of perception of Shakespeare's father; a quiet, God-fearing, thoughtful man, given to the reading of good books, avoiding quarrels with a most Christian-like fear."[9] What history did not know about John Shakespeare, glover and skin curer of Henley Street, Stratford, Mrs Stowe would supply.

On the evening of the day in which the birthplace of William Shakespeare had inspired these visions, Mrs Stowe learned from a member of her party Mr Joseph Sturge, the Quaker from Birmingham, that there was no certainty that the house in which she had been so inspired was the right house. With very good humour she accepted the possibility, but authenticity of sensation was not to be denied by historical contingency. As the Santa Casa of Loreto had been translated by angels from Nazareth to a laurel wood in Italy (with a stopover in Dalmatia) that it might be preserved from the Turk, so Harriet Beecher Stowe was translating the sacred house of Shakespeare so that it might become an object worthy of New England worship and to preserve it from Puritan contempt. Of the home of the Holy Family at Loreto, the encyclopaedia gravely states, "St. Luke is alleged to have been its sculptor; its workmanship suggests the latter half of the 15th century."[10] This delicate questioning of legend should not trouble the faithful and Mr Sturge's questioning of Mrs Stowe did not trouble her.

Surrounded by her minister relatives, Harriet Beecher Stowe led an exemplary life as daughter, wife, and mother. Her brother's life was less unsullied. His involvement with a Mrs Theodore Tilton in his last years as minister to the Plymouth Congregational Church of Brooklyn led to trial and retrial by civil and ecclesiastical bodies. Though the Reverend Beecher was never found guilty of gross immorality, he was deemed to have acted unwisely. He spent $118,000 in his own defence.[11] Notwithstanding, the brother was as deeply imbued with the religious spirit as the sister and with a correspondingly sensitive response to English impressions. Indeed they seemed at times to possess the mental equivalent of a

17. The Ruins of Kenilworth Castle

"When they rose up before me I found myself trembling, I know not why." (Henry Ward Beecher)

movie-camera so lively were their historical reconstructions and dramatic imaginings.

The first of Henry Ward Beecher's "Letters from Europe" (published in 1855) described his visit to Kenilworth, Warwick and Stratford – "Kenilworth, Warwick, and Stratford-on-Avon, all in one day! Then I am to spend the Sabbath here! I can neither eat nor sleep for excitement. If my journey shall all prove like this, it will be a severer taxation to recruit than to stay at home and labor."[12] Beecher was in England to recuperate from his efforts in Brooklyn where he had become not only the city's leading preacher but America's. Beecher practised the same popular extroversion of internal emotional experience in his travel writing as he did in his sermons. The letters from Kenilworth, Warwick and Stratford were a standard of the romantic, literary travelogue set in midmost England but with a particularly acute description of heightened psychological conditions. In his own rather overblown way he anticipated Henry James. Beecher showed the same talent for the public display of private emotion that was evident in the writing of his fellow minister-travellers. He was able, eager, indeed, to weep in print. The American maxim that it is a terrible thing to see a grown man cry does not apply to a man of God.

Beecher told his readers that he had expected no great enjoyment from Kenilworth because such enjoyment "requires a store of historical associations; and much of the sentiment of veneration; or else a lively relish for antiquarian lore; none of which have I." But the playing down of the scene only served to make the emotional climax more intense when he actually came to the ruins of Kenilworth Castle –

> I was close upon them before I saw them. When they rose up before me I found myself trembling, I know not why. I could not help tears coming. I had never in my life seen an old building. I had never seen a ruin. Here, for the first time in my life, I felt the presence of a venerable ruined castle.

Beecher's latent preparedness for the castle took him by surprise. He discovered that he had, through his reading of Scott and his knowledge of English history, a readiness for the new experience presented by the ancient castle that kept him dreaming in the ruined rooms and at the broken windows for full three hours – "as I sat in a room, upon a fallen stone, one incident after another from the novel, and from history, came to me, one name after another, until I seemed to be visiting an old and familiar place."[13]

The sensations induced by Kenilworth were but a prelude to those produced by Warwick Castle, when in the middle of his eventful day, Henry Ward Beecher moved on to see the second of the great scenes of midmost England. The intensity of his excitement was such that he experienced a kind of mystical union with a historical, a visionary landscape. It was a sensation that recalled the root meaning of the word *ecstasy*, and an experience that Beecher described with some clarity:

18. Warwick Castle

When we came fairly into the courtyard of the castle, a scene of magnificent beauty opened before us. I cannot describe it minutely. The principal features are the battlements, towers, and turrets of the old feudal castle, encompassed by grounds on which has been expended all that princely art of landscape gardening for which England is famous – leafy thickets, magnificent trees, openings, and vistas of verdure, and wide sweeps of grass, short, thick, and vividly green, as the velvet moss we sometimes see growing on rocks in New England. Grass is an art and a science in England – it is an institution. (Harriet Beecher Stowe)

My mind was so highly excited as to be perfectly calm, and apparently it perceived by an intuition. I seemed to spread myself over all that was around or before me, while in the court and on the walls, or rather to draw everything within me. I fear that I seem crazy to you. It was, however, the calmness of intense excitement.[14]

This simultaneous intuition of the psyche, as it at once filled the landscape and drew the landscape within, externalising the self and internalising the world, was a class of experience that found its analogies more easily in religious and mystical writing than in ordinary descriptive prose.

The annihilation of the sense of space achieved either through the expansion of self to fill the landscape, or through the absorption of the landscape into the self, was accompanied by a recreation of time and with it the experience of two kinds of past: the historical past covering a thousand years back to the heroic age and the personal past reaching back deep into the recesses of childhood –

I stood for a little, and let the vision pierce me through. Who can *tell* what he feels in such a place! How, especially, can I tell *you* – who have never seen, or felt, such a view any more than I before this time! Primeval forests, the oceans, prairies, Niagara, I had seen and felt. But never had I seen any pile around which were historic associations, blended not only with heroic men and deeds but savouring of my own childhood.

The little one and two inch drawings of his picture books had now risen up into great walls hundreds of feet long: "It was a historic dream breaking forth into waking reality." On the walls of Warwick Castle, Henry Ward Beecher found himself projected back to a time before the English language was formed, a time before modern civilisation was fashioned – "I stood, in imagination, and reversing my vision, looked down into a far future to search for the men and deeds which had been as if they were yet to be; thus making a prophecy of history; and changing memory into a dreamy foresight."[15] The historical perspective had given Beecher a dizzying vantage point; his post on top of the walls of Warwick Castle had given him a vertiginous delirium. Henry Ward Beecher wrote the first of his "Letters from Europe" in the room where Shakespeare was born and he wrote it, he said, on notepaper that depicted the very scene. His attempts to capture the evanescent moment and to increase for himself and his readership the authenticity of his fantasy were like those of Frederick Law Olmsted who had only a few months before been thumping the table in Chester, writing at an old desk, in an old chair, in an old room, in an old tavern, in an old city, in an old world.

Beecher's second letter from Europe was dated 4 August 1850 and he entitled it "A Sabbath at Stratford-on-Avon." He planned his first full day in Stratford (he had arrived the night before from Warwick) to include morning service in the church, afternoon service at Shottery, and evening service at the Holy Cross Church. Like Olmsted, he was going to make a great deal of his first sabbath in England. He was also making a religious matter out of a pilgrimage that might otherwise have had a distinctly secular flavour, and indeed would have been frankly disapproved of by Beecher's Puritan forefathers. There were some paradoxes involved in the nineteenth-century New Englander's celebration of William Shakespeare as their national poet; and they only fully laid claim to him some time after the Germans had begun to refer to him as *unser Shakespeare*. There was little evidence of interest in Shakespeare in seventeenth-century America: "There is no record suggesting that a copy of his work was included in any New England book collection" for that period. And though editions became widespread in the eighteenth century, the Boston sheriff came on stage himself in 1792 to close down a theatre that had opened with performances of *Hamlet* and *Richard III*. Moral opposition to playing, players, and playwrights continued into the nineteenth century (though it was less intense, but far from non-existent in New York and the South).[16] But Shakespeare the poet was exempt from much of this censure because he was considered a moralist, and it was for every virtue but the dramatic that he was first praised by American commentators. It was as a high-minded seer that he entered the curricula of the New England schools and the parlours of New England homes. He was valued for his poetry and for his characterisations, as a poet and novelist, so to speak, not as a playwright. The popularity of terms like those of "the Bard" and "the Swan of Avon" reflected the emphasis of the prophetic–poetic and played down the theatrical–dramatic. His name was linked by travellers to Stratford with those of poets. Milton was his usual companion, sometimes Spenser; very rarely were other playwrights named with him. He was known from the study not from the stage.

By planning for himself on Sunday, 4 August 1850, a full day's church-going, Henry Ward Beecher satisfied his own conscience, fulfilled the expectations of his congregation, and co-opted the spirit of William Shakespeare into the evangelical mode. The memory of the Bard was honoured by visitation to the temple not the theatre. So it was with good cheer that Beecher wrote, "As I sallied forth to church, I seemed not to have a body. I could hardly feel my feet striking against the ground; it was as if I were numb. But my soul was clear, penetrating, and exquisitely susceptible." He delighted in the suggestions of Stratford and of Shakespeare; he delighted in the children and the good people walking to the service; he delighted in the interior of the stately and beautiful church; he was moved by the well-known bust of Shakespeare and the knowledge that the dust of the poet was under the pavement. In Stratford Church, Henry Ward Beecher heard the service that had been his mother's form of worship. She had been an Episcopalian. The Godhead, Shakespeare, his mother, Stratford, Old England, and his childhood fused and another American was elevated by the transcendental, transatlantic experience:

> I cannot tell you how much I was affected. I had never had such a trance of worship, and I shall never have such another view until I gain the Gate . . . I was dissolved . . . wafted gratefully toward God . . . My soul, then thou didst magnify the Lord . . . I had risen, it seemed to me, so high. . . . O, that swell and solemn cadence . . . I trembled . . . There was a moment in which the heavens seemed opened to me, and I saw the glory of God!

This ecstasy was created by literary memory, religious excitation, and the physical scene. Description of this scene was not the purpose of the travel letter: "I am not describing anything to you as *it* was," wrote Beecher, "but am describing myself while in the presence of scenes with which through books you are familiar."[17] The sensations that he had experienced in Warwick, where tiny engravings had become hundred-foot walls, the sensation of stepping into the illustrations of childhood books and into the pages of history, were repeated again in Trinity Church. Like Alice, the traveller passed into the wonderland that lies on the other side of the mirror of common sense.

The sermon that followed the opening prayers and readings did not meet with Beecher's full commendation; he approved but with reservations. It was seldom that an American did truly enjoy English preaching. But Beecher's act of communion restored the exulted

19. The Church, Stratford-upon-Avon

The church has been carefully restored inside, so that it is now in excellent preservation, and Shakspeare lies buried under a broad, flat stone in the chancel. I had full often read, and knew by heart, the inscription on this stone; but somehow, when I came and stood over it, and read it, it affected me as if there were an emanation from the grave beneath. I have often wondered at that inscription, that a mind so sensitive, that had thought so much, and expressed thought with such startling power on all the mysteries of death, the grave, and the future world, should have found nothing else to inscribe on his own grave but this: –

Good Friend for Iesus SAKE forbare
To diGG T–E Dust EncloAsed HERe
Blese be T–E Man $\overset{T}{Y}$ spares T–Es Stones
And curst be he $\overset{T}{Y}$ moves my Bones

(Harriet Beecher Stowe)

mood that had possessed him before the sermon. It was the first time that he had ever received the sacrament in the order of his mother's church and it happened that he actually knelt with the dust of Shakespeare beneath his knees when he received the consecrated elements. "I thought of it, as I thought of ten thousand things, without the least disturbance of devotion. It seemed as if I stood upon a place so high, that, like one looking over a wide valley, all objects conspired to make but one view."[18]

In religious terms the day had begun well and it was not entirely the Reverend Beecher's fault if the rest of it did not go as planned. When he walked out to Shottery for afternoon service, he discovered that Shottery had neither service nor church and he returned to Stratford only to be in time to miss the Holy Cross evening service. But the sabbath had not been wasted or misspent. By a resolute act of will and imagination, Beecher had involved Shakespeare in the rituals of religion; Beecher had justified his worship of Shakespeare in religious terms. Thirty-five years before, Washington Irving had gone to Stratford on a poetical pilgrimage; in 1850 Henry Ward Beecher gave a literal meaning to that image. Stratford was made into a Holy Land. Beecher's final justification of his journey was to tell his readers that salvation will bring a time in which God will be as evident and sensible in the universe as Shakespeare is felt in every corner of Stratford. William Shakespeare had a Real Presence.

On Monday, 5 August 1850, Henry Ward Beecher left Stratford by the Oxford coach, sitting on top the better to enjoy the beauties of Warwickshire. The mood of the Shakespearean sabbath was still upon him and he departed in a state of terrible clerical glee – "To be sure, I maintained a grave and reserved exterior, all the way; but my heart laughed and sung at every step."[19] His holiday was doing him good. Henry Ward Beecher's Puritan ancestors had come to Massachusetts in 1637 to live in a land unpolluted by the godlessness of playwrights, to set up the city on the hill that would be above worldly pleasures. The journey of their descendant to Stratford showed that the rehabilitation of William Shakespeare in the iconography of the New England religious imagination had gone a long way. The impulse of Americans who made a religious poet out of Shakespeare was not at the bottom so very different from that of the sceptical American like William James who turned away from

20. Henry Ward Beecher

the cockneyfication of Stratford in disgust and felt the urge to take up the cause of that eccentric New Englander, Delia Bacon. She proposed her namesake in place of the man known as William Shakespeare, a rank imposter, a butcher or a glover or whatever, whose line of business was in no way to be contradicted by the narrow, provincial place in which he had lived. But for the relentless fact-finding of twentieth-century American scholars the figure of William Shakespeare must long ago have disappeared behind the relentless projections of nineteenth-century American travellers.

6

WESTMINSTER ABBEY: THE GREAT VALHALLA BY THE THAMES

"England," a land in the heart's geography, had a movable centre. The "real thing" might be round any corner but it would not, if found there, remain long. The American traveller was in a state of unending quest – his Grail moved before him. If he did not find it at Stratford he moved on. But even if he did find it at Stratford, he moved on anyway because the apprehension was evanescent. Like all higher sensations it was liable to fly from the habitual and the familiar. And though the "real thing" was so frequently found in English country lanes and English village greens, there was at least one great city that could make a powerful claim to being some kind of "real thing" – and that city was London.

For the nineteenth-century American London was the centre of the world; its identification as the heart of England was contingent upon this. The narrator of Henry James's story, "A Passionate Pilgrim", put the sentimental case as strongly as it would bear statement:

> We felt to excellent purpose the sombre charm of London, the mighty mother-city of our mighty race, the great distributing heart of our traditional life. Certain London characteristics – monuments, relics, hints of history, local moods and memories – are more deeply suggestive to the American soul than anything else in Europe.[1]

London always impressed Americans forcefully though not always so positively. A very strange and very holy Methodist missionary–preacher who came to England to convert the British to Christianity at the beginning of the nineteenth century found London the very type of that against which he would warn the world – "Surely London is more like the city of Babylon than any other city, to fill the world with her merchandise, and answers better to that mentioned in Revelation than any other." The denunciation established the fact of London's importance in this apocalyptic vision and showed how, in his own way, the Reverend Lorenzo Dow had allowed London to supplant the city of Rome which traditionally was entitled to the designation of Babylon in fundamentalist rhetoric. If its luxury and sin entitled Protestant London to comparison with Catholic Rome, its wealth and its power excited comparison with Imperial Rome. Wandering through Wapping and the Isle of Dogs in 1805, Benjamin Silliman was moved by the West India Docks to believe that "such magnificent proofs of commercial prosperity the world has never seen before." And back in the City proper, he had climbed to the top of the Monument and felt the extent of London as only the visual picture could convey it – "it is indeed a vast city; it is a world. – Southwark alone would make a great figure if placed by itself, but connected with London, it is only the hem of the garment."[2]

This vast city was spectacular in every way. Its fabulous wealth lay piled in heaps in its shop windows inciting admiration and awe, if not actual purchase. At the beginning of 1818, Richard Rush strolled from his office at the American Legation where he was Minister and did some window shopping in Ludgate Hill. In Rundell and Bridge, Silversmiths, he saw a display of dinner services costing between £30, and £50,000; a candelabra was going for £1,400 and a dress sword for 4,000 guineas. He stepped inside and found the assistants most civil, giving thanks for the purchase of "a pin for a few shillings."[3] Rush was just as impressed by the fact that though London was able to offer for sale goods of all descriptions, kinds and qualities, everything was of home manufacture; the merchandise was not, that is, as in America, imported.

It was not only the size and the wealth of London that excited visitors. Its growth was even more intoxicating – it was expanding at the rate of an American boom town. Another Methodist visitor to London, Wilbur Fisk (a man more orthodox than Lorenzo Dow) wrote of the London of 1835 that "everybody feels, when travelling over London, that it is, 'too big,' and yet when its growth will stop cannot be forseen."[4] It was generally agreed that its size was already unfavourable to piety (but that was a sentiment at least as old as William Langland and no doubt a great deal older).

London was the modern-day Rome and the idea was again put most effectively by Henry James speaking through the voice of a Roman, the Prince Amerigo, the betrothed of an American industrialist's daughter.

The Prince had always liked his London, when it had come to him; he was one of the modern Romans who find by the Thames a more convincing image of the truth of the ancient state than any they have left by the Tiber. Brought up on the legend of the City to which the whole world paid tribute, he recognized in the present London much more than in contemporary Rome the real dimensions of such a case. If it was a question of an *Imperium*, he said to himself, and if one wished, as a Roman, to recover a little the sense of that, the place to do so was on London Bridge, or even, on a fine afternoon in May, at Hyde Park Corner.[5]

London could as adequately suggest to the travelling American as it could to the fictional Roman the sense of an Imperium passed on from the ancient Roman to the modern British empire. For this reason, London did not always suggest England, the "real" England that is, discovered by Olmsted in Cheshire, or Coxe in Kent, or Beecher in Warwickshire. But the world's great capital had its own centres of intensity and one such was Westminster Abbey. The Abbey proved itself able more frequently than other places to excite the Romantic response – "How then did my heart warm," said Geoffrey Crayon in *Bracebridge Hall*, "when the towers of Westminster Abbey were pointed out to me . . . this great mausoleum of what is most illustrious in our paternal history."[6]

The kind of sentiment that the Abbey excited in some travellers was scarcely different in kind from that generally excited by the sense of London as the world's centre. The greatness of England was then the main theme of these Westminster meditations. The black man William Wells Brown gave full vent to this in his reflections on the building:

The warm panegyrics that have been lavished on [England's] constitution and laws, the songs chanted to celebrate her glory, the lustre of her arms, as the glowing theme of her warriors, the thunder of her artillery in proclaiming her moral powers, her flag being unfurled to every breeze and ocean, rolling to her shores the tribute of a thousand realms, show England to be the greatest nation in the world.[7]

Brown was a liberated slave and his identification with England was part of his rejection of America. Nonetheless the rhetorical formulas that he found to express his admiration and affection for England were remarkably similar to those of other Americans who wanted close identification with England. William Brown's reflections in Westminster Abbey might easily have been those of A. Cleveland

Coxe (had Coxe felt at ease in the Abbey which in the event he did not) or of Harriet Beecher Stowe.

On the other hand, the Abbey could work its magic on the most ardent Anglophobe. David Locke believed London to be the heart of a grand system of plunder, and he nursed a real dislike of the British, but he could not deny some measure of admiration for the Abbey. Once there he dropped his usual facetious, often bantering tone and wrote – "The wandering about among the tombs of so many illustrious dead, and the reading of so many fulsome epitaphs – albeit I know they were not altogether deserved – produced an impression, a feeling of solemnity, that no other one place in all England could conjure up."[8]

The panegyrics on England were of course something more than that. contained in these apparently humble exultations of another nation and another people was a distinct pride in the American share in the glories of that nation and people. Westminster Abbey was not merely a monumental testimony to English greatness. William Wells Brown's expression of this pride took no account of the American share in it perhaps but the white American in Westminster Abbey renewed his pride in his own people. He believed that the United States were destined to be, if not that they were already, the greatest nation on the face of the earth. It was a measure of America's greatness that she would be greater than the country reflected in the grandeur of this ancient place. This dual experience of identification and distinctiveness exulted the American in Westminster Abbey. It gave a triumphant sense of achievement and expectation both to those who loved and to those who disliked the English. It enabled the American as self-consciously aware of his intense ambivalence as Nathaniel Hawthorne to write in his notebook in September 1855 –

> And how glad I am that England has such a church, its walls incrusted with the fame of her dead worthies, ever since she was a nation – their great deeds, and their beautiful deeds, crystallizing there – turning to marble there. An American has a right to be proud of Westminster Abbey; for most of the men, who sleep in it, are our great men, as well as theirs.[9]

A posthumous grant of citizenship had been made to William Shakespeare by the New World pilgrims to Stratford; a retrospective act of annexation was made upon the royal Abbey by the citizens from the land where every man was a sovereign.

In January 1877 John Lathrop Motley's daughter Lily was married to Sir William Harcourt, M.P., in Westminster Abbey. Dean Stanley officiated. The ceremony took place in Henry VIII's chapel. There were few guests but it was a solemn occasion and the great American historian allowed himself a moment of historical awe. He permitted himself to be deeply touched, a sentiment that his professional activity usually caused him to disdain. He gave his old friend Dr Oliver Wendell Holmes in Boston a full and well-satisfied description of the event.

The party [he wrote] stood on the slab covering Edward VI's tomb, and at the Dean's back was the monument in which James I had his bones placed along with those of Henry VII . . . The tombs of Mary Queen of Scots and of Elizabeth were on either side . . . one could hardly realize amid all this ancient dust and ashes that a modern commonplace marriage was going on.[10]

The couple honeymooned at Strawberry Hill, a property of Lady Waldegrave, Harcourt's aunt. Harcourt was himself in the fullness of time to become Lord Reay.

The union was not exactly commonplace and Motley was doubtless very pleased with the response that Holmes sent him some weeks later:

The account of your daughter's wedding was like a passage from a stately drama. It was, *is*, I ought to say, enough to thrill any American to his marrow, to read of those whom he has known so long and well . . . enacting one of the great scenes of this mortal life in the midst of such shadows, treading over such dust in an atmosphere of historic immortality.[11]

Oliver Wendell Holmes pitied any American who could not be so kindled.

When many years before, in 1834, Holmes had been a medical student in Paris, he had been a little more phlegmatic about the attractions of Westminster Abbey. He had written home a stenographic, all but derogatory note on the place: "*Westminster Abbey.* A great gothic church, not half as handsome as Notre Dame outside, but finer in the interior. – the gothic arches, remarkably narrow, – fine monuments, – Poet's Corner – 1s. 3d. to pay, etc. See all tourists." The letter of 1877 showed how the memory of the Abbey and years of reading in English poets and novelists, which distinguished his years at Harvard as much as his professorship of anatomy and physiology, had made Holmes more responsive to the associative riches of Edward the Confessor's foundation. When in 1886 Holmes made the longed-for second journey to Europe and again visited the Abbey, and again visited Poets' Corner, he was moved to find there a face that he recognised, that of his old friend Henry Wadsworth Longfellow, the first American poet to be so honoured. Could there be an American who did not feel, Holmes wrote, "a thrill of pleasure at recognising the features of his native fellow-countryman in the Valhalla of his ancestral fellow-countrymen."[12]

Poets' Corner lay at the centre of intensities. And the monument to Longfellow gratified the pride of the American at the end of the century in a way unimaginable at the beginning, unimaginable when Oliver Wendell Holmes had paid his entrance fee in 1834. In 1886, he was not obliged to pay at all because Archdeacon Farrar was his guide and there was no carping, this time, at the fact that Poets' Corner was the hackneyed theme of "all tourists." Holmes now relished the sense of community, of shared and inherited emotion that the very fact of its popularity implied – "I think no part of the Abbey is visited with so much interest as Poets' Corner. We are all familiarly acquainted with it beforehand."[13]

For the nineteenth-century transatlantic visitor, Poets' Corner provided just that concentration of association, that substance of presence, that massing of effect and that familiarity of detail necessary to make real the literature of his childhood. The American found himself surrounded by beloved poets and much-imitated essayists. A. Cleveland Coxe was pleased to see the memorials to Chaucer and Jonson and even more deeply moved by "that of the stainless Spenser." Bayard Taylor's excitement betrayed him into various inaccuracies and misunderstandings, but he betrayed no uncertainty that he was coming upon the real England:

> On entering the first thing that met my eyes were the words "OH RARE BEN JONSON," under his bust . . . the sublime countenance of Milton. Never was a spot so full of intense interest . . . Every step called up some mind linked with the associations of my childhood . . . I paused long before the ashes of Shakespeare . . . What a glorious galaxy of genius is here collected.

Taylor could probably have told himself, had he been so minded, that Shakespeare's ashes were not in Westminster Abbey, that his body was buried in Stratford (to which place Taylor was in time to pay a most reverential visit) but the romantic misapprehensions caught the main idea well enough. Like Stratford, Poets' Corner excited a special sense of Anglo-American identity. It appealed in terms of the shared language. "A place so sacred to all who inherited the English tongue," as Taylor said, "is worthy of a special pilgrimage across the Atlantic."[14]

It was apparently not easy for an American *not* to respond to Poets' Corner. James Fenimore Cooper had not expected a great deal of Westminster Abbey when he visited in 1828. He warned the recipient of his Letter IV from England that he was not going to entertain him "with many cockney descriptions of 'sights'" among which he counted the Abbey. But though he had several architectural criticisms to make of the building, he found himself startled and moved by Poets' Corner. The combination of historical association and childhood impression worked irresistibly in the transatlantic spirit so that even the most hostile was subdued: "As we sat there looking over the Poets' Corner," wrote David Locke, "the deep silence of the majestic building, growing more and more profound, there came trooping through the mind constantly changing pictures suggested by the memories awakened by the vivid recollections of the once great in literature and art, science and warfare, who are still alive in the hearts of the English-speaking people."[15] He saw, placed on the grave of Charles Dickens then dead eleven years, a bouquet of fresh flowers. He learned that an unknown hand renewed it every day. It was a gesture that disarmed criticism.

Poets' Corner gave the American traveller the sense that he had found the still point at the centre of the world. But to achieve this release from the everyday world and to achieve the transcendent state of ecstatic union with "England" in the middle of the noisiest and most populous city in the world seemed a miracle of a very special order. Nathaniel Hawthorne found Westminster Abbey and St Paul's Cathedral the two most impressive places in all London for the very reason that they created their special order out of so great a chaos. The seclusion and coolness of St Paul's gave him in the hot

21. Nathaniel Hawthorne

August of 1856 an appreciation of what the Puritans had rejected – "oh that we had Cathedrals in America, were it only for this sensuous luxury." Hawthorne returned to St Paul's and to Westminster Abbey in his walks and in his notebooks repeatedly. His first visits were made on his first journey to London in 1855 and he can be seen in his notebook record to grow gradually in his appreciation of these great buildings and in particular of Poets' Corner. He wrote of his first visit with an easy familiarity – "It is a very delightful feeling to find yourself at once among [the poets]; – the consciousness (mingled with a pleasant awe) of kind and friendly presences, who are anything but strangers to you." But in 1855 he was not so awed that he did not think the thing had been rather overdone. Poets' Corner did not need to be quite so crowded as it had been made. He estimated that the poets who really meant anything could be placed comfortably along one side of the transept. But in the two years that followed Hawthorne learned something about the sympathies of the

Abbey and its power to harmonise its own disparate elements. His last visit on Sunday, 27 December 1857 (only a few days before he left for Italy) revealed a rather different response to the crowded aisles and chapels: "On the whole, I should be sorry to spare one of all these marbles; and the grandeur of the Abbey is quite capable of swallowing up all these absurd individualities, whenever it is desirable to overlook them."[16]

This attachment had developed over time and even in the month following his very first visit, Hawthorne's response to the Abbey began to develop. His willingness to allow time to make changes in him, his compulsive descriptions of places already described, give the *Notebooks* an unusual value. After his third visit to Poets' Corner in that month of September, 1855, he wrote, "Poets' Corner has never seemed like a strange place to me; it has been familiar from the very first; – at all events, I cannot now recollect the previous conception of which reality has taken the place. I seem always to have known that somewhat dim corner."[17] It was a familiar restatement of the theme of familiarity, but one made with a delicate new emphasis.

It provided the theme of his account of Poets' Corner in his written-up travel book, *Our Old Home*, where he told his readers, "it seemed to me that I had always been familiar with the spot." Hawthorne made his description of the Abbey an occasion, one taken by many Americans before and since, to write an essay about Poetry, Kingship, Fame and Time. These ancient kings had ruled a legendary land known from childhood through the descriptions of these venerable poets. Hawthorne also took occasion to tell, teach might be a better word, his readers something about the special quality of Gothic architecture, "for there is nothing in this world so fascinating as a Gothic minster, which always invites you deeper and deeper into its heart both by vast revelations and shadowy concealments." He taught them, as the building had taught him, not to allow first judgements (not only uninformed but often enough insensitive) to inhibit response to these great structures. What he had learnt by December 1857 he passed on to his readers. The Abbey melted all the allegorical absurdities in marble and all signs of decay in its own fabric "into the breadth of its own grandeur." It took Hawthorne time to realise how beautiful was Westminster Abbey, time to develop within its walls a full sensibility of its medieval beauty. "The heart aches, as one gazes at it," he wrote of Westminster Abbey in 1856, "for lack of power and breadth enough to take its beauty and grandeur in." This admission of a limited response was itself proof of how far the cathedrals had brought his Puritan spirit. The chronicle of his *Notebooks* bore out the entry made in October 1855 when Hawthorne had taken to stepping into the Abbey as often as he could – "I think I could never be weary of it; and when I finally leave England, it will be this spot which I shall be most unwilling to quit forever."[18]

The mysterious and evocative power of the Abbey, its capacity to excite the transatlantic imagination prompted Mark Twain to his singular essay, "A Memorable Midnight Experience." Twain went to see the Abbey in 1872 and while he saw all the things that every other tourist saw, he did his sightseeing by night. This gave his description a peculiarly Gothic flavour and he began more in the spirit of an adventurer than of an essayist. A friend "as reliable as he was eccentric," called upon Mark Twain at 11 p.m. one night to take him on an expedition. Twain lost all sense of direction as they passed through London's maze of streets. The greatness of the city and the disorientation of the traveller combined to give the most powerful effect to the building that came at last before him:

> I looked my inquiry.
>
> "It is the tomb of the great dead of England – *Westminster Abbey*."
>
> (One cannot express a start – in words.)

Mark Twain was thereupon handed into the care of a Mr Wright, Superintendent of the Works. Expert, intimate, and idiosyncratic, Mr Wright began at once to initiate Mark Twain.

> "Yonder is where old King Sebert the Saxon lies – his monument is the oldest one in the Abbey; Sebert died in 616 . . . Now yonder is the last one – Charles Dickens – there on the floor with the brass letters in the slab – and to this day the people come and put flowers on it. Why, along at first they almost had to *cart* the flowers out, there were so many."[19]

These same flowers, the same renewed, were there to enchant David Locke nine years later. It was in this fact of continuity, in this continuity with a past that was by the very fact of the Abbey's continuity not a lost past, that the mysterious power of the Abbey lay. This was the mystic core of the secret religion of the Abbey. There in a great church dedicated to the God of the Hebrews, the

22. Westminster Abbey

God of Time was worshipped and the spirits of the dead invoked in obsequies that were something less and something more than Christian. It was rightly described by Holmes as Valhalla, and Henry James rightly repeated the sentiment, calling Westminster the "great Valhalla by the Thames" when he attended the burial of Robert Browning in Poets' Corner in 1890.[20]

The ancient, almost pagan, undercurrent excited the reverence of the unreligious and subdued the enthusiasm of the clergy. A. Cleveland Coxe moved uneasily about the Abbey, not his usual self at all –

> With what refreshment I often turned from the royal tombs to the Poets' Corner; and there, with what reverence did I turn most frequently to the monuments of those whose high artistic inspiration was characterized by the pure spirit of the love to God. It was pleasing to behold the memorials of Chaucer, and of "rare Ben Jonson"; but with a fonder veneration I paused more frequently before that of the stainless Spenser.

The Reverend Wilbur Fisk denied that it was a place of worship at all; "it is rather a monumental temple, consecrated to eminence and genius." He was quite impressed by the funerary monuments of skeletal Death but frankly disgusted by the epitaph written by the facetious poet, John Gay for Gay's own tomb:

> "Life is a jest, and all things show it.
> I thought so once, and now I know it."
>
> Not so – by this time he has doubtless discovered that life is a momentous reality . . . What an imposition upon the living, and what an insult to the dead.

Coxe and Fisk picked their way among the tombs, ill-at-ease and apprehensive. Twain, on his midnight prowl, relished the promiscuity that upset the clerics and entered into the grave humour with delight. Mr Wright told Twain and Twain told his readers that the bodies were so closely packed in the floor of the Abbey that there were three heads which had claim to being that of Ben Jonson: "the bones are awfully matted together." And there was a delicious appreciation of Mr Wright's revelation that among the filled graves of kings, queens, knights, poets, and statesmen, there was an empty one – "'Overlooked, somehow – but,'" said Mr Wright, "'– it is a very nice place indeed, and very comfortable.'"[21]

A palpable, a familiar, a comfortable relation with the dead was what Mr Wright, as much sexton as superintendent, had to offer. What was there for Mark Twain to receive was a relationship with the past so actual that he could reach out and touch it – "on every hand dull shapes of men, sitting, standing, or stooping, inspected us curiously out of the darkness – reached out their hands towards us – some appealing, some beckoning, some warning us away." Links with the line of the great dead were what Twain wanted and what he found in the Abbey. In the royal chapels, said Twain, the American could meet face to face with "the colossal myths of history." Here in the Abbey, time and space created a sanctuary, freed of the limitations imposed by date and world: "We walked up a flight of half a dozen steps and stopping upon a pavement laid down in 1260, stood in the core of English history, as it were – upon the holiest ground in the British Empire, if profusion of kingly bones and kingly names of old renown make holy ground."[22]

As Mark Twain and Mr Wright looked at the tomb of Queen Eleanor, "we saw," said Twain,

> the vast illuminated clock face of the Parliament House tower glowering at us and point with both hands to midnight. It was a derisive reminder that we were part of this present, sordid, plodding, commonplace time, and not august relics of a bygone age and the comrades of kings . . . and with the last stroke the mocking clock face vanished in sudden darkness and left us with the past and its grandeurs again.[23]

The clock – the instrument of measured time, Big Ben –the standard of Imperial time, the clockface – the monitor of thrifty time, these were able to intrude their narrowed reality upon the holy ground and able to return the time-traveller to his point of origin at a stroke. But narrow time could not entirely deny the enriched time of the Abbey, where Time Past existed in pluralities. The curfew bell in Chester had tolled the nineteenth century away for Frederick Law Olmsted. Big Ben tolled it back for Mark Twain but the extinguishing of the clockface on the stroke of twelve acted, miraculously, to restore the palpable illusions of the Abbey's special reality and to dismiss the specious present. "A Memorable Midnight Experience" contrived its effects rather too efficiently. Mark Twain's staging was elaborate indeed. Everything happened exactly to cue; sound effects, lighting, and timing were just right. But staginess is an element of much of the best travel literature. It is the writer's duty to travel to the right place at the right time and Queen Eleanor's tomb at midnight was such a time and place.

Mark Twain used a repressed comic energy to add an element of excitement to his "Memorable Experience" but he did not allow this to disrupt the note of reverence. Even if the traveller in the Abbey was often brought to the verge of outright laughter he was usually restrained by its mysterious power as the American traveller was not restrained by the Tower of London. The idealist mood imposed a strain on the American and the golden veil that he hung between himself and shrine or landscape required a constant effort to keep in place. Like a monk in choir, the traveller was subject to sudden bursts of unexpected levity. These threatened the solemnity of those grave occasions that represented the fulfilment of a lifetime's literary dreaming. Reverence too long sustained could catch the traveller in a backwash of laughter or else in a fit of historical nausea that came as an unhappy reaction to the splendid, the noble, the ancient. As Hawthorne said of the British Museum, "It quite crushes a person to see so much at once."[24]

The crushing sensation of the Museum and the outright laughter in the Tower were an oblique tribute to the grandeur of Westminster Abbey. Neither Museum nor Tower had an overarching beauty to give harmony to the accumulations of the ages. By contrast, though the Abbey's Past was dim, it could be discovered; and as to the form of that Past, it carried a man out of himself. In Museum and Tower, the American found the Past heaped up for its own sake and he was repulsed. In the Abbey, the Past was given a context; it was given rhyme, and with rhyme, reason. The traveller had only to step back and look above him to be raised up from the oppressing or provoking burden of the ages. The Abbey harmonised, crystallised, spiritualised the Past; it provided the frame in which the traveller could learn the habit of aesthetic appreciation.

7

ENGLAND: THE AESTHETIC LANDSCAPE

In March 1869 Henry James wrote to his mother from London to explain why he had as yet shown so little epistolary appreciation of England – appreciation being after all the American strength. "The truth is" he wrote, "that the face of things here throws a sensitive American back on himself – back on his prejudice and national passions, and benumbs for a while the faculty of appreciation and the sense of justice."[1]

It was not the strangeness of the world to which he was a visitor that made James numb. He made this quite clear in his description in *The Middle Years* of his first reactions to English life. The older James wrote of the younger: "I yet felt it in no degree as strange or obscure, baffling or unrecognizing on its own side." Instead he was like a "miraculously" well-prepared guest who needed "no word of explanation before joining in" every topic of conversation. This produced in him a "very ecstasy of understanding." "Really," said the older James, "wherever I looked, and still more wherever I pressed, I sank in and in up to my nose." At this early stage, James believed himself well and truly an insider. Like other Americans before him, he seemed to have felt that he was not only well prepared but better prepared than the English themselves. The paradox of his relationship was, naturally, to be expressed better by no one than by himself: "I knew what everything meant, not simply then but for weeks and months after, and was to know less only with increase of knowledge."[2]

In 1871 James published a short story that he called "A Passionate Pilgrim." It contained an analysis of the phases of the American traveller's response to Europe and it provided an insight into the passivity that had caused James to tell his mother that England benumbed "for a while the faculty of appreciation." The narrator of the story was an unobtrusive American in Europe; unexplained himself, he was filled with the explanations of others; unobserved, he observed. Why he was in England, why he had the leisure and the disposition to take up the cause of an unknown fellow countryman who came his way, the story did not reveal. But the narrator, whatever else he might be, was a man skilled in the psychology of travel, one cunning in his fine discrimination of emotional reaction to the things seen and the things felt. There was no greater proof of this skill than the narrator's analysis of an experience of Hampton Court Green. He and his companion, Mr Clement Searle of New York, had spent the day looking at the royal palace, a place to which every touring American must needs go. They refreshed themselves after their exertions by taking dinner and a bottle of "excellent Burgundy" in a tavern near the palace gate. The scenic effects included evening light, cottage garden, red-brick palace, village green, royal park, ancient church. Wine and landscape combined to move the narrator deeply:

> There is a rare emotion, familiar to every intelligent traveller, in which the mind, with a great passionate throb, achieves a magical synthesis of its impressions. You feel England; you feel Italy. The reflection for the moment has an extraordinary poignancy . . . I had known it from time to time in Italy and had opened my soul to it as to the spirit of the Lord. Since my arrival in England I had been waiting for it to come.

The narrator believed that it might have been the bottle of Burgundy that had unlocked the gates of the senses, but whatever the cause the rare emotion "came now with a conquering tread. Just the scene around me was the England of my visions."[3]

The "rare emotion" was as much spiritual as sensual. And the narrator's experience was the reverse of Proustian. The physical scene was not rendered visionary by the act of time and memory but the visionary scene, the England of the narrator's visions, was rendered actual by the act of space and imagination. It was an act of space because the visionary had had to cross the Atlantic – his travelling conjured the "rare emotion." The opening of the narrator's soul was like that of a mystic "as to the spirit of the Lord." The single bottle of "excellent Burgundy" stood there preserving a gentlemanly restraint, a delicate consciousness of the potentially ridiculous, in a situation that might otherwise become outrageous.

Such a "magical synthesis" of impressions may have been what the sensitive American was awaiting when he wrote home to an expectant family in Boston. This synthesis certainly took place for

Henry James, as for the Pilgrim's narrator, in Italy. In October 1869 Henry James wrote from Rome: "At last – for the first time – I live!" He went to the excess of telling his brother William that he had gone "reeling and moaning thro' the streets in a fever of enjoyment."[4] The first travel sketches to make use of his "great beheld sum of things" were not written till 1872, but the synthesised impressions had already begun to flow into the letters and the James family was to get all the appreciation of the English scene that they could have wished for.

Leon Edel describes these first striking, dramatising letters sent from Paris, Rome, London, as destined "for an invisible recipient who would read them later in the American setting – himself." James told his brother William that the letters were to be used as notes. The play between the letters and James's stories, novels, and travel essays in the next seven years was strong. In "A Passionate Pilgrim," the view from the Malvern Hills was to be described as "a compendium of the physiognomy of England" and the narrator's rapturous descriptions of Worcestershire (where the hero of the tale laid claim to an hereditary estate) were fully anticipated in letters that James wrote to his family. They showed that expressed appreciation of England was triumphantly possible. And in this landscape description the language (in letters as in fictions) pressed beyond the phenomenon to express some quintessence that was non-material, a spiritual reality. The sky over Worcestershire was, James.wrote to his father: "tremendous and Turneresque, a chaos of rolling grey – a rain of silver, a heaven of tender distant blue – there is something to my eyes in a sight so wonderfully characteristic and national, so eloquent of the English spirit and the English past." The scene evoked the English spirit and the English past for James because he saw it as a composition of artistic effects "good old English 'effects'" that combined to suggest a reality that could be discussed in terms of ends sought and means used. James was as conscious as Frederick Law Olmsted that the English countryside was a product of landscape design. And the elements that the English spirit worked to evoke its past were listed by James in the letter to his father:

The other afternoon I trudged over to Worcester – thro' a region so thick-sown with good old English 'effects' – with elm-scattered meadows and sheep-cropped commons and ivy-smothered dwellings of small

23. Henry James

gentility, and high-gabled, heavy-timbered, broken-plastered farm-houses and stiles leading to delicious meadow footpaths and lodge-gates leading to far-off manors – with all things suggestive of the opening chapters of half-remembered novels, devoured in my infancy – that I felt as if I were pressing all England to my soul.[5]

The sensation that in a particular corner of England the traveller had come face-to-face with all England was the essence of the "rare emotion" to be described so precisely in "A Passionate Pilgrim." It was a Jamesian phrase for what A. Cleveland Coxe called the "sentiment and poetry" of England. The "rare emotion" was what Olmsted and others felt when they called out at last that this or that was the "real England." Henry James's thirty years of travel essays about England were the distillation of that sense into the prose of a master in a concentration that he alone could achieve. And the title of this collection, *English Hours*, spoke of the coincidence of time and place which produce the rare emotion.

It was an emotion most frequently aroused for James the traveller in a county across the border from Worcestershire, in a place that he called variously "the heart of England," "the richest corner of England," "the core and centre of the English world," "midmost England," "unmitigated England." "In Warwickshire" was the tenth of the *English Hours* and in this essay Henry James described a series of romantic landscapes that were "compositions." James made his theme the English home, and English domesticity. He described a country rectory, a home in Stratford for a scholar, a new house that became as he stood looking out of its windows suddenly, especially beautiful, and finally he described three country houses. The essay had its heroine – the English woman – and the whole became a panegyric upon her service to her husband. In Warwickshire, James told his readers in a metaphor taken from the inventive practice of American journalism, "I have been interviewing the genius of pastoral Britain."[6]

Like other essays in *English Hours*, "In Warwickshire" defied easy identification of its subject. The subject deliberately and explicitly avoided was Shakespeare – "Inevitably, of course, the sentimental tourist has a great deal to say to himself about this being Shakespeare's county," but James spoke of him as little as possible. When he mentioned Stratford it was only as it were by chance because there he found the perfect house – a newly built home with a view of Shakespeare's church and a garden fit for one of his comedies. Altogether it "seemed to me for a quarter of an hour the richest corner of England." If Stratford was deliberately not the subject of "In Warwickshire," then the home and its graceful hostess became the subject only because James insisted that the midmost point of England's midmost point must be the home. But the traveller, the writer and the reader were in Warwickshire because it was Shakespeare's county. Either consequently or coincidently, Warwickshire maintained a special relationship with the rest of the country – its "meadows are to common English scenery what this is to that of the rest of the world."[7]

James's diffidence about making Shakespeare the subject of his essay on Shakespeare's county was matched by his diffidence towards the landscape itself. Shakespeare and Stratford were about the commonest subject of American travel essays and the fastidious traveller felt compromised by the obligation to describe it. And if Warwickshire were the quintessence of "common English scenery," it might just be that it was the most "common" of all. In James's very first letters on the subject written in April 1869 he had described Warwick Castle as a showy modern house, Kenilworth as no more impressive than a local stone-mill, and Stratford as a place uninspiring to the point of humiliation. Warwickshire, Henry wrote to William James, "is in fact too monotonously sweet and smooth – too comfortable, too ovine, too bovine, too English, in a word . . . It seems like a vast show region kept up at the expense of the poor." James used this letter when he came to write the first of his Warwickshire essays in *English Hours* ("Lichfield and Warwick," 1872). There he said of Shakespeare's county: "The landscape indeed sins by excess of intuitive suggestion; it savours of larder and manger; it is too ovine, too bovine, it is almost assinine." (For publication the last adjective had replaced the private "too English.") The wit was more pointed, the syntax more subtle, and the social criticism more covert. And even in the still later essay where James celebrated Warwickshire as "the core and centre of the English world," he condescended to the landscape, and conveyed his continuing diffidence of its excesses. The sheep in Stratford fields, he wrote, "were by no means mere edible mutton; they were poetic, historic, romantic sheep; they were not there for their weight or their wool, they were there for their presence and their compositional value, and they visibly knew it."[8]

There was a great deal that the Reverend William Gilpin would have approved in this sentiment – the compositional value of landscape was the first principle of picturesque beauty. Sheep were valuable to this end not only as being picturesque in themselves but perhaps more essentially because the very tone of the landscape, that quality of the neat and the domesticated, was conserved by their cropping and grazing. Without this, say students of landscape, "grass loses its creeping habit and the surface becomes ragged and unkempt"[9] – emphatically not the Warwickshire note. But to have the sheep themselves aware of the Reverend Gilpin's principles of picturesque beauty not only made mock of the high seriousness of Gothic sensibility but mocked at (even while it engaged in) the pieties of the American pilgrim's search for the sacred spot that would be midmost England.

James ended his essay "Lichfield and Warwick" by describing a portrait by Vandyke of a Genoese lady. The picture hangs in Warwick Castle. The subject and the setting led James to contrast the "midlight of midmost England" with the glare of the Mediterranean sun: "intensity for intensity – intensity of situation constituted – I hardly know which to choose." By act of domicile, it might be said that James eventually elected for England, but in 1872, James had not finally chosen against Italy (inevitable though a retrospect of his life seems to make that choice). In discussing this great dilemma, Leon Edel says that James felt "that he could never absorb and appropriate Italy as he had appropriated London and Oxford, and indeed all England, where he had felt himself breathing the air of home." But James had written home from Rome that at last he lived; the magical synthesis had come first there; he had reeled and moaned in its streets. It might be said that Italy offered more of what the New World traveller sought in the Old than anywhere else. It was, says Cushing Strout in *The American Image of the Old World*, "inevitably the essence of the Old World for a Protestant, prosperous, industrialized, democratic country". The Italianate architectural rage in the America of the 1880s was but one of many evidences of this. Grant Allen's nineteenth-century guidebook, *The European Tour*, is quoted by Strout as advising the American tourist that Italy was the key to Europe and that England required "only a short final stay." To the extent that the American was a Protestant, a New Englander, an industrialist, and a democrat, Italy was the Catholic Church and the Catholic Church was Europe – so Henry James presented it for his character Mr Waymarsh, Lawyer, of Milrose, Connecticut meeting his friend Lambert Strether at Chester:

The Catholic Church for Waymarsh – that was to say the enemy, the monster of bulging eyes and far-reaching quivering groping tentacles – was exactly society, exactly the multiplication of shibboleths, exactly the discrimination of types and tones, exactly the wicked old Rows of Chester, rank with feudalism; exactly in short Europe.[10]

But if brave, little Chester could so effectively represent the enemy that was Rome, the case was not so clear for Italy. Strout's contention that Italy held first place in the tourist's ambition is disputed by another commentator on Americans abroad who states categorically that "the first love of the American travellers was invariably France... It was followed by Great Britain, Italy, Germany, and Switzerland." Third place is less impressive. But discriminations are possible and Leon Edel's comment on Henry James's final choice for England has already suggested the clue to the abiding attraction of England. The very fact that England was less than Italy "the enemy, the monster of bulging eyes," that it was the familiar of childhood-reading made England the more lovable. "Americans," says Margaret Mead, "are oriented towards the Europe from which their ancestors emigrated, not to the Europe which exists today."[11] And if this is true of the twentieth-century American, it was true of the nineteenth-century New Englander, and it was especially true of the New England writer. His relationship to Europe was extended through language and literature and this almost invariably meant that whatever his first love, whether Italy or France, his most enduring love was England. The continental countries were loved like mistresses; England was called the mother country. And the fact that the Americans looked to the Europe that their ancestors had left, the Europe of the past not of the present, was a testimony to the Americans' wish to see themselves in the role of legatees when they took ship for Liverpool.

In 1840 N. P. Willis returned from the social and literary successes of his European life and took his ease on a Pennsylvanian farm. He had occasion in one of his *Letters* (languidly penned in his carpet slippers and in the cool of the day beneath the shade of a bridge) to take note of a phenomenon on the banks of the Susquehannah – "This good woman, or this great lady, is the only daughter, as I understand it, of an old farmer ninety years of age, who has fallen heir to an immense fortune in England." If this woman, the wife of a local tavern keeper, ever came into possession of her English fortune, she would have lived out the fantasy of a thousand Americans and become the flesh and blood embodiment of the American claimant, a figure that achieved "the status of a literary convention" in nineteenth-century American fiction. These lost heirs, says Philip Rahv, haunted early American books. They haunted the pages of Nathaniel Hawthorne's last unfinished romances and men and women like the Susquehannah tavern-keeper's wife crowded the Liverpool Consular Office during Hawthorne's tenure of that position from 1853 to 1857. They made the liveliest impression in the opening essay of *Our Old Home*. That they were more than fictions was attested by their appearance in the pages of the *English Notebooks*. "As an individual," Hawthorne wrote in "Consular Experiences," "the American is often conscious of the deep-rooted sympathies that belong more fitly to times gone by." Any coincidence of names, a coat-of-arms on a silver mug, or a yellow document in a drawer "has been potent enough to turn the brain of many an honest republican" and make his rush to England to lay claim to a title.[12]

Those making a literal claim to title, property or fortune in England, were by Hawthorne's account a laughable, pathetic group of people – many obviously close to, if not well within, the boundaries of insanity. (English visitors to American madhouses were always sure of finding inmates who had assumed noble titles.) Hawthorne described these hopeless travellers with gentle irony and treated them kindly in his official capacity. That he had a strong sympathy for the metaphorical reality of their claims was evident in the last lines of the essay, "Consular Experiences," – "I hope that I do not compromise my American patriotism by acknowledging that I was often conscious of a fervent hereditary attachment to the native soil of our forefathers, and felt it to be our Old Home." And this was a sentiment expressed even more fervently in the *Notebooks*. Travelling through Yorkshire, Derbyshire, and Lincolnshire in 1857, he wrote, "What a wonderful land! It is our forefathers' land; our land; for I will not give up such a precious inheritance."[13]

Like James, Hawthorne referred to Warwickshire as "midmost England" and found its countryside one of the strongest and in some respects strangest evidences of inheritance. He loved to spend his holidays in the "genteel" new village of Leamington Spa, a little to the east of Warwick situated on the River Leam, a river more lazy than that of Concord, his American home: "Certainly, this river is a perfect feature of that gentle picturesqueness in which England is so rich, sleeping, as it does, beneath a margin of willows that droop into its bosom." Hawthorne found it suburban, pretentious (its street names all aristocratical); it was cosy, a little tedious; it was ideal for retreat. The "fiction of a chalybeate well" had produced the reality of a flourishing resort town, surrounded by fine hunting country, great house, and ancient castle. And by the footpaths that led into this countryside, Hawthorne was taken to farms, cottages, mills, ponds, "and all those quiet, secret, unexpected, yet strangely familiar features of English scenery that Tennyson shows us in his idyls and ecologues." These footpaths across Warwickshire were more ancient than the Romans; they belonged to the most remote past. The historical tie with this landscape was so profoundly felt that Hawthorne had to seek some profound explanation. Everything that he saw in the Warwickshire countryside seemed familiar. Bebbington Parish Church was no more strange than the Salem Meeting House – "This was a bewildering yet delightful emotion." Obviously it was generated by all the reading and talking about Old England in New England but it was so strong that he could almost believe it "a sort of innate idea, the print of a recollection in some ancestral mind."[14]

Strange indeed this sensation, known to the Irish–Americans as going back where you've never been before; Hawthorne's speculative explanation gave his sense of heritage a kind of material reality – and in this he showed his fellowship with deluded compatriots pursuing will-o'-the-wisp claims to the actual turf and sod of England. The most complete fictional representation of this figure was Mr Clement Searle of New York, who believed himself twentieth cousin of Mr Richard Searle of Lockley Park, Worcestershire, an estate to which Clement Searle made his feeble, hopeless, and romantic claim. In speaking of the matter to the story's narrator, the American Searle explained, "'There is no doubt, I fancy, that a hundred years ago, we suffered a palpable wrong.'" That would make the date, if the story was contemporary with its publication, round about 1776 – the date at which A. Cleveland Coxe sustained his wrong at the hands of George III's ministers. The narrator of Clement Searle's sad tale made no positive declaration on the rights and wrongs of the claimant's case – the case's being such that declaration on it were neither possible nor relevant but he knew the exemplum of his moral, one that he stated early in its telling:

The latent preparedness of the American mind for even the most delectable features of English life is a fact which I never fairly probed to its depths. The roots of it are so deeply buried in the virgin soil of our primary culture, that with out some great upheaval of experience, it would be hard to say exactly when and where and how it begins. It makes an American's enjoyment of England an emotion more total and sacred than his enjoyment, say, of Italy or Spain.[15]

The ethics of enjoying England were something that Henry James discussed often and he did so because he took a strong stand on doubtful ground: he believed that the American traveller should make it his business to like what he found in England. If the transatlantic visitor were to allow himself to be disappointed by the shabbiness, ugliness, even the monotony of what he found in the Old World, James believed he would fail to come up to an occasion for which his life in America had been preparing him; he would miss his aesthetic opportunity.

In his late autobiographical work, *The Middle Years*, James described the disappointment of his first adult encounter with London's dreary streets and suburbs. But he perceived something of value, something not to be missed, in the very defects of London: "I remember at least that in spite of such disconcertments, such dismays, as certain of the most thoroughly Victorian *choses vues* originally treated me to, something yet deeper and finer than observation admonished me to like them just as they were, or at least not too fatuously to dislike."[16] Fatuous dislike came as easily to the American traveller as uncritical admiration. It is instructive that James felt the first was a greater danger than the second. As he had looked at the ugliness of London (Baker Street's ugliness, specifically), James's initial visual reaction, "observation," was overruled by something "deeper and finer." The young James was held to a more penetrating and rewarding gaze so that he saw through the *choses vues*. Ugliness became a relative value, one subject to change. There was a kind of Platonism in James's response to London – a sense that the phenomena were not the final value; they were but clues to a "deeper and finer" reality. With how much greater skill did James pursue his distinctions, but they were one with those in which Olmsted revelled in Chester and Coxe

24. Baker Street

A Christmas Day or a Good Friday uncovers the ugliness of London. As you walk along the streets, having no fellow pedestrians to look at, you look up at the brown brick house-walls, corroded with soot and fog, pierced with their straight stiff window-slits, and finished, by way of a cornice, with a little black line resembling a slice of curbstone. There is not an accessory, not a touch of architectural fancy, not the narrowest concession to beauty. If I were a foreigner it would make me rabid; being an Anglo-Saxon I find in it what Thackeray found in Baker Street – a delightful proof of English domestic virtue, of the sanctity of the British home.

(Henry James)

anguished over in Cambridge. James struck a delicate aesthetic and moral balance in 1869 and he reaffirmed it in 1916. It involved elements of moral judgement that remain disturbing, and James confronted himself and his readers with the ethical dilemma of travelling in all his travel writing.

In 1877 he visited, and wrote an essay about, Oxford. His interest centred on All Souls College, an undergraduateless place of storied wealth, idleness, and pedantry. James discovered that All Souls was deemed, among Oxford's many abuses, the greatest abuse. But for the tourist, this very fact added to its charm: "one would like while one is about it, – about, that is, this business of admiring Oxford – to attach one's self to the abuse, to bury one's nostrils in the rose before it is plucked." The traveller's duty was to bury his nose in abuse – an unexpected moral imperative. All Souls and Oxford offered so unusual, so rare, a combination of elements and associations that not to take advantage of the travelling moment would appear to be an act of obtuse insensitivity, of fatuous dislike. The same compelling argument moved Henry James's pragmatic brother, William the philosopher, to the same inescapable conclusion over thirty years later. Oxford, he wrote to Charles Eliot Norton, "is an absolutely unique fruit of human endeavor, and like the cathedrals, can never to the end of time be reproduced . . . Let other places of learning go in for all the improvements! The world can afford to keep her one Oxford unreformed."[17] William James admitted that this was a superficial judgement, that Oxford was modern and, in many ways, democratic. And he did not think that he would ever want to go there again, but it was unique. To reform it would be to destroy it; it would "never to the end of time be reproduced." The liberal will was paralysed.

Henry James was less solemn in this matter than his brother. His description of All Souls and his visit to Oxford made up one part of a double-headed essay that he published under the title of "Two Excursions." The other excursion was to Epsom Downs for Derby Day. The licensed misrule of unbuttoned populace and frolicksome undergraduates, a wild boisterousness running all the way through English society, provided the unifying, but unstated, theme of the whole essay. Henry James affected a dilettante persona in "Two Excursions," as he did in other of his English travel essays. In this role, he described himself "as a mere taster of produced tastes."[18]

But this Huysman-like self-portraiture served to set in motion certain aesthetic experiments and to draw some critical fire; it disguised a more serious concern with the "disconcertments" and "dismays" that allowed the rose of abuse such full and pleasing growth. The ugly things to be seen in England were not superficial defects that could easily be done away with; it is obvious that James believed them to be in some way a necessary condition of the attraction of England. He would not and he could not wish them away.

In his great essay "London," originally published in 1888 and placed first in *English Hours* in 1905, James described a direct relationship between the charm of London and its ugliness. London generated "geniality" at the same time as it shocked by its brutalities, poverty, and gin: "And yet I should not go so far as to say it is a condition of such geniality to close one's eyes upon the immense misery." What James loved about London was its general vibration and, he said very plainly, "the impression of suffering is part of the general vibration." Henry James reversed the conclusion that Oscar Wilde had drawn from crossing the Atlantic: "In going to America," said Wilde in 1883, "one learns that poverty is not a necessary accompaniment of civilisation." Henry James's experience of England, London, and Englishmen told him that, at least in England's case, this could not be so. In January 1879 Henry James was invited to stay at Fryston Hall, one of Yorkshire's great houses and the home of Lord Houghton. On his way to this delightful place, James was distressed by the "blackened landscape and the dense and dusky population, who form a not very attractive element in that great total of labor and poverty on whose enormous base all the luxury and leisure of English country-houses are built up." To describe the great Yorkshire coalfields and the coal-grimed Yorkshire miners as a "not very attractive element" was not a reaction that met the demands of social justice and human need. On the other hand, James, like some other Victorians, English and American, seemed to have accepted the revolutionary consequences of so uneven a distribution of wealth with equanimity. A few years later in another letter to America in which he discussed the social price paid for civilisation, James compared the Britons to the Romans faced by the barbarians. But he added: "In England, the Huns and the Vandals will have to come up – from the black depths of the (in the people) enormous energy."[19] Perhaps fantasies of this retributive justice compensated to some extent for the day-to-day enjoyment of the continuing injustice.

In 1869, James had accepted the disconcertments of Baker Street (and in 1916, had reconfirmed this decision); in 1877, he had accepted the sweet-smelling abuse of All Souls; in 1879, he had accepted the blackened population and landscape of Yorkshire; in 1888, he had accepted the suffering of the poor in London's slums. What was beautiful was conditional upon what was ugly; what was good was conditional upon what was evil. Reform would only destroy; but revolution might redress injustice. In 1899, a progressive phase of the tendentious moral formula was demonstrated in a letter that Henry James sent to his nephew, Henry James, Junior. The nephew was concerned with the conduct of the United States as she made her entry to the world stage of political power. Apparently, she was about to establish an empire of her own in Cuba, Puerto-Rico, Guam, Hawaii, and the Philippines. What, the nephew wanted to know, was to be thought of America's adopting an imperial role? The answer, said the uncle, was to examine Britain's imperial role. The evils of the British Empire could not be denied but British expansion and imperialism were so much a part of England's greatness that England must be wished expansive and imperialist. The United States was a new case. Her good and evil were potential, not like England's actual. The uncle could not deny to the United States in the future the opportunity that had made England great in the past.[20] The social price of the civilised prize had been stated in a new tense, that of the future.

It is not unfair to James to point out that he had to pay little of the social price and that he enjoyed a great deal of the civilised prize. The suffering of the London poor and the dirt of the Yorkshire miners were not his suffering and dirt. The rudeness of the English he had had to endure personally, but even this was not without value. His waiter's truth to type at the Adelphi Hotel, Liverpool, in 1869 was truth to history, to poetry, to Dickens, Smollett, and Hogarth. If this included his treating a young man brusquely, it remained a "revelation," and the price could not be said to be great. He had been happy to pick such prickly and eccentric fruits of English civilisation. And when in those earlier days, he had reached London and had sought out an "eating house of the very old English tradition," he had found the Albany sordid, primitive, rude. But by a transatlantic conversion, he had turned this price into prize. He recalled in 1916, how in 1869 he had rejoiced in the place: "As one sat there one *understood.*" Understanding was deeper and finer than appreciation. "The very rudeness was ripe."[21]

The ugly things of England were not to be wished away. They were not to be refurbished, reformed, or removed. The "general vibration" depended upon them. Were England's political system to be updated, her housing modernised, her abuses reformed, and her population given social justice, England would not be worth the tourist's visiting. In England James rejoiced in a landscape which he felt that he *understood*, understood better than the American scene. In England understanding was an achievement made possible by imaginative identity with elements that were foreign but which had an associative power that made them both accessible and infinitely valuable. The English scene was one that James never exhausted; nor did it ever exhaust him. He was unfailingly refreshed and renewed by his encounters with the English landscape and the delight of his later years was to be driven about in Edith Wharton's motor car within which he rejoiced in the villages, lanes, fields, and names of rural England – "Brookland, Old Romney, Ivychurch, Dymchurch, Lydd – they have positively the prettiest names." This richness of the English scene, this connotative density, this associative intensity threw about England a sacred aura that made it difficult for the sentimental traveller to treat it in the same frame of reference with the New World from which he had come. The concentration of England was a matter of wonder to men and women from a continent that impressed by expanse, by vastness, by distance, by wilderness, by emptiness. "Just think how much of England we have here," Charles Eliot Norton wrote home from a corner of Kent that had associations with Pitt, Chaucer and the Romans. Norton found a delicacy and variety "quite unknown to our own dear country where Nature seems to have been in a hurry to finish her work."[22]

The concentration of England was so great that it gave an impression of endlessness. Towns, cities, cathedrals, castles, and estates, and all these great multitudes of people, were to be found in an area smaller than Georgia. The scene overwhelmed the eye, said Emerson; it required a hundred years to visit. For the American, said Benjamin Silliman, England was "all classical ground," and every rood was "replete with historical associations." The richness of time in space compelled response in the American. The associations of literature and history gave the land a magical quality that removed it far from the world of their own land and left moral judgement in suspense. "I wonder," wrote Harriet Beecher Stowe, "how many authors it will take to enchant our country from Maine to New Orleans as every foot of ground is enchanted here in Scotland."[23] And England was no less rich than Scotland.

E. S. Nadal, a Virginian appointed a secretary to the London Legation in 1870, felt that the most beautiful American landscapes might be more beautiful in point of scenery but that they could never for that reason match those of Britain. Nadal did not, as Henry James was to do, find the American scene oppressive. The Virginian had made it the occupation of two full years of his young manhood to lean on fences and admire the landscapes near his boyhood home. Nadal did not think, as Charles Eliot Norton thought, that Nature had been in a hurry to finish America. The difference was in the matter of humanity. "Any little nameless stream in the Shenandoah Valley is better than the Dee. But in the tavern nearby there would have been no landlady with the keys, nor the really good music of the harper, nor the table spread with tarts and berries, nor very likely the pretty girl." The density of human associations in the English landscape had an intensifying effect on all of them so that the tombstone dated 1790 meant less to Nadal in the United States than a tombstone with the same date in an English churchyard. The dead American occupant had no "constituency." He represented no one; the American past had, as it were, not got started. Oliver Wendell Holmes described this condition as "a top dressing of antiquity." In America, he said, "the soil is not humanized enough to be interesting whereas in England so much of it has been trodden by human feet, built on in the form of human habitations, nay, has been itself a part of preceding generations of human beings, that it is in a kind of dumb sympathy with those who trace its turf."[24] Ticknor's wish to kiss this soil, Coxe's welcome of it as a "sacred land," Silliman's knowledge that it was "all classical ground" were all subsumed in Holmes's identification of this loam with the very flesh and blood of his forefathers. The act of walking in England became an act of ancestor worship. And the instinct to preserve and to leave untouched a land hallowed in this fashion was made correspondingly stronger. The American had travelled in space to come closer in time to his past and it might be expected that he should appreciate what he found.

In 1817, Richard Rush docked at Portsmouth to begin an eight-year mission as Envoy Extraordinary and Minister Plenipotentiary from the United States of America to the Court of St James. He had come to England to settle certain crucial diplomatic issues. He had already negotiated the disarmament of the North American Great Lakes and was going to London to take up once again the question of the impressment by the Royal Navy of United States sailors. Five years before this had been the occasion of the war between the two nations in which the British colonial capital at York (in Upper Canada) and the American federal capital at Washington had been burnt. Rush was going to London to work out the policy agreements that led, through the co-operation of the British Government and the strategic support of the Royal Navy, to the promulgation of the Monroe Doctrine. Rush was going to London to begin the tortuous consultations that were to surround the Oregon question. The immediacies of everyday England might have been expected to have preoccupied Mr Rush when he reached Portsmouth and could see all around him the naval evidence of England's power, but it was not so. His reflections in his memoranda book were as rich in sentiment and warm glow as those of any holidaying clergyman; for these were, he said, "unrepressible feelings in an American. His native patriotism takes a higher tone from dwelling on the illustrious parent stock. Places and incidents that Englishmen pass by fill his imagination."[25]

Richard Rush was truly a son of the Revolution; these were not the sentiments of his father's generation. The father, Dr Benjamin Rush – the "Hypocrates of Pennsylvania," a devoted physician who had killed his patients by overtreatment – had been an ardent patriot and an able revolutionary. Dr Rush would not have sentimentalised England but his son found his place willingly, easily, and successfully in the Court of London as he called the Court of St James. He made no bones about reconciling the morals of a republican with the manners of a courtier, and he served his country well while doing so. He made himself a welcome guest at the tables of the great. His accounts of dinner at Apsley House, where the Duke of Wellington was his host, were filled with details of service and respect for form that make delightful reading.[26]

His mixed diplomatic and social activity made him familiar with the inside of White's. When he was there one day, someone mentioned the candles that were kept burning in the club's windows all night long: "'Yes' said a member, '*they have not been out, I should think, since the reign of Charles II.*'" How could a traveller like Rush contemplate putting out those lights? How could he be expected to wish to see extinguished so visible a link with the past? And yet the lights burning all night for close to 150 years might well be construed as an abuse. But from the perspective of Rush's world, there would be no gain and great loss if the candles were done away with. Such a traveller must side with conservative sentiment and make himself at home at White's. Rush had not gone to England like Frederick Law Olmsted or A. Cleveland Coxe or Henry James to experience the past; he had gone to shape the future, but he understood very well the hold that England might have over the American imagination: "Perhaps more of the romance of English history, is apt to linger in the mind of an American visiting England, than in an Englishman's. To the former, the whole is an abstraction – like ancient history – until he gets to England; then . . . Saxon days, Norman days, the Plantagenets, the Tudors, the Stuarts, seem to come over him in the midst of modern days, and engross his thoughts and feelings at every turn."[27]

Recognition was the most lively of the initial responses to England that the American experienced. The whole charm of England lay in the fact that it was "the abyss of the familiar." In this abyss a man might lose himself and escape everyday life. Still better, he might find himself, an earlier self, his boyhood self. Men like Washington Irving who had never been to England before felt this as intensely as Henry James who had indeed spent periods of infancy and boyhood in the country. "I traversed England," said Irving, "a grown-up child, delighted by every object great and small; betraying a wondering ignorance, and simple enjoyment, that provoked many a stare." Old world things had, said Charles Eliot Norton, "a deeper familiarity than the very things that had lain before our eyes since we were born."[28] Recognition was a crucial element in the "rare emotion."

The landscape of England had become familiar to these men and women primarily by way of their childhood reading and by the illustrations in the magazines that were taken in every American house that had children reading poetry. Recognition and *déjà vu* were diffused throughout a landscape peopled by the characters of poem, play, and novel, a landscape sacred to the memory of writers long dead, a landscape lived and breathed in by writers yet alive. Travellers moved about England excited by fantasy, pilgrimage, and homage.

In this landscape, there was only one stream more sacred than the Avon and that was the Thames. Its valley was a *campo santo* and the established point for viewing it was Richmond, "so long a favourite object of poetical eulogium." It was for most Americans exactly what they expected of (and wanted from) an English landscape – "the perfection of English scenery." The language used to describe it was almost invariably that of classical poetic diction: "charming meadows enamelled with flowers, the silver windings of the Thames, the luxuriant outlines of the foliage . . ." The view evoked the memory of no one poet though the two most quoted were James Thomson and John Milton. "L'Allegro" and "Il Penseroso" were for the New Englander the essence of English landscape poetry – more so than Thomson's *Seasons*. Milton's two idylls must "have been written on top of Richmond Hill," said John Motley. The prospect summoned up as wide a range of images as the views in the Avon Valley. And the Hill gave a descriptive opportunity quite different from that presented by Westminster Abbey. It was a painterly occasion that obliged the sentimental traveller's best prose. (He could not for that reason always give it.) The view remained, an alcoholic newspaper editor wrote to his Ohio readers, "a revelation of the absolutely beautiful in Nature."[29]

The most recurrent image used to describe England in nineteenth-century American travel literature was that of the garden. The American was impressed by the sheer number and variety of the gardens that he found in England; he was even more impressed by the fact that the whole country was "groomed," "finished," "completed" to the point that it could be described as "the very garden of the world." There was, so far as he could see, no wilderness at all. "Shropshire is called 'wild,' though to American eyes it seems almost suburban in its smoothness and finish." The domesticated, tamed quality of the landscape induced a sense of unreality. At the same time, it encouraged a selective vision that excluded anything that was ugly or disruptive: "I used to think the gardens never ended," Nadal wrote, "but lay side by side the island through, and that the sea washed them all round."[30]

The landscapes were invested with moral qualities which expressed for the traveller values inherent in the English nation – "the great charm . . . of English scenery is the moral feeling that seems to pervade it."[31] For many it lacked the vigour of the American natural scene and it spoke of England's ties with the past and with death, just as the American landscape spoke of the future and of life.

To describe the actual gardens of England, images of Paradise and of Eden were used. The types of ornamentally cultivated ground that most excited travellers were the cottage garden, the cathedral close, the London park, the formal (or "palace") garden, the college court, and the country-house park. These were a "sort of paradise," "a little garden of Eden," "Arcadia." They were places where Coxe discovered "rhyme seemed reason and fancy, fact"; places where Hawthorne believed one had "life without the trouble of living"; places where James wished "to lie down on the grass . . . forever, in the happy belief that the world is all an English garden and time a fine old English afternoon."[32]

The country or "great" house was felt to be the complement of the landscape, making a harmonious whole with domesticated nature. England, said Irving, "is studded and gemmed, as it were, with castles and palaces, and embroidered with parks and gardens." For travellers like Irving, the country house preserved the heritage and artefacts of the past, as it did the name and the wealth of the family it housed, but at its best it did far more. It preserved an ancient and honourable pattern of human relationships, a mode of being a gentleman and a lady, of being a master and a servant lost to the modern, democratic, and American order of things. The inhabitants of these houses were fitted for that landscape which was illuminated by the historical, literary, and ancestral vision. Contemplation of them roused the "rare emotion." England was most England in the gentry, the yeomanry, and the peasantry of the great estates. (England was least England in the workers, politicians, and industrialists of the great cities.) The Squire of Bracebridge Hall was a "lingering specimen of the old English country gentleman" and

25. Castle Howard

his hobby was "a bigoted devotion to old English manners and customs"[33] – it was a hobby that he shared with American travellers.

Many Americans approved aristocratic rule for England, and they did so without needing to create their reality out of fictitious elements as Irving was forced to do in *Bracebridge Hall.* Ralph Waldo Emerson came to a reluctant approval of aristocracy because he saw "a cold, barren, almost arctic isle" made into a land of plenty through the will, wealth, and administration of the aristocracy of England. But the reality so created was "factitious," said Emerson, "the whole is Birminghamized, and we have a nation whose existence is a work of art."[34] In *English Traits*, Emerson gave one of the most perceptive analyses of the land which had built "a hundred thousand palaces" and he gave one of the most reserved approbations of the artificial construction that he believed England to be.

In 1805, an American traveller reported that the great estates within easy reach of London were "so completely guarded with high brick walls that you might imagine the Barons' wars had not yet terminated." Sign-posts read "Man Traps." High walls everywhere hid Arcadian spots where life was easy indeed. A cultural objection was raised against this easy life by a handful of those few Americans who had sufficient access to country houses to become disillusioned by them. "The English when bored," said Henry Adams, "kill something." The country house, wrote Henry James to Charles Eliot Norton was a "gilded bondage." The problem for intelligent Americans was the inane conversation of fellow guests. Outsiders like Nathaniel Hawthorne thought the great house "as perfect as anything earthly can be";[35] insiders were less certain.

A moral objection was raised against the country house by many more Americans who saw in the high walls and man traps evidence of injustice. The civilisation that enabled lords to live well required labourers to work relentlessly. The price that had to be paid for the prize of civilisation troubled the conscience of many Americans who admired or enjoyed that civilisation. John Motley, who saw the inside of a large number of great houses, found them "paradises very perverting to the moral and the politico-economical sense."[36]

The moral dilemma posed by the clash of aesthetic and social values caused considerable stress for travellers, and many, having enjoyed England as much as they could, were relieved to start for home and the more simple moral condition of less civilisation and less injustice. Some, like Hawthorne, who were obliged by financial and professional constraints to remain in England, found the strain telling. Henry James chose to remain in England for good, and to live out the moral dilemma, and to see it through to a resolution. His defence of the price paid for the great prize of "high civilisation" was a theme as constant in his travel writing as his evocation of the "rare emotion." Continued enjoyment of England obliged continued expiation. The country house (despite its being a "gilded bondage") remained the focal point of the moral issue. "Of all the great things that the English have invented and made a part of the credit of the national character, the most perfect, the most characteristic, the one they have mastered most completely in all its details, so that it is a compendious illustration of their social genius and their manners, is the well-appointed, well-administered, well-filled country house." America denied the truth that production takes time, but James knew that the "flower of art blooms only where the soil is deep."[37] Conservatism had the cathedrals, the colleges, the castles; dissent and democracy had only their logic.

The sentimental traveller was instinctively conservative; he was very likely to like things just as they were when those things coincided with the abstraction that he had made of England. Henry James's admonition had had to do with the liking of the monotony of Baker Street, but this registered an aesthetic refinement of the conservative principle that did not trouble the majority of sentimental travellers. They did not expect England to extend the boundary of their appreciations. England was expected to fulfil expectations. The aesthetically suggestible traveller like Olmsted had his sympathies enlarged; the aesthetically dogmatic traveller like Coxe did not. The essentially aesthetic posture of the traveller was described bluntly by Henry Adams:

For English reforms, Adams cared nothing. The reforms themselves were medieval . . . He resented change. He would have kept the Pope in the Vatican and the Queen at Windsor Castle as historical monuments. He did not care to Americanize Europe. The Bastille or the Ghetto was a curiosity worth a great deal of money, if preserved; and so was a Bishop; so was Napoleon III. The tourist was the conservative who hated novelty and adored dirt.

Adams had been in Paris during the revolution of 1870 and "came back to London without a thought of revolution or restlessness or reform. He wanted amusement, quiet, and gaiety."[38] The ironic self-derogation could not be more complete. The feckless amorality of the traveller – identified unsparingly as "the tourist" – could not better be exposed. Adams relished the role of mocking himself along with millions of American tourists who had known the succession of sensations represented by the Atlantic, the Mersey, the Adelphi, Chester. Henry Adams sneered at himself before anyone should do it for him.

The older Adams ridiculed the younger Adams and so separated himself from the foolishness of that earnest student of life so relentlessly seeking education along with "amusement, quiet, and gaiety." Though neither were attractive personalities, the younger is marginally less irritating than the older who constantly told his readers that everyone, including Henry Adams, was a dupe, but only Henry Adams knew it. "He will not expose himself," says Ferner Nuhn, "Adams was always wrong, but no one else was right! Adams knew nothing, but no one else knew even that much!"[39] Henry Adams's presentation of himself as a diplomat, historian, and tourist in pursuit of education in Europe was as complex as Henry James's presentation of himself as a writer and tourist in pursuit of

26. Henry Adams

impressions in Europe. But *The Education of Henry Adams* did not share with *The Middle Years* of Henry James the resonance and generosity of spirit that the novelist allowed to illuminate his portrait of himself as a young man.

The young Adams had been filled with awe by Eaton Hall in 1858. He returned in 1868 to find that it "no longer impressed his imagination." The youngish man "thought he owned the St. James's Club" in 1870. He returned in 1897 to find himself the "oldest Englishman in England," dispossessed by a generation of Englishmen who no longer felt and thought as Englishmen had once felt and thought.[40] Adams had come, in 1858, like so many another American to lay claim to his English heritage. His initial exclusion from English social life had been so complete that he had experienced an agony of dispossession. He had recovered to travel a full circle through repossession and dispossession again. The eighteenth-century American had become a twentieth-century American and repudiated energetically the sentiments of the nineteenth-century tourist. The nineteenth century was never one in which Henry Adams felt very happy. In the thirty years since the descendant of Massachusetts Puritanism had embraced papacy, episcopacy and monarchy, Adams had educated himself sufficiently to realise that his tolerance was a reactionary emotion. He had become a professional historian and had achieved a professional disdain for amateur attitudes towards the past. Long experience of Europe had replaced aesthetic appreciation with moral evaluation.

PART II

AMERICA

I was roused by the voice of a kind-hearted Yankee skipper, saying, "Come, get up; there's a glorious country, and no mistake; a great country, a progressive country, the greatest country under the sun." . . . I looked in the direction indicated by his finger, and beheld, not the lofty pinnacled cliffs of the "Pilgrim Fathers," but a low, gloomy coast, looming through a mist.

Isabella Lucy Bird, *The Englishwoman in America*

8

LANDFALL AND LANDING

The speed of the ocean-going vessels of the 1830s could leave the mind of the traveller in something of a whirl so that he was as likely to be impressed by the smallness of the world as by the grandeur of the Atlantic or the mightiness of the continent discovered by Columbus. George Combe, a phrenologist, found that only thirteen days out of Bristol, the sun was four hours later than his watch, which still showed London hours. He was never before so struck by "the diminutive size of the globe which we inhabit." Thomas Grattan's arrival in Boston to take up the post of British Consul there in 1839 impressed him with similar sensations: "My voyage across the Atlantic has been so rapid that my mind cannot entertain those ideas of expanse, distance and separation, with which our friends in Europe are at this moment filled." The idea that did possess him was that here was a land with a new past, one that rushed at him in a whirlwind of associations: "Columbus and his fellow-adventurers, he had no peers – Raleigh, the red man, the pilgrim fathers, the wilderness, the frail barks, traversing the waste of waters, chivalry, adventure, witchcraft, as the mind looks back – civilization, corruption and decay as it rushes on."[1]

There was, as it were, a class of sensations, that the landfall of the New World irresistibly forced upon the responsive traveller. The elements of the scene molded the feelings of diverse personalities into similar patterns. Thomas Grattan, a fastidious diplomat and man-of-letters, who had in his own phrase a "well-informed, highly educated Tory mind," discovered in himself the incipient buccaneer: "When at last I put my foot, for the first time on the soil of the new world, I thought I could comprehend the emotions of the early adventurers who sought their chequered fortunes in this land of promise." It is, indeed, a wonderful moment. And as each traveller's ship approached the new, unknown, and mighty continent, he found himself in the grip of forces that were dictating

27. Boston Harbour

emotions, producing reactions, and controlling moods in a remarkable way. In 1835, Richard Cobden made his first visit to America and recorded his experiences in brief diary entries. One of these made a hundred miles outside New York Harbour, caught exactly the sense of the approach: "June 6 1835. Anxiety to see land increases as we find ourselves a short distance [from Sandy Hook] – rise and fall of spirits with every change of wind – . . . hopes and fears – ." The tantalising, tormenting nature of the sailing vessel's unpredictable motion forward played on the nerves. The English traveller did not savour these last days and miles of the Atlantic journey as so many American travellers savoured the approach to Liverpool. The Englishman was anxious only to get on with the business in hand. The rich and rewarding apprehension of the American was not something that the Englishman experienced as he approached America. He was an adventurer and not a pilgrim. For him the dominant emotion was excitement mixed with anxiety. He did not anticipate a fulfilment but a challenge and there is no lingering pleasure to be enjoyed by the delay of the one as there is by the delay of the other. Sea life, Cobden concluded, was not natural and the urge to have the landing over and done with increased to a torment when his nostrils were tickled by the inexpressible fragrance of the shore. To be able to smell a land that you cannot see, still less touch, to know America through your nose only, is a remarkable sensation. Anxiety and sensory stimulation set the Englishman aquiver. Cobden's diary again captured the moment: "Eager look out for the pilot-boat which approaches us – beautiful sailing craft schooner rigged – puts our pilot on board of us at 7 – not like our pilots – all eyes criticize this first American visitor."[2] Cobden's first American did not falter under the English gaze.

The eastern coastlines of America, when approached from the sea, were not for the most part impressive, but the travellers did not know what to expect and the topographical understatement of the first landfall provoked curiosity: "The indescribable interest with which I strained my eyes," wrote Charles Dickens in 1842, "as the first patches of American soil peeped like molehills from the green sea, and followed them, as they swelled, by slow and almost imperceptible degrees, into a continuous line of coast, can hardly be exaggerated." The appearance of the land that rose before the traveller and the well-known boasting of the American people were intriguingly at odds. This discrepancy was brought to the attention of Isabella Lucy Bird as she approached the American continent for the first time in 1854:

I was roused by the voice of a kind-hearted Yankee skipper, saying, "Come, get up; there's a glorious country and no mistake; a great country, a progressive country, the greatest country under the sun." . . . I looked in the direction indicated by his finger, and beheld, not the lofty pinnacled cliffs of the "Pilgrim Fathers," but a low, gloomy coast, looming through a mist.[3]

Most travellers still managed at this moment to remember that here was the New World. Mrs Sarah Mytton Maury in 1845 felt no despondency when she caught sight of New Jersey, "wooded down to the edge of the water, and looking like the garden of Eden, after an absence from the sight of land of nine and twenty days." She was planning to emigrate and hoping to persuade others to do so. Moreover, her voyage from Liverpool was one of the most unpleasant that these middle-class travellers had to record. She and a son had been among five first-class passengers on a ship that was taking nearly three hundred emigrants to New York. Smallpox had broken out. Under these conditions no doubt New Jersey did look like the garden of Eden. She was, as she told Mr Gallatin of Washington, to find "all America 'couleur de rose.'"[4]

But Englishmen and women were usually put in mind not of Adam when they saw the shoreline of America, but of Columbus. In 1806 John Lambert went on deck to find that his ship had entered Trepassé Bay and he was at once re-enacting the event of 1492:

As it was the first portion of the New World that regaled my eyes after a tedious passage, it was on that account doubly acceptable; and, barren as it appeared, I gazed on it with pleasure, while my imagination wandered from the trifling privations and difficulties of my own voyage, to those which the great Columbus encountered in search of a new hemisphere.[5]

Lambert's response to the American strand had something in common with that of Americans seeing an English shoreline for the first time. Although he was not ecstatic, his spirits, like those of Cobden and Mrs Maury, were raised by the sight of land. On the other hand it could happen, in fact it fairly frequently did happen, that the Englishman or woman was deeply depressed by the sight of America. This was very true of those who were planning to make money. Many Americans went to England for business reasons, but the great majority of these managed to convey the impression that they were getting what they wanted anyway: they were getting paid for doing what they would otherwise have paid to do. This tended to give a brisk, cheerful tone to American travel books – they shared some of the lightness of heart of the young businessman with his first expense account. Between exile and vacation there is a great division.

Fanny Kemble went to America in 1832 to raise money. In the company of her father, she hoped to redeem by a grand theatrical tour the debts that the Kembles had accumulated in London. They had no more wish to play Philadelphia than they had to play Birmingham. Fanny Kemble had left England in tears and her last act had been to snatch up a bunch of English flowers. These she would keep until she once more stood upon the soil on which they had grown. She felt she was leaving "home and all the world behind."[6] She anticipated an exile much longer than the year she and her father intended to stay in the New World. And in the event, Fanny Kemble was to stay many years in America. She married there, took up residence there, and had her children there before she was able to return (if she ever did) that bunch of flowers to its native soil.

But she did not know this when she set sail on 1 August 1832, and she did not know it when she caught sight of America before the month was out; nonetheless, she felt the chill of exile: "Hail, strange land! My heart greets you coldly and sadly! Oh how I thought of Columbus as with eyes strained and on tiptoe, our water-weary passengers stood, after a summer's sail of thirty days, welcoming their mother earth." She was taken from her sailing vessel by a steamboat when she reached New York Harbour, but was if anything still more dispirited: "I could not endure to lift my eyes to the strange land, and even had I done so, was crying too bitterly to see anything."[7]

She missed the opportunity to describe one of the favourite sights of English travellers. And even when her tears were dried and she was able to see a glorious sunset over New York Harbour some weeks later, she felt obliged to add: "I would have given it all – gold, and purple, and all – for a wreath of English fog stealing over the water." Americans in Europe tended to conceal their homesickness;

as if it were something to be ashamed of. It was detectable in more or less explicit remarks: in Hawthorne's boast that New England turnips were superior in flavour to English apples; in Henry James's admission twenty years after the fact that homesickness had inhibited his first appreciations of London; in the happy leave takings made by many an American traveller, who could not conceal his high spirits at the thought of getting back to New York or Boston. But the English travellers like Fanny Kemble made a display of homesickness; it was a way of registering their sense of their inner superiority to the people they found themselves among and a way of bolstering their inner insecurity in the face of a culture that did not assure them when they needed assurance. Fanny Kemble believed that she and her father had been accepted by London Society despite their profession; she was outraged at the laxity of American social custom that not only treated her father as a gentleman but treated everyone else as one also apparently: "Here, an innkeeper is a gentleman, your equal, sits at his table with you; you pay him, and are obliged to him besides."[8] Gentility so freely bestowed could not shore up a gentility so painfully earned. Fanny Kemble's homesickness was a sign of her genteel rank.

The English and the American attitudes towards each other's homesickness revealed an amusing mutual contempt. Thomas Grattan found the American woman's claims to have felt homesickness in Europe one of the most trying and inexplicable affectations in women whose many affectations added greatly to the misery of the years that Her Majesty's Consul spent in what he called "Civilised America." He put American homesickness down to the lack of importance experienced in Europe: "It is absolutely matter-of-course – an indispensible necessity for every American woman," he wrote, "I never knew one in Europe who did not tell me she was so. I never knew one in America who had been in Europe who did not tell me she had been so." This affectation frequently resulted in the return to America of women who had married Englishmen. These poor men were "forced to relinquish all the advantages of European life, to accompany their wives to the uncongenial soil in which they never can be acclimatized." Thomas Grattan's heart went out to such unhappy men and he took this callousness of the wives as a demonstration of the coldness in the American female heart. "Love of country is at best but a secondary passion, in comparison with love

FEATHERSTONHAUGH'S

EXCURSION THROUGH THE SLAVE STATES.

PERILS OF BUFFALO HUNTING. *See page* 129

VOL. II.

LONDON:
JOHN MURRAY, ALBEMARLE STREET.

1844.

28. Title-page of George W. Featherstonhaugh's *Excursion through the Slave States.*

of husband and children. The woman of true sentiment finds her home where *they* are. Their country is her country, and their people are her people ... Deficient in affection, she may be strong in adhesiveness; and she may be fond of place in proportion as she is indifferent to person."[9] The idea that these women might genuinely love America was not only preposterous to Grattan, but ill-accorded with the widespread European conviction that Americans were not real patriots. They were held not to be a real nation and therefore could not be expected to experience national feelings. It was vexatious that they should appear to do so.

Mr Grattan's incorrigibility found its match however in that of a Mr Mackenzie of Georgia whom Alex Mackay met on the train from Columbia to Augusta. Mackay had an easy way of engaging anyone that he met in conversation and he learnt a great deal about the United States by so doing. On route to Augusta, the journey was long and hot, he and Mr Mackenzie took up the topic of the homesickness of the European in America. The conversation became very muddled until the Georgian made clear what it was that he had in mind: "'But I meant, sick of home,' he added in a tone of great emphasis; 'for they can't be long in the midst of our free institootions without a-getting dead sick of their tyrannical governments.'"[10]

The institutions of the United States were in fact very much more likely to excite the European, though not always to admiration, than the North American coastline. William Thackeray wrote back to his daughters that he had arrived safely at Halifax in the November of 1852, "But I'm disappointed in the grandeur of the prospect," he added. "It looks small somehow – not nearly so extensive as 1000 landscapes we have seen." The same sight had more than disappointed William Cobbett many years before. His habitual conviction that his judgement was better than that of his superiors operated aboard ship as strongly as it had done and was to do again on shore: "When I first beheld, the barren not to say hideous, rocks at the entrance to the harbour, I began to fear that the master of the vessel had mistaken his way."[11]

The forbidding appearance of North America as it revealed itself to the Briton who approached by way of the semi-arctic desolation of Nova Scotia was matched by that revealed to the Briton who approached by the semi-tropical desolation of the Gulf of Mexico. This was not an unusual seaway for the European: it had distinct advantages if the traveller knew that he or she wanted to reach the American interior directly. In 1827, Mrs Fanny Trollope was one such traveller. She wanted to go straight from London to Cincinnati to open a superior general store. It was to be a great failure. Ten years later Captain Marryat passed through Cincinnati and made a special point (as did all English travellers) of going to see Mrs Trollope's building: "Mrs. Trollope's Bazaar," he wrote, raises its head in a very imposing manner: it is composed of many varieties of architecture; but I think the order under which it must be classed is the *preposterous*. They call it Trollope's Folly; and it is remarkable how a shrewd woman like Mrs. Trollope should have committed such an error. A bazaar like an English bazaar is only to be supported in a city which has arrived at the acme of luxury . . . No wonder, then, it was a failure: it is now used as a dancing academy, and occasionally as an assembly-room.[12]

In order then to reach Cincinnati to establish this ill-fated bazaar, Mrs Trollope had left London accompanied by her younger children on 4 November 1827. On 25 December her ship arrived at the Mississippi Delta: "The first indication of our approach to land was . . . this mighty river pouring forth its muddy mass of waters." The next signs of land were the beginnings of the extraordinary seascape of matted vegetation and mud that the Mississippi pushes out into the Gulf itself so that there is nothing that can be described as a coastline at all. The scale of the thing, the size of the Delta, could not be comprehended. On the mud were to be seen pelicans; with the pelicans, a pilot boat and a pilot ready to guide the ship through the maze. On that Christmas Day in 1827, it was all "utterly desolate." The base for the pilot vessels was the "most miserable station" of Balize – a kind of sea-town somehow existing on the delta cane-brakes of the Great Father of Waters. Driftwood was everywhere as Mrs Trollope's ship finally entered the system of levees that ran back 220 miles from the Delta containing the great flood of one of the world's deepest rivers.[13] Mrs Trollope's description of her arrival in the New World was among the most extraordinary and the most depressing.

She was nonetheless making her way to a conventional landing at the port of New Orleans, generally agreed to be an impressive city. "Nothing can be more imposing than its position," wrote Alex Mackay in 1847, "as you approach it by the stream. Almost the entire length of the noble amphitheatre front which it presents to you is in view." There were three miles of warehouses, a spacious promenade called the Levee, numerous vessels. Even twenty years earlier it had had enough style to satisfy the fastidious taste of Mrs Margaret Hall, a woman of aristocratic connection who liked very little in America. She wrote home to her family (in letters that were not published during her lifetime) that she admired the appearance of the New Orleans' houses "with their queerly-shaped, high roofs and iron balconies instead of the pitiful wood things universal elsewhere, for which [she had] not yet got over [her] contempt." New Orleans was generally pleasing but it did not especially please Mrs Trollope who found that it could present "very little that can gratify the eye of taste."[14]

The entrance to the northern harbour of Halifax had depressed Cobbett, Thackeray, Dickens, Bird, in fact almost everyone who used it; the entrance to New Orleans desolated Mrs Trollope. A man who made a landing, as it were midway between these extremes, one Lieutenant George Gleig, found the coastline of America little more inviting. Gleig approached America by way of Cape Charles and Chesapeake Bay and his ship made towards the land on 14 August 1814. "The coast of America," he wrote in letters home that he very definitely did see into print, "at least in this quarter, is universally low and uninteresting; insomuch that for some time before the land itself can be discerned, forests of pines appear to rise, as it were, out of the water."[15] The captain of Gleig's ship was not looking for a harbour however. Gleig, like Cobbett on his first journey, was on a troop ship but this time the British troops were planning a direct assault on American soil and had in mind the burning of Washington. Gleig's approach to America was in truth an attack but in fact his attitude towards the country and the people was much less hostile than many less military Englishmen and women.

When the navy had found a likely spot, the army made ready to land. These were crack troops who had just completed the great peninsular campaign led by the Duke of Wellington himself and it had only been after they had put to sea at Bordeaux that the men had learned that they were bound for Washington not Bristol. A more reluctant band of Englishmen never approached the shore of America. But they knew their duty and knew better than to complain. "Provisions for three days, that is, three pounds of pork, and two pounds and a half of biscuits, were cooked and given to the men; the cartouche boxes were supplied with fresh ammunition, and arms and accoutrements handed out." Ready as few passengers got ready for a landing, they moved from the warships to the boats: "Each boatload of soldiers, likewise, drew up the moment they stepped on shore, forming a line without any regard to companies or battalions; whilst patrols were instantly dispatched to reconnoitre and take possession of every house, as well as to line every hedge."

There was apparently no enemy within many miles of the place because it was to be a long time before they met their first American.[16]

Lieutenant George Gleig was to be a more successful soldier than Sergeant William Cobbett. Gleig survived the American campaign to become eventually Chaplain General of Her Majesty's Forces. When in 1846 he preached from his pulpit in the Royal Hospital at Chelsea, he did so from beneath an American standard he had captured. Nathaniel Hawthorne was to see that flag and to feel saddened to see it hung in British triumph and American shame. (Anthony Trollope felt a reverse emotion – or should it be called an identical emotion? – when he saw the British regimental standards that hang in the chapel of West Point, spoils of the War of Independence.) The tangible evidence of the military conflicts of the two peoples was a sobering experience. Disagreement meant, in the last resort, war, and war was very far from the thoughts of most travellers, no matter how disgruntled they might have become with their hosts. The mutual contempt of the two parties to the conflict of the 1812–15 War made it an unhappy model of Anglo-American attitudes. In the long run the British lost because they refused to take seriously the threat of American arms. Wellington's aristocratic command would not commit enough troops to the campaign to ensure its success. And at New Orleans, the advantages that had given regular troops at Washington ascendancy over irregular troops were reversed.

Mrs Hall, the wife of a captain in the Royal Navy, was depressed to think that such gallantry had been displayed on a field that offered the fallen heroes no honour: "How sadly" she wrote in 1828, "all those who lost friends here must have grudged their fall after escaping in safety from the long and toilsome campaigns in the Peninsula, to come to be mowed down by a parcel of American Militia." The extraordinary disparity between British and American losses was not weighed against the American defeats sustained in the early part of the campaign. British visitors to New Orleans were to be taken over the battlefield for the next fifty years. As in Washington's Capitol they were to be instructed in the barbarity of their nation, so in New Orleans they were to be instructed in the inferiority of their fighting men. "New Orleans, – for want of a better, – is the American Waterloo,"[17] wrote a Scotsman who went to the battlefield in the 1830s.

It was not until after the Civil War that Americans allowed the memory of their victory to be overtaken by time and by greater military events. But during the course of the Civil War itself the Battle of New Orleans was still thought sufficiently impressive to diminish a Britisher's national arrogance. In 1861, in the early months of the war, southern military men took William Russell to visit the site of the battle of 1815. (He dated it 1814.) The live oaks were still scarred by cannon, and shot was still to be found embedded in the tree trunks. But William Russell was no ordinary tourist. He was a veteran war-correspondent and he sized up the battlefield of New Orleans with a professional eye, and gave the readers of his *Diary* a complete technical analysis of the errors of the British attack. One of the most telling conclusions of this was his estimation of the nature of the American defence. Russell believed that the pride of the Americans was "erroneously" based on their small losses. "It is," he noted caustically, "one of the events which have created a fixed idea in their minds that they are able to 'whip the world.'"[18]

One of the most painful ironies of the Battle of New Orleans was that this battle "with all its attendant carnage and woe, was fought," as Mrs Hall's husband wrote in *Travels in North America, in the Years 1827 and 1828*, "by two nations who were at that moment at peace." The peace negotiations that had led to the Treaty of Ghent were signed on 24 December 1814 and the Battle of New Orleans was fought on 8 January 1815. This was of course far too short a time to get the news from Ghent to this particular Aix. The news did not in fact reach the British until 14 February. "And I shall not deny" wrote Gleig "that it was received with much satisfaction."[19]

That the battle was fought when the two nations were technically at peace pointed up the representative value of this whole action in terms of Anglo-American attitudes in the first half of the nineteenth century. War was the real outcome of the special hostility that existed between the two nations. And war remained a real possibility for some years to come. War remained as a rhetorical possibility to the very end of the century. Anglo-American hostility could find no more terrible expression but it was the kind of encounter that induced some Englishmen to temper their ready

29. "Thackeray's Works, Sir!"

contempt for the Americans. "We who only seven weeks ago had set out in the surest confidence of glory, and I may add, of emolument, were brought back dispirited and dejected," wrote Gleig. "Our ranks were woefully thinned, our chiefs slain, our clothing tattered and filthy, and even our discipline in some degree injured."[20]

Lieutenant Gleig's trip to America must represent a low point in Anglo-American relations and it can hardly stand as a model for the average tour. He had, nonetheless, in common with many fellow Englishmen the hope of what he called, discreetly, "emolument." Few of those who set sail for the United States in the nineteenth century expected to take their reward at the point of a bayonet, however. At the very least, other Englishmen would offer the Americans a lecture in return for their gold. So William Thackeray planned in 1853: "I shall carry away near 1000£ from here alone," he wrote of New York. "It is a little rain of dollars. Pray heaven to send plenty of rain." But in fairness to the lieutenant and to the lecturer, there were motives other than gain. Gleig's first ambition was glory and Thackeray was certainly after the writer's equivalent: "The first name I heard in the railroad going hence from New York was my own by a pretty child selling books," he wrote from Boston, "So – here it is after fifteen years thinks I, here's the fame they talk about."[21]

9

THE SEABOARD CITIES

Glory and plunder, fame and dollars, these represented the dual purposes of many Englishmen in the New World, and William Makepeace Thackeray's approach to his opportunities by way of New York Harbour represented the most commonplace, and at the same time one of the most splendid, ways of reaching that World. The English may have been disappointed by the coastline of America but those who landed at New York were seldom disappointed by the scene that greeted them when the pilots brought the ships up through the Narrows and into the great bay that gave shelter to half the ocean's shipping. "Man's imagination can fancy nothing so beautiful as [New York's] bay and port, from which two immense rivers sweep up on the sides of the land, on which the city is," wrote William Cobbett in 1818. "These rivers are continually covered with vessels of various sizes bringing the produce of the land . . . The city is a scene of opulence and industry: riches without indolence, and labour without grudging."[1]

Cobbett was accused of promoting his section of America for commercial reasons but no one ever laid that charge against Mrs Fanny Trollope. Nonetheless, New York Harbour was praised as highly by her as it was by William Cobbett: "My imagination is incapable of conceiving anything of the kind more beautiful than the harbour of New York," she wrote towards the end of *Domestic Manners of the Americans*. It rose, like Venice, from the sea. "New York, indeed, appeared to us even when we saw it by a soberer light, a lovely and a noble city."[2] Mrs Trollope was feeling that relief which came to the English whenever they returned to (or in her case at last reached) the city that in all America was most European. Her contemporaries in travel, her equals in anti-democratic hauteur and her superiors in social rank, Captain and Mrs Basil Hall, both experienced a renewed admiration for New York and its beautiful situation after they had been to New Orleans and back.

30. New York Bay

They first came to New York when their ship passed the Sandy Hook Light House at sunset on 15 May 1827. They had entered the harbour in the dark and missed seeing the beauties of the approach as a result, though these were described rapturously by fellow passengers. But Captain Basil Hall had spent twenty-three years at sea with the Royal Navy and knew exactly what he wanted when he came to port: a good, shore-cooked meal and this was exactly what he got. The next morning, as soon as he arrived at his New York hotel, he ordered a breakfast of shad, an American fish reputedly excellent. With his shad he was given "a great steaming, juicy beefsteak . . . flanked by a dish of mutton cutlets . . . To these viands were added a splendid arrangement of snow-white rolls, regiments of hot toast, with oceans of tea and coffee."[3] The captain's imagery was never original but he did enjoy his food. Others might complain but he showed that an Englishman in 1827 could still enjoy a beefsteak for breakfast.

They returned to New York for the last time on 25 June 1828. Here they completed a great journey that had taken them south to New Orleans, and north again by steamboat, coach and packet boat: "As I came up the bay," Margaret Hall wrote to her sister, "some little recollections of the dreamy feeling I had when I first looked upon New York thirteen months ago crossed my imagination, but the feeling was very short; then all was imagination, now all was certainty and I walked up to the hotel almost as if I were at home." The Halls had not the same hearty spirits that had been theirs when the captain had attacked his shad, beefsteak and mutton cutlets the previous year, but they were feeling better than they had for months. They were of course less than thirty days away from England – they reached the Isle of Wight on 22 July – but New York itself had taken on something of the colouring of home. The imaginative uncertainty of the first appearance of the city had been replaced by a homely familiarity. This was the Halls' third entry to the bay and they were now contrasting New York not with London but with the towns, villes, burgs, and cities of the dreadful Mississippi Valley. New York looked very different and almost inviting. This changed relationship with the city should not be exaggerated. Margaret Hall did not become sentimental; safely at sea, she wrote to her sister, "I cannot say that I feel at all sorry or that I have the smallest regret on leaving New York, or indeed America

31. Basil Hall

. . . We had quite a gay setting-out as there was no one there whom it cost us a tear to part with."[4] It was unlikely that the Americans shed any tears either as the Halls, Eliza, their daughter, and their maid pulled past Sandy Hook eastward bound.

Even if the Halls had left New York without regret, the city had lost some of its foreignness and they had begun to feel at ease there. The Halls believed that the dreamy feeling that New York had induced in them when they had first landed in May 1827 was to a great extent caused by the fact that they were in a city that was at once very like and very unlike the cities of their own country: "As we passed along," Basil Hall wrote, "many things recalled the seaports of England to my thoughts, although abundant indications of another country lay on all hands." He was also reminded very powerfully of London, "yet there was more or less of a foreign air in all we saw, especially about the dress and the gait of the men.

Negroes and negresses also were seen in abundance on the wharfs. The form of most of the wheeled carriages was novel; and we encountered several covered vehicles, on which was written in large characters, ICE." Despite these differences, "there was so much about it that looked like England, that we half fancied ourselves back again; and yet there was quite enough to show in the next instant, that it was a very different country. This indistinct, dreamy kind of feeling, lasted for several days; after which it gradually faded away before a different set of impressions." New York City was foreign and familiar at the same time and the effect was disturbing. Where every sign was in English it was difficult for the nineteenth-century Englishman to accept that he was not in some part of England or some extension of the Empire. "English names are plentiful around you," wrote Alex Mackay of his landing in New York in 1846, "and many objects have an English look about them. Yet, when the Englishman steps ashore, it is on a foreign, though a friendly land."[5]

The reaction of the English travellers to New York was to some extent a match to the reaction of the American to Liverpool, for both sets of travellers recognised the likenesses of the two seaports. This recognition did not have exactly the same effect on the two sets of travellers, however. The American response was primarily one of disappointment. The feeling of being cheated played only a small part in the English response.

When John Lambert reached New York in 1807 he found it "an exact epitome" of London. In 1818, William Cobbett wrote,

> blindfold an Englishman and convey him to New York, unbind his eyes, and he will think himself in an English city. The same sort of streets; shops precisely the same; the same beautiful and modest women crowding in and out of them; the same play-houses; the same men, same dress, same language: he will miss by day only the nobility and the beggars and by night only the street-walkers and pickpockets.

Cobbett made no pretence of the fact that he hoped to encourage the farmers of his beloved Hampshire to emigrate to Long Island to live again the life of the old Golden Age. In *A Year's Residence in the United States of America*, Cobbett directed his readers to a fine description of the once happy state of England made by the writer Fortescue. This passage, said Cobbett, "describes the state of England four hundred years ago; and this, with the polish of modern times added is now the state of the Americans. Their forefathers brought the 'English hospitality' with them; for when they left the country, the infernal *Boroughmonger Funding system* had not begun."[6]

How Frederick Law Olmsted and Oliver Wendell Holmes would have liked to have been able to believe that! But even if the Golden Age of English rural life could not be expected to exist in the hinterland of a foreign city, Cobbett was not creating his political fantasy out of nothing. Travellers in the 1830s repeated his claim that New York was an English town. Thomas Hamilton did so in terms that made an almost exact counterpart to Benjamin Silliman's comment on the likeness of Liverpool to New York:

> In visiting a foreign city, a traveller – especially an English one – usually expects to find, in the aspect of the place and its inhabitants, some tincture of the barbaric. There is something of this, though not a great deal, at New York. The appearance of the population, though not English, is undoubtedly nearer to it than that of any city on the continent of Europe; and but for the number of blacks and people of colour . . . [there is little] to remind a traveller that the breadth of an ocean divides him from Great Britain.

A fellow Scot, the phrenologist George Combe, had much the same comment some years later (in 1838), "The time since we left Bristol, appears to be so short, and the dress, manners, and language of the upper classes are so similar, to those of the same rank in England, that it is difficult to 'realize,' as the Americans express it, the idea of being so far from home." But he made an interesting qualification: a man had only to pick up a newspaper or to overhear a conversation to "realize" only too well that England and America were two different worlds. This was a notion that Frederick Marryat chose to explore in the opening pages of his *Diary in America*. He had discovered that the likenesses and the differences between New York and an English city were deceptive: "On my first arrival I perceived little difference between the city of New York and one of our principal provincial towns"; he wrote, "and for its people, not half so much as between the people of Devonshire or Cornwall and those of Middlesex." But this was not an impression that survived the length of his eighteen-month tour. Marryat became more and more impressed by the differences between the two countries. "Even at New York, the English appearance of the people gradually wore away . . . and I found that there was a great deal to reflect upon and investigate, and that America and the American people were indeed an enigma."[7]

By the end of the 1830s the visitor from England was not always struck by the likeness of New York to English cities. A traveller, who came to New York only a few months after Captain Marryat had departed, wrote that he did not find it like England at all, "my first impression of the city, as we drove through some minor streets and a portion of Broadway, being that it looked half Dutch, half French, something between Paris and Rotterdam." Thomas Grattan had spent the previous decade living in continental Europe, mainly in Brussels but partly in the two cities with which he compared New York. This may have influenced his reaction to the American port but it was not at all uncommon for those English visitors who knew France and the north of Europe, especially Holland, to compare New York of the 1830s with those countries rather than with England. Grattan went on in a later chapter of *Civilized America* to identify what it was that created for him the un-English quality of American cities: the fashion of the young men's clothes, the appearance of the houses (even the brick ones); the small shops "with narrowed-paned windows"; above all, the colour and display. "There is an over-abundance of glaring sign boards, gilding, and green paint."[8]

The signboards or hoardings were to become an ever more prominent feature of the New York cityscape but the brightness of colouring (to which Grattan objected) was not in itself a result of the advertising energy of the American city. In 1832, Fanny Kemble had noted in her journal that in New York, "the houses are almost all painted glaring white or red; the other favourite colours appear to be pale straw colour and grey. They have all green venetian shutters, which give an idea of coolness, and almost every house has a tree or trees in its vicinity, which looks pretty and garden-like." One of the things that Nathaniel Hawthorne most disliked about the city of Liverpool was its gloomy, colourless quality and in his *Notebooks* he contrasted the grime of both Liverpool and London with "the cheerful glare of our American cities." It was a difference between New York and Liverpool that struck an Englishwoman, a resident of the English port, in exactly the same way: "The clearness of the atmosphere, and the absence of coalsmoke" in the city of New York were particularly pleasing after "the dingy mud coloured walls of the

32. "Broadway Fashions"

houses in Liverpool". The immediate cause of this difference was not simply that the English liked dirty paint and the Americans liked gaudy colours, though some travellers were contented to attribute these differences (along with all others) to the perversity of their hosts. Other travellers were aware of the difference between the coal burnt in New York grates and that burnt in the Liverpool ones. In New York, wrote Miss Bird, "anthracite coal is almost universally used, so there is an absence of that murky, yellow canopy which disfigures English towns." This supply was to last another thirty years, that is into the 1880s, and to give eastern American cities clear atmospheres where the English cities had smog. Charles Lyell gave the readers of his *Travels in North America; With Geological Observations* a pretty full account of the geological reasons for this in the section of his book in which he discussed the Allegheny Anthracite Coalfield and he reverted to the point when he and his wife arrived at New York by way of steamboat from New Haven: "At length we seemed to sail into the very suburbs of the great city itself, passing between green islands, some of them covered with buildings and villas" and everything was crystal clear in New York's bright skies. This was not the least of the qualities that made for the stunning effect that New York Bay had on travellers newly arrived there. "It was a splendid autumnal morning"; wrote George Combe of his arrival in New York at daybreak on 25 September 1838: "the air was clear, fresh, and bracing, and the sun brilliant . . . all around was land, beautiful in its outlines, and studded with houses, white as snow, and embosomed among trees."[9]

The sky above the bay of New York reminded Lady Emmeline Stuart Wortley of Italy and the comparison was one that she was to make again about the American skies in general, "so exquisitely clear and transparent." Clear, bright prospects were not only to be found in New York – the continental eastern seaboard did not have skies like those of a small seabound western island. And the bright clear skies of Italy should not have been quite so unexpected in a city that shares a latitude with Naples. Indeed the same brightness of aspect was to be found much further north and the city of Boston, close to the latitude of Rome, could produce the same effects on the newly arrived Briton as did New York. "When I got into the streets upon this Sunday morning," wrote Charles Dickens of the day following his arrival one Saturday in Boston and the New World,

> the air was so clear, the houses so bright and gay; the signboards were painted in such gaudy colours; the gilded letters were so very golden; the bricks were so very red, the stone was so very white, the blinds and area railings were so very green, the knobs and plates upon the streets so marvellously bright and twinkling; and all so slight and unsubstantial in appearance – that every thoroughfare in the city looked exactly like a scene in a pantomime.[10]

The intensity of Dickens's reaction to this phenomenon matched the excitement of Frederick Law Olmsted in the city of Chester where he felt that the sight before him was a stage set and that at any moment stagehands would clear it all away. Dickens, like Olmsted, used the same rhetorical technique of accumulation of effects to convince the reader, and himself, of the reality of the "slight and

33. “On the Commercial Wharf, Boston”

unsubstantial” world that lay before him. Where Olmsted thrust before his reader old things – chair, table, room, tavern, city – Dickens thrust new things – signboards, bricks, blinds, railings, knobs, plates. The clear, bright atmosphere revealed a world that lived up to the promise of “New.”

Dickens continued the exploration of his New World in the same spirit of theatrical excitement for the rest of that first day: "I never turned a corner suddenly without looking out for the clown and pantaloon, who, I had no doubt, were hiding in a doorway or behind some pillar close at hand. As to Harlequin and Columbine, I discovered immediately that they lodged . . . at a very small clock maker's one story high, near the hotel." Dickens was not at all troubled by the sensations of hypersensitivity to visual impressions as Basil and Margaret Hall had been when they found their common sense of things disturbed by the onset of new stimulation after the blank and deprivation of the Atlantic. A wave of impressions like that which floated Henry James all day when he arrived in New York in 1904 lifted Charles Dickens off the ground when he arrived in Boston in 1842. Both novelists were simply delighted by the opportunity that this presented to the creative imagination. The "subject" took them by storm; they did not have to search for material; the fear was as James put it more that "the assault of suggestion is too great; too large, I mean, the number of hares started, before the pursuing imagination."[11]

So Basil Hall had enjoyed his "dreaming sort of feeling" while it had lasted but had welcomed the return to common-sense perception when it came, and the majority of British travellers were more like the Halls than like Dickens. They strove to bring themselves back to earth, slightly mistrusting the euphoria and lightheadedness that came with the arrival in so distant a land. The Americans in England handled their euphoria rather differently since they tended to identify it with a higher rather than a deranged state of consciousness. The England they had been dreaming about was a fantasy place so it came as less of a surprise that the real England was fantastic. Dickens for his part was not especially euphoric on the morning of his first walk through Boston, not especially euphoric for Dickens that is. He was always capable of becoming highly excited by the object described. His letters, essays, and speeches no less than his travel books and his novels demonstrated the same passionate concern with things and words. The rhythmic, repetitive prose that made things in Boston "so clear . . . so bright and gay . . . so very golden . . . so very red . . . so very white . . . so very green . . . so marvellously bright and twinkling . . . so slight and unsubstantial" might be found just as hard at work describing the miserable dullness of Bleeding Heart Yard or the monotony of Islington's streets. In fact an image that Dickens was to use to describe the outskirts of London in *Our Mutual Friend* cropped up at the end of his account of his first walk into the New World. He eventually reached the limits of Boston and so set himself to describe the suburbs:

The suburbs are, if possible, even more unsubstantial-looking than the city. The white wooden houses (so white that it makes one wink to look at them), with their green jalousie blinds, are so sprinkled and dropped about in all directions, without seeming to have any root at all in the ground; and the small churches and chapels are so prim, and bright, and highly varnished; that I almost believed the whole affair could be taken up piecemeal like a child's toy, and crammed into a box.[12]

If it had not been that the whole passage reflected Dickens's usual perception of the world as an unusually immediate, very present reality, then Dickens might have been thought to have been overtaken by the distorted perception that frequently overtook travellers in a new land. However since Dickens's remarkable description of Boston was in no way beyond his common high writing, it might be concluded that the common traveller sometimes achieved through the disorientation of travel the perceptive mechanism of the uncommon traveller, the writer of genius.

But even for Dickens the New World was never again to be quite so bright as it was on that first day in Boston; the special excitement expended, it was not easily achieved again, so the arrival of Charles Dickens in New York Harbour was a less colourful occasion than had been his arrival in Boston. It was still the custom in the early 1840s to take both boat and train in the journey from Boston. The through-rail link had not been organised to anything like the same degree of efficiency, so travellers found it convenient to take the train as far as some port like New Haven, and complete the journey by way of Long Island Sound. Dickens's entry into New York Harbour was by this back-door route, where the Sound narrows down to the East River and the ships come up between the islands on which New York and Brooklyn stand. "Soon," wrote Dickens, "we shot in quick succession, past a lighthouse; a madhouse (how the lunatics flung their caps and roared in sympathy with the headlong engine and the driving tide!); a jail; and other buildings: and so emerged into a noble bay." But compared with Boston, said Dickens, in New York, "the houses are not quite so fresh-coloured, the sign-boards are not quite so gaudy, the gilded letters not quite so golden, the bricks not quite so red, the stone not quite so white, the knobs and plates upon the street doors not quite so bright and twinkling." Fifty pages on Dickens produced a complete verbal echo of the description of Boston, diminishing New York's glitter point by point. The same rhetorical technique of accumulative syntax created anew the same emphasis but not the same excitement. Dickens was not finding New York as visually stimulating as he had found his first American city. In fact he found that New York's back or by-streets were as neutral as those of London and that the "Five Points" district was as filthy as Seven Dials itself. Dickens actually responded to this aspect of the city as much as he did to the poverty and depression of London: he visited the lunatics, the imprisoned, the orphaned in New York (and in all the cities of his North American tour) as much as he possibly could. It was an enthusiasm he never lost. On his return to America in 1867, he again found time to visit the slums and to describe the activities of those who preserve law and order: "I have nowhere, at home or abroad," he wrote to John Forster from Boston on 22 December 1867, "seen so fine a police as the police of New York; and their bearing in the street is above all praise . . . Let me add that I have been tempted out at three in the morning to visit one of the large police station-houses, and was so fascinated by the study of a horrible photo-book of thieves' portraits that I couldn't shut it up."[13] All his life, wherever he found himself, Dickens could not repress his interest in crime and punishment. These early examples of mug shots must have been a rich find.

Dickens's instinct to compare districts of New York with those of London in 1842, and, it might be conjectured, the likelihood that in 1867 he compared the faces of American criminals with English ones, reflected the habit of the English traveller to refer all back to the country that he had left behind him. America was constantly seen as being like or unlike England; one effect of this habit was that America tended to be praised, though by no means automatically, when it corresponded to England. Captain and Mrs Basil Hall made this the explicit standard of their judgement of the country. Since, like Captain Marryat, they found that in the long run there was more that was different about America than identical, the Halls were repulsed by the country. But even those who were not naively or grotesquely prejudiced against the American ways, and who theoretically at least wanted America to be different (and Isabella Bird, Charles Dickens, Sarah Maury, were such travellers), even they tended to judge America by an English standard, and were likely to find America failing their test even when they had no explicit purpose that America should so fail.

This observation would be more of the truism it suggests itself to be, if it were not for the case of the American travellers in England. They did not automatically judge the country visited by the country vacated. They had supplied themselves with an alternative standard by which to judge the England before them by judging it against an England "conceived from far back," as Henry James said of the England anticipated by his heroine Milly Theale, an England, "conceived from the tales of travellers and the anecdotes of New York, from the old porings over *Punch* and a liberal acquaintance with the fiction of the day."[14] In this fashion, England became the measure used by both sets of travellers. But while the American was comparing the country that he was visiting to the England of his imagination, the Englishman was comparing the country that he visited to the England of his memory; in the circumstances, this led to the Englishman's having on the whole a less agreeable time in America than the American had in England. The Englishman's searching out what reminded him of home could make his travelling become an exercise in self-contradiction; he would sometimes have done better, obviously, to have stayed at home if it were home that he was looking for. It did not necessarily make his travel book any the less entertaining or any the less instructive that it was written in a spirit of criticism rather than appreciation.

Finding a likeness to something in England became then the habit of these travellers and the pattern of their travel books. In this respect the comparison of New York to Liverpool was merely a particular example of the general tendency. Since it was also a pattern of American travel books about England it must be supposed that the English making the comparisons were responding to a suggestiveness in the scene that was very strong. But the Englishman in search of England abroad was not content with establishing this identity the once; he kept his paradigm – London – before him at all times and submitted each city as it came before him to the scrutiny that the comparison demanded: each city, that was, that could justify comparison with the great model. New York was automatically accorded this dignity, as was Boston; Philadelphia and Baltimore were also admitted to the competition.

Washington before the Civil War did not merit serious consideration; "The first appearance of Washington is exactly what I expected," wrote Margaret Hall in January, 1828, "as unlike the capital of a great country as it is possible to imagine, excepting the very first building of all, the Capitol . . . one is tempted to ask even in the heart of the city, 'Where is Washington?'" Lieutenant Gleig had spoken of it fondly as a city in its infancy, but in 1814 it possessed, he said, "no leading features"; those it had he helped to burn down. Washington remained for decades a species of joke in the Land of Promises. The most grandiose ideas of Democracy were reflected in its great outline – "They have," said Alexis de Tocqueville, "already rooted up trees for ten miles around lest they should interfere with the future citizens of this imaginary metropolis." That was in 1831; thirty years later Washington was still, as William Russell put it, "all suburb and no city" and it was not until the 1880s that its wilderness of mud was to be transformed into what James Bryce described as "one of the handsomest capitals in the world," one that cultivated "the graces and the pleasures of life with eminent success . . . a winter resort of men of wealth and leisure from all over the continent."[15] It took almost a hundred years for the American people to realise the promise and the pretension of their capital city. The great metropolitan monument to the democratic principle did not suggest, once it was completed, comparison with any European capital city: Washington remained, as it had always been for the European visitor, an anomaly, with the difference that the European now stayed to admire and not to laugh.

Towns further south than Washington were seldom considered in the comparison with London even when they were much admired by English men and women. "Tranquil" Savannah, "Oriental" Charleston, "picturesque" New Orleans, fascinated travellers but seldom invited comparison with what had been left behind. The scene with stepping stones outside St Michael's Church, Charleston, put William Thackeray's travelling companion and secretary in mind of "one of the old prints of our squares (where some of these stepping stones still survive) a hundred years ago", but generally the southern town was too exotic to suggest (or merit) direct comparison with England in point of landscape. Washington represented some sort of divide. When the Halls left it behind to travel into Virginia and the real South, they found the land so tropical that "almost for the first time we felt fairly on our travels." Had they been in Washington in the summer time they might have found that the tropics reached further north than Virginia but their southern exposure forced that reappraisal of New York that made them identify it with home. It "resembles England so much more that returning to it now we should wonder how we had ever found it different."[16]

English travellers of the Halls' political and social persuasions – that is, Tory and traditional – did often, though by no means always, find an identity between the English class system and the caste system of the South but there was very little else that was identifiably English beyond the Potomac. Englishness was essentially a feature of the northern seaports and the English traveller delighted in playing the American game of comparing cities, keeping in mind a standard that the Americans themselves did not necessarily take into account. In 1837, Captain Marryat made his play in this field by summing up the "fine city" of Boston as a place where the people "are more learned and scientific . . . than at New York; though not more so than at Philadelphia; but they are more English than in any other city in America." In the October of 1803, the Earl of Selkirk, in North America to establish a settlement on Prince Edward's Island for his emigrating crofters, found the general appearance of Boston "very much like an English Country town – making allowances for the wooden houses when they occur." This was a quality that Boston preserved for the next thirty years when Thomas Hamilton, like Selkirk a Scot, noted of Boston that "There is nothing very handsome about the town, which is rather English in appearance, and might in truth be easily mistaken for one of our more populous sea-ports." He found the houses to be built predominantly of granite and brick. The streets were narrow, crooked but clean. It was, he thought, a more finished city than New York: "There is in Boston less of that rawness of outline, and inconsistency of architecture, which had struck me at New York." One of the reasons for this was that New York had increased in size nine times in the last thirty years and a good half of it had been built in the last ten. New York was a young giantess; Boston was a staid matron. The constant building and rebuilding of New York and, to a lesser extent, of all the seaboard cities throughout the nineteenth and on non-stop into the twentieth century made them lose their English appearance. Wood, not brick and stone, became the predominant building material; brick remained the building material of the English city and gradually the difference grew. By 1849, the port of Liverpool had begun to lose the raw, fresh look that made Americans feel they had come to an American city. The city fathers had nearly completed their great programme of building docks, basins, and warehouses – and they had built in granite: "The gray stone piers and docks, the dark look of the magnificent warehouses, the substantial appearance of everything around causes one to think himself in a new world instead of the old," William Brown wrote of his arrival there in 1849. "Everything in Liverpool looks old, yet nothing is worn out." This impression of permanence was exactly the quality that Benjamin Silliman had not discovered in 1805 when he found the English port to look if anything more raw than its American equivalent. Permanence was exactly the one impression that New York did not give to the English visitor of the 1830s: "New York always gave me," said Fanny Kemble, "the idea of an irregular collection of temporary buildings, erected for some casual purpose, full of life, animation, and variety, but not meant to endure for any length of time; a fair, in short."[17] This was the note that New York was to strike, at least when seen from the bay and rivers, to the end of the century, and beyond. In 1904, Henry James was to wonder why the generally shabby and rundown appearance of the New York docks, piers and warehouses did not share in that romance which generally attaches itself to the waterfront of any European port. New York had long before achieved its condition of permanent impermanence; Europeans waited for it to be finished but not New Yorkers. Were Henry James to return in 2004, he would no doubt be able to pose the same question about the New York waterfront. But American delapidation is dynamic.

Fanny Kemble's comment that New York was like a fair caught at the reasons for this. The Americans were not building with any idea of permanence in mind. There was and is no tradition of repairing and restoring. It was always more profitable to pull down the old and set up the new; even better, where land was available, was to build a new structure right alongside the one that was falling down. If this

34. "After the Fire, New York"

did not help the look of the city, it was not the city's look that the businessman had invested in. For this reason, American cities always proved themselves so disaster-resistant; their growth like that of American forests was, in the nineteenth century at least, only stimulated by the great fires that periodically burnt down the business sections. The more complete the destruction, the more certain seemed the recovery. All the English travellers of the 1820s, 30s and 40s, had spirited descriptions to give of this phenomenon, and New York in particular was favoured with what appeared to the English as a remarkable number of fires. Fanny Kemble noted in her *Journal* during one visit to the city, that a fire was raging outside her hotel and that "this is about the sixth fire since yesterday evening. They are so frequent here, that the cry, 'Fire, fire!' seems to excite neither alarm nor curiosity."[18] She, like most English women and men, had high praise for the New York fire-fighters, the most ancient and most honoured of the city's uniformed brigades.

Boston was not much better. Lady Emmeline was woken by the

alarms of fire every night that she stayed in the city in 1849. She claimed on a second visit to the city that the fires were so frequent that they had become a means of lighting the streets. This may have been an example of traveller's gullibility, pardonable exaggeration, or Yankee wit, but it suggested the dimension of the problem, though neither in Boston, Gloucester, nor New York did Lady Emmeline ever take fright so many, bold, and ready were the bands of volunteer firemen.[19]

Most travellers concocted some theory to account for the frequency of these fires. Among the more popular were to blame the negligence of Negro servants, the American indifference to the loss of human life, and the practice of arson by insurance agents. But the English enjoyed these fires as much as any New Yorker or Bostonian and did not fail to note how readily the wooden houses burnt. "I was in very great luck in the spectacle I witnessed," Margaret Hall wrote. "There were four houses destroyed. They burnt as if they had been made of paper." Mrs Hall relished a good show; Harriet Martineau had the serious misfortune in this direction of missing by no more than a few days the Great New York Fire of 1834. This destroyed all of the Wall Street area: "The New York fire broke out at eight in the evening of Wednesday, the 16th of December," she reported in *Society in America*. "Every one knows the leading facts, that 52 or 54 acres were laid waste; many public buildings destroyed, and property to the amount of 18,000,000 dollars." When the fire was at its height, news was brought of the absolute lack of water because of the freezing up of every standpipe in the city – worse was the fact that there was no gunpowder to be had closer than the town of Brooklyn. The fire could not be fought and breaks in the housing could not be made. Harriet Martineau was not insensible to the human tragedy that lay behind the great spectacle of such a fire and she repeated a moving detail of the catastrophe: a lady and gentleman spectator "took their stand in a square, in the centre of which an immense quantity of costly goods was heaped up. It was strange and vexatious to see the havoc that was made among beautiful things; – cachemere shawls strewing the ground; the horses' feet swathed in lace veils . . . After [the lady] had left the place, the houses caught fire, all round the square fell in, and burned the costly goods in one grand bonfire."[20]

But despite the individual tragedies, the fires were not bad for

35. Wall Street

At right angles with Broadway was Wall Street, the often-described business centre of New York, of which the sketch gives some notion as it existed at that time. As you entered the Merchants' Exchange in that thoroughfare you heard the voices of eager auctioneers, seen gesticulating, each of them in their individual stalls fixed circularly round the inner Rotunda. (Eyre Crowe)

business. It was as true for New York in 1836 as the Earl of Selkirk had discovered of Boston in 1803: "every considerable fire has tended to the improvement of the city & very generally the ground has sold for more than the old houses would have done before the fire often 30 per ct."[21] Harriet Martineau witnessed the first signs of the rebuilding of New York's business area and travellers' reports were soon enlivened by details of the fabulous real estate transactions that followed the fire. The commercial energy that was making the boom town one of the most startling features of the American landscape, creating cities out of wilderness overnight, always seized the opportunity to create a new downtown out of new havoc.

If New York was "that city which seems to be more plagued with fire than any town in the world," that might in itself have been an index of its commercial activity and success. One of the effects of the burning was a constant rebuilding. The constant rebuilding (the fires were only one cause of this) made New York progressively less like London all the time. The pace of building (and of fires) was a little slower in Boston, partly because it had lost its eighteenth-century commercial equality with New York, consequently it reminded English visitors more frequently of home. "The houses," said Fanny Kemble, are like English houses: the Common is like Constitution Hill; Beacon Street is like a bit of Park Lane; and Summer Street, now that the chestnut trees are in bloom, is perfectly beautiful." Boston created a most favourable impression on that critical diplomat, Thomas Grattan, not least because it was "far more English-looking than New York." He too liked the Common, comparing it to a London park, "one of the finest of its kind" which he had ever seen. And the poet and scholar, Arthur Hugh Clough, found some consolation in Boston for his over-hasty resignation from his appointment as principal of University Hall, London: "I like Boston," he said in a letter to England dated 11 November 1852, "there is a sort of park, 'the Common' with iron railings, and houses something like the Piccadilly row above the Green Park, only all residences without shops . . . [one of these belonging to General Hancock] quite an old-fashioned George II. house; the others later, of red brick, with balustrading and carving, many of them. It is really very tolerably English in the town." Boston was attractive to the English and attractive because it was "English." Charles Lyell experienced the pleasant surprise of this likeness when he landed there in 1841: "I am astonished, after having traversed the wide ocean, at the resemblance of everything I see and hear to things familiar at home." And he and his wife responded to Boston's congeniality to the extent that after they had been in and around the city for some weeks (while Lyell lectured on the principles of geology), "we often reflected," he wrote, "with surprise in how many parts of England we should have felt less at home."[22]

This sensation of feeling "at home" abroad, a sensation searched out by the English traveller, was to be achieved to some extent in the city of Philadelphia but the regularity of its street plan, the grid laid down by its Quaker founders, was felt to be characteristically American and by the same measure quite un-English: "Philadelphia," said Thomas Hamilton, "is mediocrity personified in brick and mortar. It is a city laid down by square and rule, a sort of habitable problem, – a mathematical infringement on the rights of individual eccentricity, – a rigid and prosaic despotism of right angles and parallelograms." The majority of English visitors found this regularity wearisome. George Combe liked the Philadelphia grid – "Nothing can exceed the convenience and elegance of this plan," he wrote in *Notes on the United States of North America during a Phrenological Visit*; but Combe, as the title of his book made clear, was something of a scientist. Philadelphia put at defiance the expectation of most transatlantic visitors of what a city should be; it overruled all notions of picturesque beauty and usually proved visually distressing. It was agreed to be a comfortable town, nonetheless. Its clean, spruce appearance also set it apart from European cities in the 1830s. Fanny Kemble felt that the city had achieved some special distinction in this regard: "'Cleanliness,' says the old saw, 'is near to godliness.' Philadelphia must be very near heaven." This even held true for the market which Fanny Trollope found very perfection: "The neatness, the freshness, and entire absence of everything disagreeable to sight or smell, must be witnessed to be believed." This was as unlike London as the street plan, though the prices could be compared. They were lower than London's, higher than Exeter's, and about the same as those of Paris in 1830. Mrs Trollope found that the regularity of the street plan and the good order of the market extended to the behaviour of the citizens so that they were all in their homes by ten o'clock and the city was dark and silent on a lovely, cool evening that would have found Regent's Street in London or the Italian Boulevard in Paris filled with people, light and noise. Philadelphia had a tamed quality that was especially in contrast with New York, a quality that made it seem very provincial. The English always had great difficulty in understanding the pretensions of Philadelphia society for this reason, though the Philadelphians practised a pattern of social snobbery that would have appeared to have been something like that of London itself: "There is no American city in which the system of *exclusion* is so rigidly observed as in Philadelphia. The ascent of the parvenu into the aristocratic circle is slow and difficult."[23]

All those English travellers who had assumed that American claims to have created a society in which all men were equal meant that all men and women were equally welcome in the Philadelphian home were distressed to find that this was not so: "The European is at once amused and annoyed," wrote Fanny Kemble (no liker of democratic manners herself), "with the assumption of a social tone and spirit at variance with the whole *make* of the country." The English liked their Americans to be democratic just as the Americans liked their English to be aristocratic. A woman like Harriet Martineau who actively espoused a liberal philosophy found the "caste" system of Philadelphia quite intolerable. She discovered that in Philadelphia (as in London) certain young ladies simply could not be brought to meet certain other young ladies. Miss Martineau for her part was unable to distinguish in any way between one group and the other. When in her painstaking, but in this instance perhaps not entirely disingenuous, way she enquired why this was the case, she was given various answers: "One person told me that a stranger could not see into the usages of their society," she wrote in *Society in America*. "Another said that the mutual ignorance was from the fathers of the Arch Street ladies having made their fortunes, while the Chestnut Street ladies owed theirs to their grandfathers." It was the kind of distinction that would have been perfectly satisfactory in Manchester, but the English liked to let it worry them in Philadelphia. Even Harriet Martineau, usually so skilled in her analyses of American motivation, allowed herself to be too irritated by the surface facts to search beyond them to the kind of sociological truth that had led the Count Alexis de Tocqueville to conclude a few years before that political equality naturally divided Americans into small private circles. They mixed freely in the market and in congress but for that reason were careful to separate in their homes.[24]

William Thackeray found Philadelphia society insupportable – "I think there's nothing to say except that I'm well through a week of awful Philadelphia hospitality," he wrote to Mrs Carmichael-Smith in the January of 1853. "They dine at 4 and sup at 10. They're offended if you don't come and God help the man whom nature has endowed with a good appetite." But he recognised that he was in a city not quite so different from London as this might suggest for he wrote from Philadelphia to another correspondent, Lady Stanley, that "I find wonderful little difference in manners – an accent not quite like our's but why need it be?" And though this was to find the English note in the people rather than the place, the city itself could evoke that sense of home, because Fanny Kemble paid the city a tribute that was quite out of keeping with the general pattern of her first book about America, a book in which she deliberately set out to blow the country up: "I am sorry to leave Philadelphia," she wrote in her *Journal.* "There is an air of stability, of well to do, and occasionally of age, in the town, that reminds me of England."[25] (Among the socially eligible young men of the city she discovered one who made her a husband. This made even Philadelphia attractive for a time no doubt.)

10

PICTURESQUE LANDSCAPES: NEW ENGLAND AND THE HUDSON

The English looked for English effects in American cities and they looked for English effects in the American countryside. American landscapes most readily appreciated were those that were most picturesque; these were also the most English. Travellers responded, as might be expected, to what was most familiar and to what was most conventional, and satisfactory landscapes were to be found in New England and New York – traditionally the most "English" regions of the Americas. "Who is it that says that America is not picturesque? I forget," wrote Fanny Trollope, "but surely he never travelled from Utica to Albany. I really cannot conceive that any country can furnish a drive of ninety-six miles more beautiful or more varied in its beauty." Of this region Alex Mackay wrote a decade or so later: "I had seen nothing in America which in appearance so nearly approximated a fertile rural district of England." To say that a valley was English was to say that it was picturesque and very beautiful. At the beginning of the century, John Lambert travelled by coach from Boston to New York and noted in his *Travels*: "Through the whole of this journey of 240 miles . . . I had passed over a most beautiful tract of country, which . . . afforded a variety of the most beautiful landscapes, and strongly reminded me of England." This kind of compliment to the New England and New York landscapes became a commonplace of the literature. Even the caustic Basil Halls were not immune to the charms of these regions and Mrs Hall wrote home in her second letter a warm description of Long Island comparing it favourably with the model landscape: "The part through which we drove is prettily wooded and has altogether an English appearance, altho' the trees are very small."[1]

There were to be found numerous pretty and neat farms on Long Island, in the Mohawk and the Genesee Valleys, in the Connecticut Valley and outside of Boston. And in all these places there were also to be found towns and villages where, said John Lambert in 1808, "a remarkably neat and indeed elegant style of architecture and decoration seems to pervade all the buildings." The white clapboard, green venetian blinds, grey shingles that he found in 1808 were just as bright when Charles Dickens saw them in 1842: "every house is the whitest of the white; every Venetian blind the greenest of the green; every fine day's sky the bluest of the blue." One village especially was singled out for praise, Canandaigua on the lake of that name, a lake that feeds the Mohawk River. Of this and other villages, Basil Hall wrote: "The word town would seem more appropriate, as these villages are not composed of cottages clustered together; but of fine houses, divided by wide streets, and embellished by groves of trees and flower gardens." Canandaigua was praised by Thomas Hamilton and by Richard Cobden; and in 1848, Alex Mackay wrote of it that visiting its broad, breezy streets with elegant white houses, "You are apt to forget that such a thing as poverty exists." "Faultless cleanliness" marked this village as it did all "the small towns, which so profusely dot the surface of Western New York . . . in every respect the most charming of their kind in the Union." This area he pointed out had long been settled and was loveliest along the road between Lake Erie and Albany. Coach travel had been superseded by the canal boat but travellers by the old road had a special reward: "The aspect which the country on either side presents is more like that of an English than an American landscape."[2]

Travellers along the Erie Canal itself enjoyed not only the visual delights of this beautiful Mohawk Valley but endured the visual onslaught of the peculiarly American phenomenon, the boom town, in the examples of Rochester and Buffalo. Of the first, Basil Hall gave a splendidly spirited description when the great Canal had only been open a year. Building was going on everywhere; streets were being cut through the forest, and settlers were all the time arriving; Hall relished the heady mixture of the new and the primeval. There was "not to be found in 1827 a single grown-up person born there," he wrote with some satisfaction. There were in all 800 inhabitants. Three years later, Thomas Hamilton reported that "Rochester is a place worth seeing. Twenty years ago there was not a house in the neighbourhood, and now there is a town containing thirteen thousand good Americans and true . . . Such a growth is more like forcing in a hot-bed, than the natural progress of human vegetation."[3]

Rochester, like Buffalo, was distinguished by its very activity and life; its unfinished, reckless appearance was redeemed for most of its visitors by the very promise of success. This was a landscape that spoke of the future and as long as it did so with confidence it had a kind of lurid fascination for the English visitor even though he was used to the finished quality of the cities of his own country and was more naturally attracted to the established village like Canandaigua. But the less prosperous settlement was always distressing. Of these, Basil Hall wrote: "The houses are generally left unpainted, and being scattered about without order, look more like a collection of great packing boxes, than the human residences which the eye is accustomed to see in old countries."[4] The image of the packing box implied not only a less careful society but a less caring society – a society that disposed of its human beings as material goods. The image was oddly at variance with the relative poverty of the Old and the New Worlds and it took no account of the housing provided for the urban populations of England but the image nonetheless spoke to a difference in perceived values.

For Charles Dickens looking at the landscapes created by another canal, one in Pennsylvania, the impressions were those of a culture that was indifferent to visual effect and spiritual value alike: "The eye was pained to see the stumps of great trees thickly strewn in every field of wheat, and seldom to lose the eternal swamp and dull morass, with hundreds of rotten trunks and twisted branches steeped in its unwholesome water. It was quite sad and oppressive, to come upon great tracts where settlers had been burning down the trees, and where their wounded bodies lay about". The images of slaughter and death were more impressive than the sight of settlement and growth. The reason why, as George Combe put it, "many objects in America appear unfinished" was well enough understood by reflective travellers – labour was so much more expensive than materials that, compared with England, finish and upkeep were neglected on houses, farms and estates. But understanding was not sympathy, and travellers from England were unable to keep aesthetic judgements separate from moral ones. The slovenly, unkempt appearance of most American landscapes was identified with a slovenly, reckless attitude presumed in the inhabitants of that landscape. In frontier New York, hard by the settled and domesticated western New York, Basil Hall found the absence of typical features of the English landscape dispiriting: "Not a single hedge or wall was to be seen in those places, all the enclosures being made of split logs, built one upon the top of another in zig-zag fashion, like what the ladies call a Vandyke border. These are named snake fences, and are certainly the most ungraceful-looking things I ever saw." Ten years earlier William Cobbett, farming in Long Island, had voiced a similar complaint, concerning the otherwise beautiful landscape. There was one principal disfigurement, "namely, the fences; and indeed . . . the general . . . slovenliness about the homesteads, and particularly about the dwellings of labourers."[5]

The limitations of the American labourer in these respects made a major theme of the book that Cobbett called *A Year's Residence in the United States of America*, the lengthy subtitle of which described it as (among other things) "treating of the face of the country, the climate, the soil, the products, the mode of cultivating the land . . . and of the usual manner of living, of the manners and customs of the people." By and large, he found that the people's manners and customs left a great deal to be desired in point of good husbandry. Cobbett contrasted the untidy American homesteads with the neat, "fairy-land" farms of England: "We here see the labourers content with a shell of boards, while all around him is as barren as the sea-beach . . . This want of attention in such cases is hereditary from the first settlers. They found land so plenty, that they treated small plots with contempt. Besides, the example of neatness was wanting. There were no gentlemen's gardens, kept as clean as drawing rooms."[6]

On Cobbett's rural rides through America, rides that were for the most part made in Long Island, New Jersey and Pennsylvania in 1817 to 1818, what he loved above all were fine, prosperous farms that displayed their success in the form of handsome, commodious buildings and well-ordered, neat fields. The image of the good farm and the pattern of good farming were those that he carried from his childhood; in the general preface to his book on American agriculture, he offered these images as his credentials: "As to farming," he wrote, "I was bred at the plough-tail, and in the Hop-Gardens of Farnham in Surrey, my native place, and which spot, as it so happened, is the neatest in England, and I believe in the whole world. All there is a garden." The English gentleman's garden remained the model of agriculture for Cobbett and the garden-like landscapes of England were those that he looked for in America; this was true even though he was in many ways a most practical man and his book on Long Island farming was as much a treatise on agricultural methods as a description of country, manners, and customs. William Cobbett was typical of those English farmers whose methods Harriet Martineau found were a source of amusement to Americans: "English farmers settling in the United States used to be a joke to their native neighbours," she wrote in *Society in America*. "The Englishman began with laughing, or being shocked, at the slovenly methods of cultivation employed by the American settlers; he was next seen to look grave on his own account; and ended by following the American plan." He learnt that careful farming led to ruin – "he has got to a place where it answers to spend land and save labour."[7]

William Cobbett did not remain in America long enough either to fall into the slovenly habits of the Americans or to learn the nature of their economies. He returned instead to England and eventually to Parliament to take up the last great work of his life, his investigation of the English farm and of agricultural England. His great book, *Rural Rides*, gave full expression to the radical conservatism that had directed his life on his much loved Long Island farm. Cobbett's antagonism to the American rural landscape where it did not remind him of his beloved native England was exceptional only because he developed it so self-consciously into an issue of national political consciousness. He had a mission, if not to convert the Americans, at least to convince the English that English ways, "old" English ways were best. Where he found the Americans better than the English, he did so because the Americans had preserved manners and customs that had fallen into disuse in England – he saw American hospitality as a relic of a once Merrie England. Where he found the Americans inferior to the English it was because new climates and new conditions had seduced them from the good manners and customs of their forefathers. But in searching out "English" effects Cobbett was in fact following the pattern that was typical of the English traveller in America.

The commentary on the slovenly homesteads of the American

farmer that filled Cobbett's journal found a close echo in the journal of a traveller who had no farming connection of William Cobbett's kind. In 1832, Fanny Kemble's theatrical tour brought her to New Jersey and there she noted that "The farms had the same desolate, untidy, untended look [as the farms of Irish and French peasants]: the gates broken, the fences carelessly put up, or ill repaired; the farming utensils sluttishly scattered about a littered yard." She contrasted this pattern to that of the English labourer: "who, after, 'sweating in the eye of Phoebus' all the day, at evening trains the fragrant jasmine round his lowly door, is the same man who, in other circumstances, would have been the refined and liberal patron of those arts which reflect the beauty of nature."[8] This remarkable linking of the English peasant and English lord was intended to suggest a moral and cultural identity between the English cottage gardener and the English landscape gardener. The English park and the English garden, the two features of the English landscape most enjoyed by the American traveller in England, were the two features most missed by the English traveller in America. In New Jersey, Fanny Kemble found snake-fencing in place of England's "hedge-rows green." Fanny Kemble did not look in vain for her idealised landscape; along the banks of Schuylkill near Philadelphia, she found what were for her most attractive houses, gardens and farms. "It was," she said, "a bit of England." But the Schuylkill landscape was not the typical American landscape, and in the various Atlantic States that she visited she looked everywhere for the peculiarities of the English countryside. Not finding them, she despised what she did find – the resourceful snake-fence, the energetically cleared forest and the demanding settlement living. The fact that in parts of Pennsylvania and elsewhere in America, she was able to find "a bit of England" only confirmed her contempt for the American experiment in living and landscape. She concluded that the American high and low refused to refine life in the way that the Englishman high and low refined life; she further concluded that this refusal by the American arose from deficiencies in moral and aesthetic sensibility.

In later years, following marriage to an American and life in various parts of America, Fanny Kemble was to moderate her contempt for the American, but in 1832, at the height of her own personal success and in the extravagance of her own self-esteem,

36. Fanny Kemble

this young woman gave unqualified expression to that unquiet self-satisfaction that made the English traveller regard English manners, customs and character as in all ways superior to other manners, customs, and character.

Fanny Kemble's *Journal*, the record of her first two years in America, was a document of self-congratulation. The reader was intended to take away a high opinion of the sensibility that produced the *Journal* and to conclude that Fanny Kemble represented the most admirable kind of Romantic spirit in contact and conflict with a most un-Romantic reality. America and the American served to provide an antithetical statement of these values. Fanny Kemble gave her readers a great deal of the reflective and the introspective in her *Journal*; she spoke a great deal of poetry, of Shakespeare, of the high impulse and the Romantic occasion; she spoke disparagingly of the profession of acting and warmly of the aspiration of drama. She placed before the reader the image of herself as one in whom the most refined impressions of art and of nature were to be found; she placed before the reader the image of the American as one in whom the least refined impressions of these things were to be found. "The utter insensibility of the generality of Americans to the beauty and sublimity of nature is nothing short of amazing; and in this respect they literally appear to me to want a sense. I have been filled with astonishment and perplexity at the total indifference with which they behold scenes of grandeur and loveliness that any creatures, with half a soul, would gaze at with feelings almost of adoration."[9] The reader could not but infer that Miss Kemble had a whole soul. She had that "sense" that the American lacked; the reader was to understand that his guide through the American landscape had the wholeness of sensibility that distinguished the Romantic soul, a sensibility that made it capable of responding to the high call of beauty and sublimity.

Fanny Kemble was moving her argument and her *Journal* away from the merely pleasing landscape to one that spoke of higher or of deeper values. These were landscapes that went beyond "a bit of England" though they required the developed sensations of the English sensibility to appreciate them. At the much praised Canandaigua in western New York, Fanny Kemble reached, as she believed, the limits of the American faculty for appreciation. She and her party had been taken up to the observatory of their inn to look down on the village and lake, and she wrote, "the view was perfectly enchanting. The green below screened in three sides with remarkably fine poplar trees, and surrounded by neat white houses, reminded me of some retired spot in my own dear country."[10] This scene of England in America was one appreciated by her hosts, by the innkeeper who had thought it worthwhile to provide a viewing point, one that the inhabitants of Canandaigua might be presumed to appreciate because they had created and preserved it. It was not typical of the American landscape but it was the best that the Americans could offer and at this best the Americans had by labour and long cultivation been able to suggest England.

The Americans achieved such a landscape only rarely; sluttish and slovenly habits made the land look more commonly like Ireland and like France. This was the primary conclusion of Fanny Kemble's *Journal* but it was not the only conclusion. Canandaigua lay mid way between two special landscapes, neither of them man made, but both going beyond the limits, as Fanny Kemble perceived them, of the American capacity for appreciation. These landscapes were those of the Hudson Highlands and Niagara Falls. These were for Fanny Kemble outstanding examples of the beautiful and the sublime. These she maintained were beyond the American, who almost everywhere showed himself insensitive to landscape. She was so taken by that of the Hudson that she questioned the failure of the Americans, as it seemed to her, to respond in the proper way to what they saw. "Is it possible," she asked, "that a perception of the beautiful in nature is a result of artificial cultivation? – is it that the grovelling narrowness of the unusual occupations to which the majority addict themselves has driven out of them the fine spirit, which is God's altar in men's souls? – is it that they become incapable of beauty? Wretched people!"[11]

Fanny Kemble's *Journal* provided in fact good examples of the kind of fine writing, refined feeling and Romantic response that the American people were trying to emulate in their own writing about the British landscape. *Sketches of Society in Great Britain and Ireland* by C. S. Stewart, M.A., of the U.S. Navy, published in the same year as Fanny Kemble's *Journal*, showed in its descriptions of the Scottish Highlands an appreciation for landscape that came close to matching Fanny Kemble's own. The American is never as forceful and never as original as the Englishwoman but he understood what had to be felt and said. But the English traveller was unaware of the finer souls among the Americans; the anti-Romantic American seemed to be the kind who made his presence felt when the English traveller was attempting to commune with Nature. When Fanny Kemble went to Weehawken to enjoy the view of the Hudson Palisades, the pine-clad cliffs through which the river cuts its lower passage, she discovered that "the effect of the whole was very sad and beautiful; and had I been by myself I should have enjoyed it very much. But I was in company, and moreover, in company with two punsters who uttered their atrocities without remorse in the midst of all that was most striking and melancholy in nature."[12]

The pun was the figure of speech least likely to give expression to the soulful feelings of the Romantic sensibility, but the unpoetical nature of the American character was further revealed, and more certainly and more damningly in Fanny Kemble's opinion, by the names that the American had given to the lovely hills of the Hudson

Valley. "Even the heathen Dutch," she protested, "among us the very antipodes of all poetry, have found names such as Donder Berg for the hills, whilst the Americans christen them Butter Hill, the Crows Nest, and such like." This down-to-earth quality, not softened at all by distance of time or tongue, exacerbated the roused sensitivity of a writer who was deliberately seeking out the Romantic as the occasion for proofs of her own strength of feeling and the superiority of her national sensibility. The Romantic poets were after all an English phenomenon; English sensibility was for a brief, unique moment guiding the world. It appeared to Fanny Kemble remarkable that a nation that shared the English tongue should be so wayward in this field of achievement. "Where are the poets of this land?" she challenged;[13] not without satisfaction, she discovered that there were none.

When the English traveller moved beyond the familiar, the pleasing, the "English" landscape in America, the first step was always towards the beautiful conceived in terms of the Lake poets and for this reason the Hudson River with its great glacier-cut valley never failed to excite a powerful response. It became an occasion for a set piece in landscape description and always evoked comparison with the Scottish Highlands or the Rhine Valley. A European model was available as an aid and response was immediate. Fanny Kemble rose to this challenge and presented very full descriptions of the Hudson Valley in her *Journal*, at all points from New York City to Albany – the town where the traveller's journey turned west along the Mohawk Valley towards the even greater challenge set to the Romantic sensibility by Niagara Falls. In terms of landscape descriptions, the first volume of Fanny Kemble's *Journal* was dominated by the glories of the Hudson as the second was dominated by the sublimity of Niagara.

The poetic mode that Fanny Kemble employed for her descriptions was Wordsworthian; in this she was like all other English travellers: "and rock and river, earth and sky," she wrote, "shone in intense and dazzling brilliancy." The prose instinctively took up the rhythms, the diction, all but the rhyme of Wordsworth's verse. As her steamboat bore her up river, Fanny Kemble allowed her readers to experience with her the growing intensity of her mood, the steady heightening of sensibility. "Far away the distant summits of the Highlands rose one above another, shutting in the world, and

37. Military Review at West Point

almost appearing as though each bend of the river must find us locked in their shadowy circle, without means of onward progress." The boat, Fanny Kemble and the reader moved through what became a series of lakes in the progress north. Each sequent lake provided a new landscape and a new experience: "At every moment the scene varied; at every moment, new beauty and grandeur was revealed to us."[14]

This mode of language was moving beyond the picturesque and preparing the reader for a more profound experience of the landscape than the principles of picturesque beauty could provide for. Fanny Kemble's Wordsworthian preliminaries make the reader ready for a full-scale Romantic moment, the encounter with the awesome. This translation from the picturesque through the beautiful to the sublime could only be guaranteed by one landscape – that was Niagara. It was in that certain knowledge that Fanny Kemble approached the great falls and it was to that climax that the second volume of her *Journal* led. But Niagara was only the *certain* occasion of sublime experience not the *only* occasion. So it was that Fanny Kemble was blessed with her encounter with the sublime amidst the growing beauties of the Hudson. At West Point, at the most famous spot overlooking the river, she and her reader had their reward. Everything conspired to the moment as Fanny Kemble, at last freed from the company of the "wretched people," and the miserable punsters, walked splendidly upward to take the view: "I looked down, and for a moment my breath seemed to stop, the pulsation of my heart to cease – I was filled with awe. The beauty and the wild sublimity of what I beheld seemed almost to crush my faculties, – I felt dizzy as though my senses were drowning, – I felt as though I had been carried into the immediate presence of God."[15] More than that a traveller could not ask of a boat trip.

West Point was capable of stirring Romantic longings and reveries in travellers far less susceptible to Romantic impressions than was Fanny Kemble. Four years after her divine encounter, Captain Frederick Marryat was climbing to the viewing point and he too was richly compensated: "A more beautiful view I never gazed upon," he wrote, "It is what you may imagine the Rhine to have been in the days of Caesar, when the lofty mountains through which it sweeps were not bared and naked as they are now, but clothed with forests, and rich in all the variety and beauty of undisturbed nature." The glories of the Hudson were in fact as well established for the tourist's pleasure as those of the Lake District and the Scottish Highlands. And they had come to the attention of the connoisseurs of these things at about the same time. Emerson thought of Scott's poetry as no more than "a rhymed traveller's guide to Scotland," and this had begun to bring the Scottish landscape to Romantic attention at the beginning of the nineteenth century. In 1807, John Lambert was celebrating the beauties of the Hudson in a florid prose that ran three pages at a time and he quoted a Romantic poem about the river that was in a verse not very much worse than Scott's own. "The river," Lambert wrote, "affords some of the noblest landscapes and scenery that are to be found in any part of North America."[16]

Fanny Kemble was writing in the same tradition, though not all prose descriptions of the Hudson attempted the mystical plain. Three years before Fanny Kemble was at West Point, Thomas Hamilton was there preparing a long purple passage that reflected more the principles of picturesque beauty than the Wordsworthian sublime. "What struck me as chiefly admirable," he wrote, "was the fine proportion of the different features of the landscape." He went on to call the Hudson "one of nature's felicities," and he praised the Hudson landscapes because of their "perfect subordination of parts."[17] This judicious measuring of elements was much closer in emotional terms to the gentlemanly enthusiasms of the eighteenth century than to Romantic ecstasy. The landscape was pleasing rather than inspiring and this was perhaps closer to the common response of travellers than Fanny Kemble's effusions.

The emotional condition to which she laid claim was nonetheless the state to which many travellers felt they ought to aspire. The diplomat, Thomas Grattan, travelled from his consulate in Boston with a firm purpose of appreciating to the full and in the proper manner the beauties of the Hudson River and of the Catskill Mountains. He warned that he was of a class that loved nature "from the impulse of genuine and listless love." The reader was thus prepared for the genuine article which proved to be "the murmuring rill, the sighing breeze, the singing birds." Grattan's enjoyment of Nature suggested a well-dressed hippopotamus engaged in the waltz. "It was thus that I wandered about the Hudson in irregular and 'truant disposition'," he wrote with a delightful pomposity. Grattan ended his tour of the region well satisfied with the "deep draughts of true religion and philosophy"[18] that he had taken in the Catskills.

The well-turned, conventional language of Lambert, Hamilton and Grattan showed them to be at ease with their feelings and subject. They knew what they must say and how they must say it; their descriptions make pleasant reading. The animosity that Hamilton and Grattan usually felt towards the men and manners of America was placated; the distress often caused by the slovenly and sluttish farming methods of the Americans was not provoked – partly because of the prosperity of the Valley and partly because the scale of the views precluded close observation. At the same time the scale of the views was not so great that they could not be enjoyed by those used to the European landscape. If the traveller had been to the Rhine, or to the Scottish Highlands, he had anticipated these Hudson views quite satisfactorily. As Charles Stewart said of Loch Lomond: "In its general features, it is not unlike some points in our principle rivers, and scarce rivals in beauty, the more bold and romantic sections of the Hudson."[19] Consequently in the 1830s the Briton writing about the Hudson Highlands and the American writing about the Scottish Highlands tended to sound very much alike.

11

THE FALLS OF NIAGARA: A DANGEROUS SUBJECT

In 1804, Thomas Moore wrote home to say, "We must have new combinations of language to describe the Falls of Niagara." He did not find them but he did tell his family that he had seen the Falls and was "all rapture and amazement."[1] The poet was set a challenge; it was one that was taken up by successive nineteenth-century writers, with greater or lesser success, but none of them found a new combination of language to do the job. Writers instead took refuge in the device of describing the Falls as indescribable. Moore's notion that something new in language must be found suggested that it was a job for the original talent of the poet but he was the only *bona fide* English Romantic poet who actually travelled to the Falls.

Nonetheless, Niagara was the ultimate in Romantic landscapes; it all but guaranteed an encounter with the Wordsworthian divine; those who could not get in touch with this emotional reality elsewhere could by way of travelling to Niagara give themselves the awful moment. It was an occasion when the most prosaic of men and women might become poetical. Richard Cobden visited it both times that he went to America and his journal, usually devoted to matters of business, politics, trade and railroads, took flight for a paragraph or so. On his second visit, in 1859, he wrote:

> The great and glorious cataract seems alike unchanged in its grandeur and minutest features. – It is a spectacle suggestive of ideas of eternity & omnipotence. – One is almost brought to kneel and pray. – I wish Byron had seen this most sublime of moving scenes that he might have given us a companion verse to his description of Mont Blanc which is sublimity in repose.[2]

Unlike the landscapes of the Hudson, this one could not easily be anticipated in Europe; there were few ways of preparing emotion and language in advance and travellers felt their deficiencies strongly, humbly turning their attention to details that could be described, fondly imagining what the great poets would make of the scene, and above all indignantly turning upon those who did not feel the profundities of the occasion and upon those who had built hotel, souvenir shop, and power mill to exploit the "great and glorious cataract." Fanny Kemble's general disdain of an unpoetical, "wretched" people was an emotion that in this particular place became one shared by the most pedestrian of English travellers. The search for the new combinations of language made for strain. The writer felt stretched to his limits by Niagara and there was none of the easy presentation that often made the descriptions of the Hudson Valley bland.

Anthony Trollope, speaking of the good landscape, said that "size has but little to do with it," but this did not address itself to the problem of landscapes that were too big to be appreciated. Trollope was thinking only of the fact that sheer size was not in itself a guarantee of beauty. And in fact the principles of picturesque beauty were very much concerned with narrowing down landscapes to comprehensible size. Nature, as William Gilpin explained, works on a vast scale, and "the immensity of nature is beyond comprehension."[3] Niagara posed a special problem: its scale was vast but it was visually comprehensible. It was exactly at the limits of landscape art. If it was beyond the limits of the picturesque, it was still within the limits of the sublime.

Travellers took up the challenge of Niagara and they attempted to act out the ritual of Romantic response in the face of a landscape that reminded them more frequently of the sea than of anything they had ever seen on land before. In crossing the Atlantic, it had befallen many of them to experience the violence of Atlantic storms, storms which they described in language that became appropriate for Niagara: "I saw," wrote George Combe of the great swell following a sea storm, "the sublimely moving masses of water rolling slowly yet irresistibly on, embodying the very spirit of gigantic power." It was to these storms that he compared Niagara. Niagara was beyond words, so was the Ocean. Charles Dickens endured a series of storms on his way out to America and he attempted to convey the power of the final storm by means of denying the power of language to express his meaning. "To say that all is grand, and appalling and horrible in the last degree, is nothing. Words cannot express it. Thoughts cannot convey it. Only a dream can call it up again, in all its fury, rage and passion." And Alex Mackay approached the might of the Atlantic with the same reverence and the same sense of superior occasion that he was to bring to his visit to Niagara. As his royal-mail steamship, the *Hibernia*, left Liverpool to begin a winter passage of the great ocean (in January 1846) he commented: "Before us lay the broad Atlantic, foaming and turbulent. I do not envy the man who could look, for the first time, on such a scene without emotion."[4]

The sea provided an image of the sublime and gave practice for emotions that were to be overexercised by many aspects of the American landscape where the wilderness provided so strong a contrast to what the Briton left behind. The American in the English landscape felt the reverse effect and turned to the sea to give him some flavour of that wilderness. E. S. Nadal found that English scenery was always "pleasing" but that this left him with a sense of incompleteness. "Nature," he said, "has been chased out of England into the sea," and the ocean alone was "sublime." James Russell Lowell wrote of the sea from Whitby to Mrs Leslie Stephen, "Thank God, they can't landscape-garden *him*."[5]

The sea, especially the sea in storm, provided an anticipation or a parallel for Niagara. Niagara was also anticipated by the various falls that the traveller saw on route to Niagara. These were particularly plentiful and splendid in western New York. Fanny Kemble, already keenly anticipating Niagara found the falls at Trenton impressive: "The several falls are very various in their height and forms," she noted in her *Journal*, "but they are all beautiful, most beautiful; not a place to visit for a day, but to live the summer away in." In sensing that falls required time in which to become fully appreciated, Fanny Kemble voiced one of the most frequent reactions to Niagara itself. Frederick Marryat experienced at the Trenton Falls a whole series of feelings that he was to feel again very shortly at Niagara: "As I stood over them in their wild career, listening to their roaring as if in anger, and watching the madness of their speed, I felt a sensation of awe – an inward acknowledgement of the tremendous power of Nature."[6]

At all these falls in western New York, "acknowledgement of the tremendous power of Nature" took all too literal a form from the point of view of the romantically minded tourist. The falling water was used to power mills, bringing people, factories, and visual blight. At the Genesee Falls, Thomas Hamilton was unable to enjoy the natural beauty at all: "The vicinity of sundry saw and corn mills has destroyed the romantic interest which invested [the uppermost fall] in the days when 'the cataract blew his trumpet from the steep,' amid the stillness of the surrounding forest." Towards the end of a volume in which Hamilton described the falls at Trenton, Genesee and Niagara, he concluded: "We feel that nature has been defaced, and that utility has been obtained at the expense of a thousand picturesque beauties and romantic associations."[7] But this destruction of the beauty of the very thing that the tourist came to see was something in which the tourist had a large share. The drinking shop, souvenir stall, and hotel put up to accommodate him were a major source of distress, especially at Niagara. It produced a complicated frame of mind in the English tourist, one compounded of romantic reverence and national irritation.

Fanny Kemble described the Trenton Falls in some detail before moving her *Journal* forward to Niagara. Her last comment on the lesser falls was to say that she was told that the greater falls would "sweep Trenton clean from our memories," but she added, "I do not think it." And she went forward eagerly to describe in detail the Niagara River as it flowed into the Falls. She described in greater detail her own sense of expectation of the Falls: "My mind was eagerly dwelling on what we were going to see: that sight which — [her *Journal* did not provide personal names] said was the only one in the world which had not disappointed him. I felt absolutely nervous with expectation." At this point the reader realised that her book was nearly over – what of the description of Niagara? ". . . down, down I sprang, and along the narrow footpath, divided only by a thicket from the tumultuous rapids. I saw through the boughs the white glimmer of the sea of foam. 'Go on, go on; don't stop,' shouted —; and in another minute the thicket was passed: I stood upon Table Rock. — seized me by the arm, and without speaking a word, dragged me to the edge of the rapids, to the brink of the abyss. I saw Niagara. – Oh, God! who can describe that sight?"[8] Here she ended her book.

This anti-climactic climax constituted a bold solution to describing the indescribable. Fanny Kemble was not obliged to do what others did, declare the task impossible and then try to do it. It was a solution that strongly appealed to Captain Marryat. (He referred to Fanny Kemble as Mrs Butler because she had by then married the young American who nameless had dragged her to the abyss.) "Perhaps," wrote Marryat, "the wisest, if not the best description of the Falls of Niagara, is in the simple ejaculation of Mrs. Butler; for it is almost useless to attempt to describe when you feel that language fails." Marryat obviously felt that Fanny Kemble's originality was not one that could be copied; he provided his readers with a four-page set piece on the Falls. And obviously it would have been impossible for a whole succession of English travel writers to have come to the brink and said no more than "Oh God! who can describe that sight?" However, Captain Marryat did not find a better description of Niagara because after first being moved to become one with the scene his next impulse was to make it into a steam boiler: "I wished myself a magician, that I might transport the falls to Italy, and pour their whole volume of waters into the crater of Mount Vesuvius; witness the terrible conflict between the contending elements, and create the largest steam boiler that had entered into the imagination of man." This was among the strangest of thoughts to occur to any traveller anywhere. Marryat rounded out his description on a more conventional note by invoking the deity: "Yes, it is through the elements that the Almighty has ever deigned to commune with man, or to execute his supreme will . . . it is through these that the Deity still speaks to man; yet what can inspire more awe of him, more reverence, and more love, than the contemplation of thy falling waters, great Niagara."[9] Solemnities were not necessarily better than absurdities.

Moore called for new combinations of language; Cobden called for Byron; Marryat appealed to Fanny Kemble. Just after Fanny Kemble had been to Niagara a minor poet by the name of Alfred Domett came to the Falls by way of Canada. He had left Cambridge without a degree but did not appear to think himself much disadvantaged by that fact. He was however wary of failing in a degree of good taste and he knew that Niagara posed traps: "It is said," he wrote in his diary, "to be bad taste to attempt a minute description of the falls of Niagara, and perhaps correctly so. Nevertheless a few words may serve to give some idea of the relative situation of at least the prominent parts." It was not a promising start, and his imagery confirmed him as no more poetical than Frederick Marryat: "It is," he said of Niagara, "as when you look at a foxhunt or an army in full march." If Domett could not recognise bad taste in himself, he looked for it in others and took the occasion to make sport of travellers who had gone before him: "Even that bold bazaar-keeper, the racy Mrs. Trollope, wept when she first saw the Falls; Hamilton talks of bounding blood, maddened veins, and throbbing pulses; Stewart gravely falls to calculating the number of tons of water discharged per minute; I forget Hall's feelings on the occasion; and the worthy Mr. Duncan says he was disappointed – God only knows what he must have expected." The Falls grew on most people, but Domett shortly became bored with the whole scene; this he admitted with a hint of self-congratulation: "It was something to learn that it was possible to look with a listless eye even at this cataract of cataracts, to yawn in the face of Niagara."[10]

Another poet had come to and gone from the Falls without capturing them in language. Poets in general did not seem to be up to the task even though, as Charles Dickens discovered, they were given a ready opportunity. In what he called a "disgusting circumstance" on the American side of Niagara, he came across numerous volumes of visitors' verse displayed in a guide's cottage: "I turned a few leaves," he wrote, "and found them scrawled all over with the vilest and filthiest ribaldry that ever human hogs delighted in." It was another instance of humanity's failing to meet its occasion and Dickens was further disgusted not only that this verse was written within sight of the Falls but that it was so carefully preserved. "I hope," he concluded somewhat ungraciously, "few of these entries have been made by Englishmen." Actually it could just have been that he was reading among others, the work of his compatriot, Richard Cobden. In his 1835 diary, Cobden copied out a miserable piece of verse that appeared to be his own. Attached to it is the legend: "Written in the book at the falls which is full of attempts at rhapsodical praise of the scene."[11]

Dickens did not quote any of this filthy verse – it might be doubted that it was actually obscene – but it represented a low of bad taste, obviously enough, in the business of describing Niagara. The strain was too great for the common man; unable to find suitable words, he had recourse to unsuitable ones. Such verse was painful to contemplate for travellers who believed in the elevating, and cleansing influence of the sublime landscape. All that water had, as it were, gone over their heads. Dickens, a man ultimately more interested in the common man than in uncommon waterfalls, noticed another example of the failure of Niagara to effect elevation of thought. Mrs Dickens was accompanied on her tour of the United States by a maidservant called Anne Brown. "She never looks at a prospect by any chance or displays the smallest emotion at any sight whatever," Dickens noted in a letter. "She objects to Niagara that 'its nothing but water,' and considers that 'there is too much of that'!!"[12]

This was a splendidly Dickensian observation. Fanny Kemble's question concerning the nature of American reaction to landscape – "Is it possible that a perception of the beautiful in nature is a result of artificial cultivation?"[13] – had obviously to be asked of the English reaction. But neither Fanny Kemble nor Charles Dickens would have expected their sensibilities to have been the same as their servants'. This was true despite the generous human sympathies of which both writers were so eminently capable. "Perception of the beautiful in nature," that is, the enjoyment of landscape, was essentially a middle-class preoccupation; and the poor did not go on tour except in the service of men and women like Mr and Mrs Dickens and Mr and Miss Kemble (she was touring with her father). The English tourist took the insensibility of his servants for granted.

Charles Dickens's own reactions to Niagara in contrast to those of his maid were very much what his readers, both private and public, expected of him: "It would be hard for a man to stand nearer God than he does there," he wrote to his most trusted friend, John Forster, "from its unfathomable grave arises that tremendous ghost of spray and mist which is never laid, and has been haunting this place with the same solemnity – perhaps from the creation of the world." A few months later Charles Dickens prepared these thoughts for publication, relying as he did very much on the letters that he had written home, reiterating the solemn and the portentous note:

> Then, when I felt how near to my Creator I was standing, [he wrote in *American Notes*] the first effect, and the enduring one – instant and lasting – of the tremendous spectacle was Peace. Peace of mind, tranquility, calm recollections of the Dead, great thoughts of Eternal Rest and Happiness; nothing of gloom and terror. Niagara was at once stamped upon my heart, an Image of Beauty; to remain there, changeless and indelible until its pulses cease to beat, for ever.[14]

Despite the conventionalities of the language and the sentiments, the prosaic effort to render the Wordsworthian sublime, it would be wrong to accuse Charles Dickens of simple Podsnappery in his letters home and in his published writings. The Victorian in Dickens was struggling hard to express a Romantic sentiment and he groped painfully for big words with which to express it. But he was undoubtedly moved by Niagara more deeply and more finely than Anne Brown who thought it "'nothing but water,'" more so than those writers of ribald verse. Charles Dickens made claim to his having received an "indelible" image of beauty from Niagara. This to some extent he confirmed by his reactions to the waterfall a quarter of a century later. Again he wrote at length to his old, trusted friend, John Forster, though this time there was no plan to produce a second series of "American Notes." But again there was the same rehearsal of sentiment:

I shall never forget the last aspect in which we saw Niagara yesterday [he wrote from Rochester on 16 March 1868] . . . The majestic valley of the Falls, so seen through the vast cloud of spray, was made of rainbow. The high banks, the riven rocks, the forests, the bridge, the buildings, the air, the sky, were all made of rainbow. Nothing in Turner's finest watercolour drawings, done in his greatest day, is so ethereal, so imaginative, so gorgeous in colour, as what I beheld. I seemed to be lifted from the earth and to be looking into heaven. What I once said to you, as I witnessed the scene five and twenty years ago, all came back at this most affecting and sublime sight. The "muddy vesture of clay" falls from us as we look.[15]

At Niagara Dickens experienced the quasi-religious moment; he was raised upward much as Frederick Law Olmsted was raised up in Chester Cathedral. The rainbow mist of Niagara produced a veil through which more base realities were filtered; the buildings usually so distressing to spectators at Niagara were caught up, along with the bridge, into the ensemble of natural elements – banks, rocks, forests, air and sky. Discordant accidentals were incorporated into the total pattern of things by the unifying beauty of the mist. The mist operated like the organ music in Chester Cathedral to induce the oceanic, to bring the traveller nearer to his God. It was not entirely true to say that North America had nothing like the Gothic cathedrals of Europe; the natural cathedral could serve a similar purpose for the tourist, and Niagara was the greatest of these. The American traveller complained that the English landscape had driven out the sublime but "sublime" was the term he used more frequently to describe York Minster, "that dream of beauty realized," as Margaret Fuller called it in 1846. "The whole is sublime," said Coxe of York. "Its own vastness," said William Wells Brown, "impress the observer with feelings of awe and sublimity." Within its "glorious arches," Harriet Beecher Stowe was moved to declare that "this sublime mystery of human power and skill is only a shadow of some eternal substance, which in ages to come, God will yet reveal to us."[16]

These feelings corresponded closely with those of the nineteenth-century visitor to Niagara. The Falls had the power of the cathedrals to overcome doubt, to realise expectations, to make mundane reality numinous, and to make the material man spiritual. But the visitor to Niagara, like the visitor to the cathedral, felt frustration as well as fulfilment; the glory of the thing to be described went beyond the ability of the writer to describe it. This contradicted the whole purpose of the travel writer who planned to put into language his experience of the world. It brought him into painful confrontation with problems of meaning, consciousness, text, and communication that travel writing could usually avoid quite successfully, by its reliance on a record of personal fact and a retailing of general information. Fanny Kemble's solution, the throwing up of hands, was one that could be variously labelled as a gesture of proper piety, as an admission of deep personal failure, as a pose that was irresponsible and cowardly.

On his last visit to Niagara Falls (that of 1868), Dickens took the precaution of not going with his servants to look at "the majestic valley." He told Forster he had chartered a separate carriage for his men "so that they might see all in their own way, and at their own time." He was wary of having the occasion spoilt by the cheerful, lively spirits of men who might think Niagara "'nothing but water.'" He approached the waters only in the company of those whom he could rely upon not to dispell the solemnity of the occasion. The same awful preparations and precautions were taken by Mrs Fanny Trollope, Alfred Domett's "bold bazaar-keeper." She spent as long a time as she could at the Falls in the May and June of 1831 and only left when, she said, "'We had to do it,' as the Americans say."[17] Mrs Trollope was quite as reverential about the Falls as Dickens.

For Mrs Trollope it was as though she were present at the Creation: "God said, let there be a cataract, and it was so." From this event, she was only to be drawn by the most pressing of schedules.

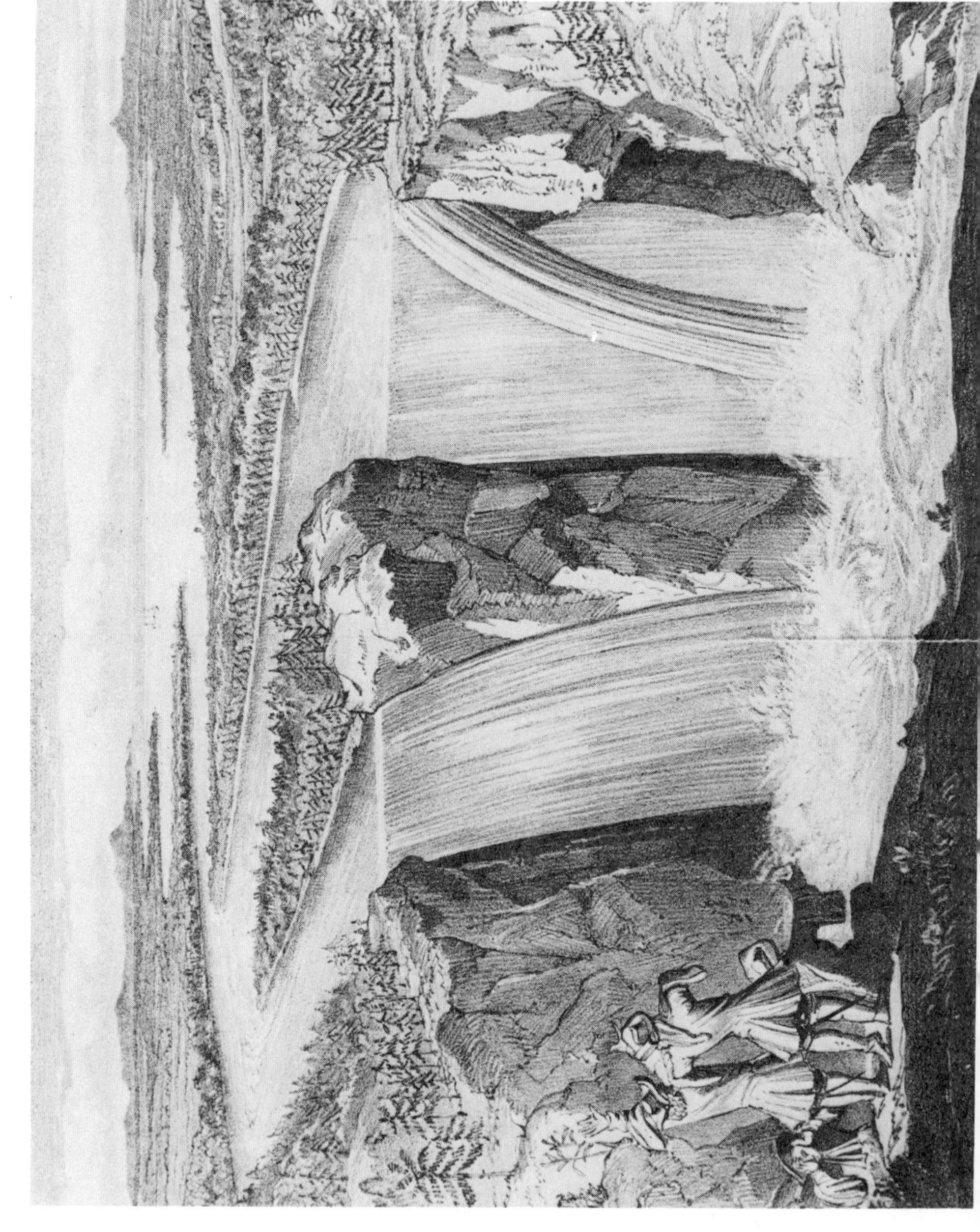

"There is," she wrote, "a shadowy mystery hangs about it which neither eye nor even imagination can penetrate; but I dare not dwell on this; it is a dangerous subject, and any attempt to describe the sensations produced must lead direct to nonsense." Mrs Trollope boldly called her subject "dangerous." She did so because of the several kinds of vertigo that its contemplation could induce. First, there was the dizziness that staring into the abyss could produce. This inclined several people to wish to throw themselves off their viewpoints and all travellers were aware of the fate that befell anyone who did fall in – something that seemed all too easy. Mrs Trollope was also aware of an inner vertigo; the viewer seemed likely to topple into an inner abyss; from this there might be as little hope of recovery as from the great whirlpool itself. There was further the danger of tempting the Almighty power by attempting description of something that came so near it; penetration behind the "shadowy mystery" might bring a fall from grace as terrible as those into the waters or into insanity. There was yet another danger of the subject; a plunging into bathos that would leave the writer damned utterly before his or her public. The nature of this fall into the ridiculous was very well illustrated by a temptation put before Harriet Martineau; it was one that she resisted with her customary good sense: "A lady asked me many questions about my emotions at Niagara, to which I gave only one answer of which she could make anything. 'Did you not,' was her last inquiry, 'long to throw yourself down, and mingle with your mother earth?' – 'No.' "[18] By the time the traveller came to write his travel book this was, of course, the only danger that remained; no longer in the presence of "the glory, and the thunder, and the majesty, and the wrath of that upper hell of waters" in the words of Mrs Trollope's son, other forms of vertigo no longer threatened.

It was perhaps as well to leave such a chance to a fellow writer rather than incur it one's self, and though Fanny Trollope did not – unlike Fanny Kemble – opt out of the business of description altogether, she did preface her words by a disclaimer that offered a fellow writer who might incur the liabilities inherent in the "dangerous subject" more readily than herself. She had had the good fortune, she wrote, to meet at Niagara an English gentleman, who had been introduced to her party in New York. "If any man living can describe the scene we looked upon it is himself, and I trust he will do it."[19] In a footnote, she identified him only as: "The accomplished author of *Cyril Thornton*." *Men and Manners in America* when it was first published in Edinburgh and London was described as being "By the author of *Cyril Thornton, etc.*" It was Thomas Hamilton who wrote the now virtually unknown "*Cyril Thornton, etc.*" Mrs Trollope was justified in her expectations to the extent that Thomas Hamilton attempted the "dangerous subject" at very full length in his book on America.

Mrs Trollope had expectations of this gentleman because Captain Hamilton had already established himself as a man capable of romantic expression. A Scots army officer, he had retired on half pay in 1818 having fought in the Peninsula and having had postings among other places in Nova Scotia and New Brunswick. He then became "a valued member of the *Blackwood* writers." He married and became a neighbour and friend of Sir Walter Scott. After his trip to America, he was to marry again and become a friend of William Wordsworth. He was eventually to die, like Fanny Trollope, in Italy.[20] With these credentials, at least those he had acquired by 1831, Mrs Trollope believed him as capable as any of realising the great ambition of describing Niagara, and living, so to speak, to tell the tale. He took over fifteen pages of the second and final volume of his travels to do the job.

Hamilton approached the Falls from the Canadian side, the favoured approach, and the outstanding impression that he sought by every means to convey to his readers was that of the sublimity of the Falls. Thomas Hamilton did not try to be original in his reaction, nor did he try to be original in his descriptions; as in most of the better accounts of the Falls, Hamilton's method was to stick to his task relentlessly and hope that the sheer weight of pages and repetition would convey to the reader that here was a subject of unusual proportions. He first presented: "the impenetrable mass of vapour with which [Niagara] is sublimely and mysteriously encanopied." "The effect produced by the overwhelming sublimity of the spectacle, it is not possible to embody in words," he wrote on the next page. The usual figure of the inadequacy of words introduced the passage that Domett mocked in his diary, one in which Hamilton tried by way of describing what happened to the spectator to suggest how far beyond and above the ordinary was the scene before him: "His blood ceases to flow . . . The past and the future are obliterated . . . He gazes on a scene of splendour and sublimity far greater than the unaided fancy of poet and painter ever pictured." There was little or no impressive detail of description; instead the language twisted and turned upon itself, in and out of comparisons that referred back to language and allied arts, and in self-reflexive fashion to the spectator himself. Of the view close into the Horseshoe Falls, he wrote: "the sublimity . . . undoubtedly extends to the very verge of horror." To describe the rapids of the Niagara River he likened them to the Falls and the Falls were in turn referred back to the rapids of the Niagara River: "The grandeur of these rapids is worthy of the cataracts in which they terminate . . . Never was there a nobler prelude to a sublime catastrophe."[21]

The failure of comparative imagery suggested only that the Falls were like themselves and like no other thing. The word *sublime* reverberated through Hamilton's account with an incessant and insistent force that finally deprived it of any noticeable effect upon the stunned senses of the reader. "The sound is that of thunder in its greatest intensity, deep, unbroken, and unchanging."[22] This was Hamilton's description of the noise of the water. It might serve as a general comment on the prose of the earnest line of the nineteenth-century writers who laboured so hard to describe the Falls. During the harshest winter, the inhabitants of Niagara Falls City will occasionally be woken up by silence. Huge ice floes in the rapids block the flow of the river and for a few hours will stop the Falls. The thunder goes unheard until it stops; but it is thunder nonetheless. Niagara prose had similar effects.

The nineteenth-century travel writer liked to believe that he was communicating facts about a real world and that such communication was very possible; this was a main source of his frustration when it appeared, as it appeared at Niagara, that language would not do the job. When language had done its uttermost, the traveller could, if he were as resourceful as Captain Hamilton, take to practical experiment. The last two pages of his description of Niagara were given to record a demonstration of the size of the Horseshoe Falls: "About a quarter of a mile above it," he wrote, "the stream had deposited a number of huge trees, and I employed several men to launch then successively into the stream, while I stood on the extreme point of the Table rock to observe their descent . . . the forest giants floated slowly onward to the brink of the precipice when they were seen no more."[23] This gentlemanly diversion did not prove very much perhaps; Hamilton's conclusion that "nothing which enters the awful cauldron of the Fall, is ever seen to emerge," is not in fact true. Objects floated over the Falls reappear a mile or so downstream often intact.

This giant game did at least show that Hamilton had reached the end of his useful delay at the Falls and his final comment on the "dangerous subject" was a footnote giving some advice on how long a person should best stay at Niagara. "For some days," said Hamilton, "the impression of their glory and magnitude will increase; and so long as this is the case, let him remain. His time could not be better spent. He is hoarding up a store of sublime memories for his whole life." This returned the reader to the effect of the Falls on the inner life of the spectator, the Niagara Falls of the imagination, and whatever kind of exterior reality the Falls might have for the individual tourist they became imaginary once he had left their roar behind. As Hamilton's footnote suggested, the nineteenth-century traveller followed through the logic of his Romantic approach to landscape and it was a commonplace of the Niagara literature to expound a Wordsworthian doctrine of recollected emotion. This again emphasised the special dual effect of the Niagara impression – it would make itself felt upon the dullest soul on the one hand; it would make itself felt with a peculiar intensity upon the impressionable on the other. The man or woman who would not usually take away any impression of a landscape would on this occasion feel as the sensitive habitually felt in the presence of the romantic scene: "a visit to the Falls galvanises the most matter of fact person into a brief exercise of the imaginative powers," as one writer put it. The sensitive man or woman would take away an impression that would be equally extraordinary: "It becomes henceforth a part of one's intellectual being," wrote Alex Mackay, "not the plaything of his imagination, but the companion of his thoughts. You can recall at pleasure every feeling and emotion which it conjured up on first beholding it. As I saw Niagara and heard it then, so I see and hear it now."[24]

Mackay's account of the Niagara experience was as thorough as his treatment of every other kind of experience in his ever-thorough *Western World.* His was among the best of many descriptions of the Falls that continued to be written by travellers to the end of the century and beyond. There was no end in the nineteenth century of writers of all degrees of reputation who presented themselves as contenders to describe the indescribable, who were willing to undertake the "dangerous subject." Though there were dissenting voices from the beginning, like that of Domett who yawned in the face of Niagara, the dominant tone was that of reverence before the power of Nature and the presence of the Sublime. The accounts tended to become longer, at least until the 1860s, as writers measured themselves against the work of those who had gone before and realised that they had to thunder longer if they were to make any impression at all. They ran the risk then, of course, of making the reader yawn in the face of Niagara. Among those recitals that may stand comparison with Alex Mackay's is the one by Lady Emmeline Stuart Wortley, who always followed closely where Mackay had gone before, and that by Anthony Trollope who in this instance, was following in the steps of his mother.

For Mackay, Niagara was as he put it, "the goal which I had set to my long and varied wanderings, and it was some time ere I could assure myself that I had really reached it."[25] Like many travel writers, Mackay brought the travelling section of his book to its climax at Niagara. The best was kept to last and only the details of departure or the chapters of general summary might follow. Fanny Kemble's *Journal* provided the extreme form of this structure; Fanny Trollope's book was the more commonplace as she allowed herself only with a great show of reluctance to be drawn away from the scene of Creation to end her days for ever in the New World.

Since Niagara was the most famous of landscapes in the western world if not indeed in the whole world, it was one that many of the travellers had set their hearts on seeing. In this respect, it shared the quality of the long-anticipated landscapes that Americans fondly stored for themselves in preparation for their journey to England and to Europe. Generally speaking there was little of this "latent preparedness" in the English approach to America, still less to specific American scenes, but here Niagara was an exception. The American frequently referred to his childhood as he approached and explored England; when he came to long-dreamt-of scenes he had difficulty in believing all was real, in believing that fancy had given way to fact. This was exactly how Mackay felt at Niagara: "it was some time ere I could assure myself that I had really reached it."

And this was because as a child in Scotland he dreamt like the children in America: "The dream of my childhood was then realised! How often, and how fondly, had that moment of unutterable ecstasy been anticipated by me; when oceans, plains, lakes, and mountains yet intervened between Niagara and me!" This was very like the reaction of the American to the English landscape made familiar by imagination, literature, and etching, but Mackay qualified the reality of Niagara in a way that was not common for the American encountering his long-expected landscape: "In all that you have hitherto seen there is nothing to prepare you for Niagara. It has no compeer."[26] Though dreamt of in Europe, it was beyond European expectation.

English travellers could nonetheless form a tolerable idea of the Falls beforehand if so minded. In *The Englishwoman in America*, Isabella Bird (later Mrs Bishop, first woman fellow of the Royal Geographical Society) spoke of her childhood anticipations of Niagara: "Somehow or other, from my earliest infancy, I had been familiar with the name of Niagara, and from the numerous pictures I had seen of it, I could, I suppose, have sketched a very accurate likeness of the Horse-shoe Fall." When she eventually reached the scene, she reported with great satisfaction: "One wish of my life had been gratified." She also confirmed that the Falls were unique in possessing this particular hold over the English imagination since the English believed that if you had not seen the Falls then you had seen nothing of America.[27]

A divine transport was obviously not something that could profitably be speeded up no matter how rapidly the tourist had reached the scene that promised sublime experience; and the more profound and the more elevating the experience was believed to be, the more necessary it became to demand that time be given to allow the scene to work its effects. The traveller who took several weeks to reach Niagara from New York or Pittsburgh might be expected to prepare himself for the return journey. But how long would the traveller stay who took no more than days to reach Niagara? How long the traveller who took only a matter of hours? Niagara would not be rushed. Of his visit in 1847, Alex Mackay wrote: "No one should stay for less than a week at Niagara." He had visited the Falls in all on four separate occasions averaging five days each time, he told his readers, "and left it each time more and more impressed with its magnitude and sublimity." He was anxious to dispel any influence of the many who were disappointed by a first view of Niagara; something those who stayed to write long descriptions blamed on the viewers and not on the waterfall: "no one remains long enough about Niagara to become familiar with it," wrote Mackay, "without feeling that the reality is far grander and more stupendous than he ever conceived it to be." Lady Emmeline discovered after her second and third look at Niagara that "it is far more magnificent than I had anticipated it to be, though my expectations were of the very highest order." But on the issue of height, she could not but admit that she was slightly disappointed. This was a reaction that she should have anticipated from her reading of Mackay because he had already pointed out that people have pictured it from below and usually first see it from above; and then "one's preconceived notions of it are outraged."[28]

If the Falls were given time to work their effect, these writers were quite agreed on the nature and the power of that effect. Again the pattern of the Wordsworthian natural experience provided the model, contemplation of the landscape bringing about a loss of immediate sensory experience until a state of oneness with the thing contemplated superseded the consciousness of separate self and landscape. "You identify it with yourself," Mackay wrote of Niagara, "until you feel as if you were part and parcel of each other; and unwelcome indeed is the incident which recalls you to the consciousness of your separate existence." Here lay the root of the all but universal irritation with the ever-present guides of the Falls, men it appeared to the tourists whose aim in life was to destroy appreciation of the natural wonder. They always obtruded themselves at the least opportune moment. The same was true of any other Americans, fellow Britons, indeed close friends. It was essentially a personal experience and the loss of self could not take place, paradoxically, until the self was entirely alone. Alfred Domett was interrupted by "a stout shopkeeper-resembling Briton" who told the poet "'If you tumble down there, it will be a long time before you get up again.'" Isabella Bird's sensibility was constantly affronted by vociferous, drunken "drosky-drivers" badgering for her custom, by friends insisting that she see the Falls from every angle and elevation, by perfect strangers, interrupting her meditations with comments like "'Well, stranger, I guess that's the finest waterpower you've ever set eyes on.'" Man intruded not only in the form of his person but in his buildings too of course, and these, objected to from the beginning of the century, were never satisfactorily dealt with; they became in fact worse. Their problem remains. In 1862, William Russell complained that, "It was distressing to find that Niagara was surrounded by the paraphernalia of a fixed fair. I had looked forward to a certain degree of solitude. It appeared impossible that man could cockneyfy such a magnificent display of force and grandeur in nature. But, alas!"[29]

Nonetheless, if the visitor stayed long enough, the Falls were able to work their effect upon him despite all the intrusions, interruptions and irritations. "One becomes here, indeed, utterly Niagarized," wrote Lady Emmeline, "and, the great cataract goes sounding through all one's soul, and heart, and mind, commingling with all one's ideas and impressions, and uniting itself with all one's inner most feelings and fancies." Even Isabella Bird was able at last to find herself alone at Niagara: "I was not distracted by parasitic guides or sandwich-eating visitors; the vile museums, pagodas, and tea-gardens were out of sight: the sublimity of the Falls far exceeded my expectations . . . It was so very like what I had expected, and yet so totally different." The spiritualising moment came to each visitor in turn and each in turn rendered it into prose and instructed the next visitor in his turn how he must respond: "To realize Niagara you must sit there till you see nothing else than that which you have come to see," wrote Anthony Trollope, "You will hear nothing else, and think of nothing else. At length you will be at one with the tumbling river before you. You will find yourself among the waters as though you belonged to them."[30]

One by one the visitors became "Niagarized" – a new combination of language that suggested the special condition induced by steady and solitary contemplation of the rush and the roar of the great cataract. It suggested a form of intoxication, a detachment from sober reality that was anticipated by a Scotsman in Richard Cobden's party "who waited till dusk when he was *fou* for seeing the falls."[31] From such intoxicated study of Niagara, the visitor had to wake up and it was then that he might turn his mind to practical consideration of the power of the falling water and this led to a statistical appreciation of the Falls.

Two pages after Lady Emmeline had commingled her ideas and

impressions with the cataract that went sounding through all her soul and heart and mind, she was calculating that the reason for all this water's flowing past her was that the Great Lakes were estimated to contain one half the fresh water on the surface of the globe. As a result, Niagara could sustain its extraordinary flow indefinitely. How extraordinary it was, she went on to demonstrate by quoting the various estimates of the flow: "The quantity of water precipitated over the Falls is estimated by Professor Dwight to be 11,524,375 tons per hour: by Darby at 1,672,704,000 cubic feet per hour, and by Pickem at . . . 18,524,000 cubic feet per minute."[32]

There is a poetry in numbers and numbers were to offer one way in which the traveller could come to terms with otherwise incomprehensible landscapes. The landscape that could not be visualised required some intellectual mode of comprehension. Niagara could of course be taken in by the eye and the quotation of statistics could not but seem rather banal. They supplanted rather than supported other, higher modes of comprehension. At the same time the traveller is concerned with facts as well as with impressions; he is concerned with curiosities as well as profundities. His is an eclectic genre well able to accommodate a great variety of materials and subjects. It should not be surprising therefore that Lady Emmeline repeated the figures that she found in local guidebooks; facts and figures had moreover a special charm or fascination for a period and a people that were excited by their material conquest of nature. Niagara was somehow summed up by the work of Dwight, Darby and Pickem. In the same fashion, Isabella Bird not only reported at great length the legend of the death of the Indian Maiden, a historical curiosity concerning the Falls, she also gave full details of the new suspension bridge that had been opened in 1854 across the Niagara River. It could, she told her readers, take a train of 400 tons, 230 feet above the river which was itself at that point 250 feet in depth. In addition, she reported, "The view from it is magnificent."[33]

In fact some of the most pedestrian expositions of Niagara contained the kind of detail that made its size and magnificence more apparent than many invocations of sublimity and divine power. One of the most striking passages from Alex Mackay's lengthy account of the Falls transplanted them from their distant American setting to the centre of London. Mackay earnestly requested the reader to follow him in this stolid imaginative act: "Let him suppose a ledge of rock, nearly as lofty as its towers, commencing at Westminster Abbey, and after running down Whitehall, turning, at Charing Cross, into the Strand, and continuing to Somerset House. Let him suppose himself on Waterloo Bridge, whence every point of the mighty precipice could be seen. Let him lastly suppose an immense volume of water falling over the whole of it, with the exception of a portion extending, say, from the Home Office to the Admiralty, which is left dry, – and he may have some notion of the extent of the cataract."[34] This was in some measure ludicrous enough, especially that splendidly positioned "say, from the Home Office to the Admiralty," but it would have created a most instructive double exposure in the mind of any reader who faithfully followed through the stages of Mackay's solemn game. The idea of 1,672,704,000 cubic feet of water pouring into Whitehall and the Strand every hour created a scene as dramatic as most imaginable scenes and the reader would need to turn to the first book of *Paradise Lost* or the last book of *The Dunciad* to get anything better.

Niagara was an epic subject and it reached to the limits of poetic imagination and statement; beyond it lay, as Fanny Trollope had so rightly said, nonsense, the nonsense of the laughable as well as the nonsense of the ineffable. Though it was just within the bounds of Romantic statement, just within the language of the landscape artist, it was pressing forward to a region where traditional modes of describing landscape had to be abandoned. One of the most dependable descriptions of Niagara was that written by Charles Lyell, F.R.S., author of *The Principles of Geology*. The greatest geologist of the nineteenth century published his *Travels in North America; With Geological Observations* in 1845 and his second chapter was entirely devoted to the Falls. For his first three pages he spoke of the matters of beauty, grandeur and personal feeling but then for some twenty-five pages he presented the reader with the results of several days of exploration, providing a full geological survey and full geological history. He described the course of the river above and the course of the river below; he penetrated calmly and enthusiastically at least one element of Niagara's mystery. Lyell's report made very satisfactory reading, placing Niagara within the greatness of geological time and the vastness of stellar space. The

39. "Bird's-Eye View of the Falls of Niagara and Adjacent Country"

report was not without its own numinous dimension: "The geologist may muse and speculate on these events," Charles Lyell wrote,

> until, filled with awe and admiration, he forgets the presence of the mighty cataract itself, and no longer sees the rapid motion of its waters, nor hears their sound, as they fall into the deep abyss. But whenever his thoughts are recalled to the present, the tone of his mind, – the sensations awakened in his soul, will be found to be in perfect harmony with the grandeur and beauty of the glorious scene which surrounds him.[35]

The nineteenth-century scientific imagination was as powerful a perceptive organ as the nineteenth-century Romantic imagination and more landscapes were within its comprehension. Nonetheless the Niagara Falls were a great stimulant to that imagination; they provided an example of sublimity found elsewhere only in the sea. They were a crucial test of the sensibility of writer and reader.

12

THE MISSISSIPPI: THE NIGHTMARE LANDSCAPE

The term "Father of Waters" is, by-the-by, a very free rendering of the Indian name of the great American river. In the language of the Choctaw tribe, MISSAH and SIPPAH, are two words very commonly used; the former meaning "old big," the latter "strong." It would be very difficult to find a more appropriate name for the mighty stream which drains a whole continent than the compound of these two adjectives, Missah-sippah, or Old-big-strong.

Captain Flack, *A Hunter's Experiences*[1]

Coming to the banks of the Mississippi, the Englishman knew that he had reached the real America. The amateur should go no further and the amateur seldom did till well after the Civil War. In 1860, Richard Burton reached St Louis, on the Mississippi just south of the Missouri confluence; there he crossed the great river without hesitation, but Burton described St Louis as "the turning-back place of English sportsmen." The scale of everything was so beyond what most of his fellow countrymen could stomach that the explorer was fairly certain of not having to meet many compatriots once he had crossed into Missouri. (He was rather hostile to those whom he did meet.) To Burton's delight, this scale was reflected in the hyperboles of western language. The word *creek* pronounced locally as "crick," was applied to streams dignified by the term *river* in Europe. Were the Thames or the Seine to run into the Mississippi, they could go by no other name. On the other hand, the Mississippi itself was not called a river. A drink was any river in Missouri, Burton told the readers of *The City of the Saints, and Across the Rocky Mountains to California*; the Big Drink was the Mississippi.[2]

Captain Flack's "Old-big-strong" and Captain Burton's "The Big Drink" both suggested a flavour of the local and the familiar mixed with the respectful. Flack was an Englishman who lived with a band of hunters for a year on the Texas range. Captain Burton was an Englishman who had sought the world over men living close to the elemental realities of wilderness and desert. Native Indian and western American spoke languages that appealed to hunter and to explorer.

The Indian name, long and flowing, fitted the river better than any European title and its etymology was variously explained. In 1815, Lieutenant George Gleig offered a source different from Flack's and was contented with the traditional translation: "The Mississippi," he wrote in Letter XVII of *The Campaigns of the British Army at Washington and New Orleans*, "(a corruption of the word Mechasippi, signifying, in the words of the natives, 'the father of rivers,') is allowed to be inferior, in point of size and general navigability, to few streams in the world." In New Orleans in 1861, William Russell discovered that Creole society circularised and gazetted its members by means of a paper called *La Misachibee*. This, Russell explained, "was the primitive Indian name of the grand river, not improved by the addition of silibant Anglo-Saxon syllables."[3] From which remark, it was not clear whether he felt that the Indian was improved or was not improved by the English representation.

The first Frenchmen in the New World had presumed to give the river a French name and Alexis de Tocqueville was one of those who preferred the old voyageurs' name for the river and called it the St Louis. "The Indians, in their pompous language, have," he said, "named it the Father of Waters, or the Mississippi." It was seldom that de Tocqueville so lapsed in the wisdom and catholicity of his judgements. His error in preferring the provinciality of European nomenclature for the poetry of Indian description can be forgiven, perhaps. William Makepeace Thackeray's treatment of the river's name was less forgivable. For him it became the "Mrs. Sippy." The only excuses that can be found for this egregious (and characteristic) lapse of taste was that he committed his pun in a letter to his little girls. He had been travelling and lecturing hard through the Carolinas and Georgia and was hoping that things would improve: "I shall find the spring a month hence when I get to St Louis up the Mrs. Sippy,"[4] he told daughters Anne and Harriet.

When Thackeray reached the broad bosom of "Mrs. Sippy," she gave him no happiness. He had thought of the Alabama River as a tributary of the Styx, and the Mississippi offered "the same dreariness on a wider scale." The huge, dirty, southern rivers put him in mind of death. They were mournful, dreary, funereal. They were the rivers of an underworld rather than a New World and they made him long for those of other continents, the rivers of Africa, of Europe, of Asia: "I had," he wrote from the Mississippi, "the keenest pleasure in the lonely beauty of the Nile and the generous Rhone charmed me and my native Ginga I remember quite well and the sense of its being friendly and beautiful."[5] There were to be no more childish jokes: "Mrs. Sippy" had become the Angel of Death and the novelist dreamed, on the slow passage of his steamboat north, of happier days and happier rivers.

The journey down the Alabama River had brought Thackeray to Mobile where like other travellers he took a sea-passage to New Orleans. The land and river journey through the southern slave states was only undertaken by tough travellers. Many, like John Lambert in 1808 or Thomas Hamilton in 1830, preferred to travel south by the sea routes from New York, Boston, or Washington. And the most usual port of destination was Charleston. In 1808 the reason for this was very obvious. With any luck, the journey from New York could be made in three or four days. It might take as many weeks and more to travel overland and was more dangerous, although the sea journey had its own hazards.[6]

With the development of the railroads, a combination of boat and train became the sensible choice and in 1846, Alex Mackay travelled all the way from Boston to Milledgeville, Georgia – some 1,200 miles – by steam power. Already by that date the railroad link between Boston and New Orleans was nearly complete, and the building of the stretch from Macon south would make it so.[7] But it was by no means a through line; constant changes had to be made, and many rivers had to be crossed by ferry. Once the steamboats had begun to work the western and southern rivers, most New Orleans bound travellers made their way from Charleston across Georgia to the Alabama River and continued south.

From Mobile travellers had the choice of two sea routes – before the building of the railroad link no greenhorn could make the land journey – to New Orleans. One way was to approach the city from the North by way of Lake Pontchartrain; the other, more difficult, was to enter the city by way of the Mississippi Delta itself. (This also was the route that would naturally be chosen, despite its hazards, by any ship from New York or Liverpool.) A high-sided riverboat was likely to roll over once it had left the shelter of fresh water and steamboats making their way from Mobile to New Orleans kept close to the shore, making their way along the shallow, sandy passages that lie between the shore and the screen of low islands that run from Pensacola to the Mississippi.[8]

There was, however, something very special about the Delta approach and it rewarded in its own way those who had chosen it over the more cautious sea-island route. It was a sight like no other. "It seems," said Thomas Hamilton, "as if the process of creation were incomplete, and the earth yet undivided from the waters." The traveller was indeed watching the process of creation because the river was making land where before there had been water. This process was explained for Basil Hall by the pilot of the ship that took him from Mobile into the wilderness of *bayou*, swamp, *freshes* and *crevasses* that made up the approach to New Orleans. All around the ship there were logs; the pilot told him that "in February, and in the beginning of March, the quantity of these logs was so great, that not only the river itself, but the sea for several miles off, was ... completely coated over with them." The logs became forced together to form enormous rafts that settled on the mud as the waters subsided. "In a short time a rank sort of cane or reed springs up... This is called a cane brake." It was not comforting nor consoling to be present at the creation: "A sort of scum on the waters," wrote Miss Martineau, "betokened the birth-place of new land."[9]

The great flood of water in muddied, flat river beds meant that the old rivers were forever reshaping and retaking courses. In December 1834 on the Arkansas, the Reverend G. W. Featherstonhaugh, F.R.S., a geologist, saw where the river had gouged away part of a plantation. Flooding had "ploughed up the whole of the soil with cotton and maize growing upon it to the extent of forty acres, and deposited it in a mass on a beach lower down." This was how the rivers went about the process of destruction and creation, of continuously renewing the New World. This was why the rivers of the Mississippi Valley were found to be filled with logs and trees and how these trees gave rise to one of the most dangerous hazards of river navigation. The whole tree, roots and all, would be floated into

40. A Mississippi Riverboat

The weather was warm and bright, and we found the guard of the boat, as they call the gallery that runs round the cabins, a very agreeable station; here we all sat as long as light lasted, and sometimes, wrapped in our shawls, we enjoyed the clear bright beauty of American moonlight long after every passenger but ourselves had retired. We had a full complement of passengers on board. The deck, as is usual, was occupied by the Kentucky flat-boat men, returning from New Orleans, after having disposed of the boat and cargo which they had conveyed thither, with no other labour than that of steering her, the current bringing her down at the rate of four miles an hour. (Frances Trollope)

midstream and it frequently happened that those roots would become caught into the river bed. Then said Basil Hall, "they lie like a lance in rest, concealed beneath the water . . . Sometimes, however, they vibrate up and down . . . which peculiar motion has given them the name of sawyer." (These sawyers gave Samuel Clemens the name of one of his most popular heroes just as the cry of the Mississippi rivermen taking soundings of the perpetually changing river bed gave him his pen-name. As a young man, Henry Morton Stanley heard the same cry on the Missouri: "'By the mark twain,' 'Quarter less three,' 'Nine and a half,' 'se—ven feet,' the boat proceeding still slower till the cry is heard, 'no-o-o-o bottom.'") As sawyers, planters, or snags, trees were a constant danger and steamboats were fitted with "snag-chambers" – a watertight bulkhead at the front of the boat – to take the deadly impact of the sawing, floating or concealed obstacles. As deep-sea sailor of great experience, Captain Basil Hall was particularly fascinated by the business of navigating the Mississippi; he loved talking to the pilots of the high-sided vessels and was appreciative of the volume of water passing through the relatively narrow banks of the river. He gave his readers five pages of Mississippi statistics, an early expression of the poetry of numbers, a poetry which was to become an increasing preoccupation of nineteenth-century visitors to the United States. Readers of *Travels in North America, in the Years 1827 and 1828* learned from Captain Hall that the width of the river at New Orleans was 746 yards and that at high water it was 852½ yards broad and that it preserved this "most wonderful uniformity in width" for more than 1,200 miles upstream from the Delta. But the depth of the river not its width was its secret. "It is the depth which gives this mighty stream its sublimity." At Natchez it is 70 feet and by New Orleans all of 168 feet deep.[10]

By the time that Basil Hall travelled north from New Orleans on his steamboat, the *Philadelphia*, the peoples of the North American continent were well started on the conquest of their environment. Eighteenth-century technology had mastered the controlling of rivers and the digging of canals. Like the building of the railroads of the middle nineteenth century and the routing of the highways of the twentieth, the "navigating" of these waterways across the continent was undertaken in a spirit that defied terrain. Navigating contributed as much as any technology to the American's sense of his triumph over "Nature" and to his pride in his conquest of the land. The levees of the Mississippi had, by 1828, been built up well above the level of the surrounding plain and that plain had been cultivated and made prosperous. Captain Hall did not begrudge the inhabitants of Louisiana – French and American – their victory.

> During the greater part of that day, [Hall wrote, taking his leave of New Orleans] the surface of the water along which we were moving, could not be less than six or eight feet above the level of the ground on both sides. The district . . . is everywhere thickly populated by sugar planters, whose sunny houses, gay piazzas, trim gardens, and numerous slave villages, all clean and neat, gave an exceedingly thriving air to the river scenery.[11]

The river was not of course tamed and the bright appearance of Lower Louisiana in a peaceful April concealed a multitude of perils that thaw, flood, and sun unleashed at less temperate seasons. It was not very much further up river to Natchez that the *Philadelphia* came upon a stretch of the river that caused her pilot to protest, "'Why, sir, this is the most scandalous bit of river that ever any man had to come up.'" The levees extend only a hundred miles above New Orleans and after that the pilot had to rely on his charts, his leadsman, and his intuition to keep his boat off the mud flats. Twenty years after Basil Hall, Alexander Mackay reported that beyond the levee system the course of the river was so unpredictable that planters had gone to sleep in Mississippi and woken up in Arkansas. In the alluvial plain, the sinuosties of the river led not only to annual changes in the main course but to a constant succession of new cuts so that islands appeared and disappeared more rapidly than they could be named. It was the pilots' custom to give them numbers, only the largest and most permanent could warrant names. Beyond the limit of the levees, the river upstream was as much engaged in the processes of destruction and creation as it was in the Delta. And downstream the levees extended but fifty miles beyond New Orleans. Though the building of this embankment for 150 miles on both sides of the river was an earthwork that might rival the achievement of the most ancient cultures in the Old World, 150 miles was not much in the 2,000-mile course of the whole river. Even within the levee system the Mississippi was too powerful to be fully within men's control. In New Orleans itself Lady Emmeline Stuart Wortley discovered that boats had to be used to get about the city whenever the banks failed. Cellars and graves all had to be elevated above flood levels if citizens were to lie easy in their beds when alive and secure in their coffins when dead.[12]

The landscape of the Mississippi found no counterpart at all in European experience and the European traveller could not prepare himself for the impression that it was to make on him. One result was that travellers seldom enjoyed the journey from New Orleans. Thomas Hamilton was struck to the point of dumbness by "the dreary and perpetual solitudes," "the huge alligators," "the trees, with a long and hideous drapery of pendent moss," "the giant river rolling onward the vast volume of its dark and turbid waters."[13]

In the face of this fearful experience, the English traveller sought some term to apply to the unexpected landscape before him and his own unanticipated response to it. It was not certain that the Mississippi displayed nobility or grandeur, but it offered an experience far above, at least far beyond, the ordinary. It was not enough to say that experience was merely awesome, it was quite often terrifying. It was not easy to describe the prospect seen from the steamboat as beautiful, and it was not possible to describe it as picturesque, but it could be described as sublime. It was true that the Romantic sensibility, used to expect rocks and mountains in sublime landscapes, looked in vain for rocks and mountains in the first thousand miles of the Mississippi's northward course, but this deficiency could not detract from the claims of the river to some special consideration: "Rocks and mountains are fine things undoubtedly but they could add nothing of sublimity to the Mississippi ... It could brook no rival, and it finds none." The colossal singularity of the river forced the Romantic traveller to redefine for himself the nature of aesthetic response. It caused him to make up the definition of his terms anew. The Mississippi did more than dominate the landscape. It was horizon and foreground in one; it went beyond the limits of vision; it stretched unchanging beyond the limits of imagination. It was out of sight.

"The imagination is perhaps susceptible," Hamilton wrote of the view from his steamboat deck, "but of a single powerful impression at a time. Sublimity is uniformly connected with unity of object." And unity of object was what the Mississippi so distinctly provided. The Falls of Niagara did so because Nature had arranged things in such a way that there was absolutely nothing else to be seen and yet what was to be seen could be contained in a single set of perspectives. The Mississippi had to be seen in time as well as in space. The traveller had to travel not only to it but along it. It was in no one place and yet it was all one thing. It had to be endured as well as enjoyed. "The prevailing character of the Mississippi," Hamilton concluded, "is that of solemn gloom." Thomas Hamilton's credentials as a man of sensibility and of Romantic feeling were very sound ones, but he showed himself to be much tried by the Mississippi: "I have trodden the passes of the Alp and Appenine, yet never felt how awful a thing is nature, till I was borne on its waters, through regions desolate and uninhabitable ... our vessel, like some huge demon of the wilderness, bearing fire in her bosom, and canopying the eternal forest with the smoke of her nostrils."[14]

But still, from time to time, appeared the hut of the wood-cutter, who supplies the steamboats with fuel, at the risk, or rather with the assurance of early death, in exchange for dollars and whiskey. These sad dwellings are nearly all of them inundated during the winter, and the best of them are constructed on piles, which permit the water to reach its highest level without drowning the wretched inhabitants. These unhappy beings are invariably the victims of ague, which they meet recklessly, sustained by the incessant use of ardent spirits. The squalid look of the miserable wives and children of these men was dreadful; and often as the spectacle was renewed, I could never look at it with indifference. Their complexion is of a blueish white, that suggests the idea of dropsy; this is invariable, and the poor little ones wear exactly the same ghastly hue. (Frances Trollope)

The last image suggested that Thomas Hamilton was frightened by the Mississippi landscape and though fear sharpens the physical senses, it tends to deaden the aesthetic. Awe and fear extended over a long period of time weigh the spirits down and the monotony of the unfamiliar can become very depressing indeed. Hamilton, like other travellers, seemed to pass through stages of visual overloading into those of visual deprivation as the forest and stream rolled by: "Conversation," he wrote, "became odious, and I passed my time in a sort of dreamy contemplation." Only in the Delta itself was

Hamilton able to stimulate his flagging imagination into some kind of response appropriate to the elemental chaos of earth and water that greeted him. Though he could hardly be said to have become uplifted, he was able to rise to something of the occasion. In the Delta of the Mississippi, the traveller, Hamilton wrote, "becomes conscious of the full sublimity of *desolation*."[15] Captain Hamilton struggled unsuccessfully but he struggled nonetheless with the challenge of the Mississippi. He pointed to the high ground of sensibility, as it were, from which the river might be enjoyed even if he did not reach that high ground. He did not blame the river for the failure of artistic response, for the aesthetic opportunity lost. There was no Walter Scott or William Wordsworth to do for the Mississippi Valley what the novelist had done for the Highlands or the poet had done for the Lake District. There was no great soul from New Orleans, from Natchez or from Vicksburg to show the way, and there was to be none for some time to come. The result was that Hamilton's description of the Mississippi Valley sounded an uncertain note; sensibility was subdued.

Hamilton could not let himself go in the face of the new emotional opportunity posed by the Mississippi landscape. *Men and Manners in America* seemed on the point of enjoyment in the Great Valley but always some reservation, some contingent qualification prevented its writer and with him its reader from going beyond conventional dismay.

The Lady Emmeline Stuart Wortley showed, by the verse that she contributed to her travel books, that she was not a good poet, but she did show a softness for full sentiment and a claim to a Romantic sensibility rather more strongly developed even than that cultivated in Thomas Hamilton by his dwelling in the neighbourhood of Scott. Lady Emmeline was disposed to like what she saw in America and she was not cast down even by the dark waters of the Mississippi. She, like Hamilton, entered the Mississippi from the Ohio. The river looked sullen and sober but was so variable in fact that navigation was very difficult. But if the captain found things unpleasant, his passenger did not: "I have been most agreeably disappointed with the Mississippi, which has, in general, the reputation of being monotonous and wearisome," she wrote. "I am on the contrary, quite delighted with it, and watched and gazed on it, day after day, and hour after hour, with ever-newly kindling interest and admiration." She entered into the landscape with an imaginative grasp of its fullness that made it possible for her to overcome its monotony, to deny in fact that it was monotonous at all: "That the banks are flat for hundreds and hundreds of miles, I own; but those forests are so grand, so boundless – the breadth of that astounding river is so imposing – its bends and curves so glorious and beautiful – that I could not find it at all monotonous." The scale of the river did not oppress her but stimulated her imagination to speculation on the boundless, to contemplation of the infinite that is more commonly provoked by the sight of the ocean or the night sky: "the mighty current of that marvellous river, sweeping on like the flow of unpausing Time, carrying all before it, I thought sublimity itself!"[16]

This respect for the river was not diminished by her continuing exposure to it and her love of and admiration for it seemed only to grow on her journey south to New Orleans. She saw river after river flowing into the stream of the Mississippi and though these tributaries were themselves splendid in their size and volume, including the great Ohio itself, she saw the Mississippi receive them "with a magnificent unconcern and disdainful indifference." With each contribution, the Mississippi became deeper but it became no wider. "In the very absence of change here, is there not something sublime?" she asked her readers. By night her river became alive with fire and noise as exhilarating and provocative in its own fashion as its curves and reaches were by day: "Imagine," she exhorted the armchair traveller, "steamer after steamer coming sweeping, sounding, thundering on, blazing with these thousands of lights, casting long brilliant reflections on the fast-rolling waters beneath; – (there is often a number of them, one after the other – like so many comets in Indian file)!"[17] Lights on the shore and the great wood fires burning in the night as signals of fuelling stations made a romantic and exciting scene that Lady Emmeline wished would delight her reader as much as herself.

She was so exhilarated by what she could see and hear that even the menace of the landscape did not diminish her enjoyment of it. Captain Hamilton found the Mississippi sublime but was awed, even cowed by it; Lady Emmeline found it sublime and was sufficiently excited by it to relish the very real dangers that the night travel, so fiery and fine, promised and delivered. The river was filled with "hideous" trees and her steamboat was snagged again and again. The first time a tree was driven through a paddle box so firmly that it stopped the wheel. The next time, at night, a tree was driven through the side of the boat causing panic and uproar among the horses and mules tethered on that deck; a third time the boat was pierced on the other side so that they were in the word of the crew, "skewered." These were the major incidents of the journey, but Lady Emmeline reckoned that they hit a snag every fifteen minutes on that particular stretch of the river.[18] (To run into a snag on the Mississippi gave rise to a new idiom in the language.)

Lady Emmeline loved the Mississippi so much that she was forced to ask herself why it was that other travellers had been so consistently hostile to its landscape. The fault, she believed, lay in their false expectation of what its grandeur might imply: they "had pictured to themselves a totally different scene, and expected a sort of exaggerated Rhine, or a magnified blue Guadalquiver." But no conventional image of any European scenery could prepare the traveller for the Mississippi and for the majority of travellers the enjoyment of landscape required a fulfilment of expectation not a total denial of expectation. In this as in some other ways Lady Emmeline proved an unconventional traveller because she found nothing to disappoint her in the Mississippi landscape and believed that it would take all of twenty-one journeys from St Louis to New Orleans before she would find it monotonous. Even at that she had her doubts because her captain (she made friends with most people) told her that he "'had never seen it any two voyages alike.'" As she had travelled from the snow and storms of Missouri to the sun and heat of Louisiana on one voyage, she could quite believe him.[19]

Captain Hamilton had tried to like the Mississippi; Lady Emmeline had succeeded but even she had had to admit that her success ran against the grain of travellers' experience. Captain Frederick Marryat called the river a "vile sewer"; Charles Dickens called it "an enormous ditch"; William Russell of *The Times* called it "a huge trench-like canal." Though all three men were distinctly post-Romantic in sensibility, they preferred their landscapes to show evidence of conventional Romantic attributes. In the absence of varied prospects and meadowed meanderings, rocks and mountains, their imaginations flagged; restlessness gave way to intense boredom. "The Mississippi is assuredly the most uninteresting river in the world," Russell wrote, ". . . not a particle of romance . . . can ever shine from its depths, sacred to cat and buffalo fish, or vivify its turbid waters."[20] By calling it a ditch, a sewer, a canal, they denied that the river was natural and excused their own refusal to pay Romantic tribute.

For many nineteenth-century travellers, the Mississippi was a naturally polluted river, an ecological contradiction because the polluting villain was not some filthy industry or some grotesquely expanded population. In 1860 Captain Burton took the river passage from St Louis to St Joseph and there he discovered the source of the great pollution, the Missouri River.

The "Big Muddy" as it is now called – the Yellow River of old writers – venerable sieve of snag and sawyer, displays at this point the source whence it has drawn the dirty brown silt which pollutes below their juncture the pellucid waters of the "Big Drink." It runs, like the lower Indus through deep walls of stiff clayey earth, and like that river, the waters it supplies when filtered (they have been calculated to contain one eighth of solid matter) are sweet.[21]

*Sweet*ness of water is a condition coincident with clarity, so much so that *sweet* and *clear* are synonymous in the language of English river poets. The Missouri too could then be sweet, it might have been a "pellucid" river but it had chosen to run its course through the great plains and had become fouled, muddied, dirty, polluted in consequence. Day and night, it carried away the waste of a continent; the winds off the Great Plains, the High Plains, the Bad Lands, the Black Hills, and the Grasslands, combined with the rivers that flow east into the stream of the Missouri; the Yellowstone, the Knife, the Heart, the Little Missouri, the Cannonball, the Grand, the Moreau, the Cheyenne, the White, the Niobrara, the Platte, the Kansas, the Black Water, the Osage, the Gasconade; winds and water together shifted the soils of Montana, the Dakotas, Nebraska and Kansas to spread them in the alluvial plain of the Mississippi and forever to extend the Delta into the Gulf of Mexico.

The dirty nature of the Big Muddy gave it a bad name and it was held to blame for debauching the Mississippi. Captain Hall broke his journey northeast to take the steamboat *Illinois* past St Louis just to see how "the clear light blue" Mississippi was dirtied by the Missouri, "as thick as peas soup." And at the point where the act took place, the Captain saw extraordinary turbulence of the waters

42. The Upper Mississippi – St Paul, Minnesota

and how for a long way the streams run parallel between two banks as if the pure northern river refused to mix with its filthy western partner. It was on sound geographical grounds Captain Hall persuaded his readers that the river running south from Minnesota was called the Mississippi. It was the rightful name because the river runs straight. It was also the rightful name, in the opinion of other travellers because the cleaner river was obviously the superior river. "It will, I hope, be a long day," Richard Burton wrote "before this great ditch [the Missouri] wins the day from the glorious father of Waters."[22]

Travellers who explored the Upper Mississippi, that is, the Mississippi north of the confluence with the Missouri, found a river very much to the European taste. In its scenery, Anthony Trollope found all the elements of the Romantic landscape. The bluffs that everywhere improved the lines of its banks he likened to castles. The clear water, the broken land, the scattered trees, the happy accident of the Fall colouring (he was travelling in the October of 1861) gave the landscape from La Crosse north to St Paul the appearance of English parkland. Parkland was for Trollope, as for other English travellers – and indeed for American travellers – the most perfect of landscape patterns: "I protest," wrote Trollope "that of all the river scenery that I know, that of the Upper Mississippi is by far the finest and the most continued. One thinks of course of the Rhine; but according to my idea of beauty, the Rhine is nothing to the Upper Mississippi."[23]

Very few English travellers went beyond St Paul but those who did rejoiced still more in the beautiful and the clean land that they found there. They found "the Mississippi light-coloured, and clear like the Minnesota river itself, which gives its name to the territory, – the literal meaning of the Indian word Minnesota being 'The territory of the sky-coloured water.'" But only explorers like Laurence Oliphant and Frederick Marryat reached so far, and they both came by way of Canada. For most Englishmen, the Mississippi was the river made filthy by the Missouri, a river to be abhorred: "Indeed, its waters are but liquid mud," Sir Lepel Griffin wrote in 1883 "and the scenery, in the lower part of its course, is chiefly composed of swamps and sand banks . . . after its junction with the Missouri, the river has become a superb volume of pea-soup; and thence pursues a thoroughly uninteresting and unlovely course to the sea, doing as much mischief as it can on the way."[24]

One of the most disgusting of these acts of mischief was the pollution of the Ohio River. For the part that the Mississippi played in the corruption of La Belle Riviere was exactly that part which travellers ascribed to the Missouri in the pollution of the river that flowed out of the "'territory of the sky-coloured water.'" Now the Mississippi was to blame and the British loved to castigate the Father of Waters. Those who have travelled all the way north from New Orleans were especially ready to revenge themselves on the river that had depressed and distressed them for so long. In February of 1828, Mrs Fanny Trollope reached the confluence of the rivers. Up to this point the only American scenery that she had seen was that of the Mississippi River and she could bear it no longer: "But we were now approaching," she wrote, "the river which is emphatically called 'the beautiful,' La Belle Riviere of the New-Orleans French; and a few days took us, I trust for ever, out of the stream which is as emphatically called 'the deadly.'" When her steamboat entered the Ohio, Mrs Trollope was almost as pleased with what she found as her son was to be pleased with the Upper Mississippi Valley. Cliffs, hills and mountains began to vary the

43. The Falls of St Anthony on the Upper Mississippi

scene and it only needed a ruined abbey to make the picture perfect.[25]

Thomas Hamilton travelled in the opposite direction and was most impressed by the confluence, catching sight as he did of the Mississippi a good way before his boat reached it: "About five miles distant, the Mississippi, sailing along in dark and solemn grandeur, became distinctly visible." The full size of the river that he was entering became evident when he realised that the Father of Waters received the contribution of the great Ohio without presenting any "visible augmentation of its volume." And though he thought the Ohio scenery good, he found it unhappily uniform. "The great defect of the scenery of the Ohio is want of variety," he complained. "During the first day I was delighted, but on the second something of the charm was gone; and at length its monotony became almost tedious. A thousand miles of any scenery, with one definite unchanging character, will generally be found too much."[26] Were the Wye Valley a thousand miles long, would it have attracted the attention of William Gilpin and William Wordsworth? Travellers whose sensibility had been cultivated by the smaller scale of English landscape had to strive hard to enjoy the American scene. It was perhaps significant that just as Fanny Trollope enjoyed the Ohio so much more than the Mississippi, Thomas Hamilton was far more impressed by the Mississippi than the Ohio. The experience of the scale of one river was itself enough to retrain the traveller's sense of perspective and revise his notion of what to expect.

Since the reaction to these gigantic landscapes required time as well as space, experience of them could be very much affected by the traveller's willingness to remain inactive while the panorama unfolded before him. For Harriet Martineau it was "holiday travelling to have such a succession of pictures as I saw made to pass noiselessly before one's eyes" and she rose at dawn every day of her journey east from Cincinnati. But Thomas Hamilton became bored and Charles Dickens was driven almost frantic: "Hour after hour," he wrote "the changeless glare of the hot, unwinking sky, shone upon the monotonous objects. Hour after hour, the river rolled along, as wearily and slowly as time itself." Restless, nervous, obsessively hard-working, Dickens was exasperated by the enforced idleness of steamboat travel. And he felt no change of spirits when he left one river for the other. The meeting point of the two rivers represented for him the grim reality in store for those who gave in to the great American promise of wealth, liberty and happiness. Those who invested their hopes and their money in the land of opportunity were bid fair, in Dickens's opinion, to end in bankruptcy, grief, death. He looked with fascinated horror at the city of Cairo that stood at the point where the Ohio joined the Mississippi. This desolated spot was, he said, "vaunted in England as a mine of Good Hope, and speculated in, on the faith of monstrous representations to many people's ruin."[27] By Cairo Dickens had become as thoroughly disillusioned with America as he had at Liverpool been enthusiastic in his support of the "Model Republic."

It became the tradition among British travellers that Dickens had had Cairo in mind when in the next year (1843) in his novel, *The Life and Adventures of Martin Chuzzlewit*, he described the American township of Eden. In a letter dated from Cairo in March 1856, William Thackeray seemed fairly confident that he was at the town where Martin and his companion Mark Tapley had been before him: "Where do you think this is written from?" he asked and answered in the same unpunctuated sentence, "the place they say was Martin Chuzzlewit's Eden Cairo at the confluence of the Ohio & Miss. such a dreary Heaven abandoned place! but it will be a great city in 5 years." John Forster used to assert that the Eden chapters of *Martin Chuzzlewit* had not been inspired by Cairo but were based on

Dickens's experiences in Pennsylvania. No one who had seen Cairo believed this. Anthony Trollope was there in the winter of 1861 when this "most desolate of towns" was a sea of mud, twelve feet below river level, without trade and supporting a Union army that was being destroyed by dysentery. Had Dickens visited Cairo then, said Trollope, "his love of truth would have forbidden him to presume that even Mark Tapley could have enjoyed himself in such an Eden." But Trollope like Thackeray and like almost all visitors except Charles Dickens saw signs of hope in this miserable place:

> Men will settle here . . . and leave their bones among the mud. Thin, pale-faced joyless mothers will come here, and grow old before their time; and sickly children will be born . . . But the work will go on, for it is God's work; and the earth will be prepared for the people, and the fat rottenness of the still living forest will be made to give forth its riches.[28]

Charles Dickens did not believe in the future of these river settlements. The very promise of places like Cairo made the fact of them more terrible. Dickens had Martin Chuzzlewit view his prospective settlement for the first time by way of a wall map in the office of a real estate agent. A Phiz illustration showed the scene: "The thriving City of Eden as it appeared on paper." The place looked so built up that Martin, an architect, feared that there might not be any work left for him to do. His fears were allayed: "'Well! it ain't all built,' replied the agent. 'Not quite.'" Some time later the hero and his companion arrived at the scene of their ambitions: "The Thriving City of Eden as it appeared in fact":

> As they proceeded further on their track, and came more and more towards their journey's end, the monotonous desolation of the scene increased to that degree, that for any redeeming feature it presented to their eyes, they might have entered in the body, on the grim domains of Giant Despair. A flat morass, bestrewn with fallen timber; a marsh on which the good growth of the earth seemed to have been wrecked and cast away, that from its decomposing ashes vile and ugly things might rise; where the very trees took the aspect of huge weeds, begotten of the slime from which they sprung, by the hot sun that burnt them up; where fatal maladies, seeking whom they might infect, come forth, at night, in misty shapes, and creeping out upon the water, hunted them like spectres until day; where even the blessed sun, shining down on festering elements of corruption and disease, became a horror; this was the realm of Hope through which they moved.

44. "The Thriving City of Eden as it appeared in fact"

At last they stopped. At Eden too. The waters of the Deluge might have left it but a week before: so choked with slime and matted growth was the hideous swamp which bore that name.[29]

Dickens shared the disillusionment of his characters. Disillusionment made him dislike what he saw just as what he saw made him disillusioned. He hated Cairo; he despised the Mississippi: "What words shall describe the Mississippi, Great Father of Rivers, who (Praise Heaven) has no young children like him! An enormous ditch, sometimes two or three miles wide, running liquid mud, six miles an hour: its strong filthy current choked and obstructed everywhere by huge logs and whole forest trees." Dickens was a writer capable of only the most strong reactions but the Mississippi drove him to an excess of rhetorical effort and the depression that he experienced going northwards to St Louis was matched only by that experienced coming southwards to Louisville. "For two days," he told the readers of *American Notes*, "we toiled up this foul stream." Though he drank the unfiltered waters of the river because it was "considered wholesome by the natives," the gruel-like appearance nauseated him and he did not relax until his party "passing a yellow line which stretched across the current, were again upon the clear Ohio, never, I trust, to see the Mississippi more, saving in troubled dreams and nightmares."[30]

13

AMERICA: THE STATISTICAL LANDSCAPE

The theme of Alex Mackay's *The Western World* was the Mississippi Valley. It celebrated the river that flowed through that valley and the peoples who would live along its shores. This was the river that Lady Emmeline Stuart Wortley in her *Travels in the United States* called the "Long Sea" and in her lengthy description of the Mississippi she repeated many of the points that Alex Mackay had already made.[1] They joined in seeing the Mississippi as a great force of nature and an even greater stimulant to commerce and civilization. The duke's daughter and the journalist joined in a hymn of praise to Commerce for it was only the worshippers at that shrine who became fully charged with the romance of the Father of Waters. In this Alex Mackay and Lady Emmeline sided with the high talking and grand boasting of western rhetoric, a literary and oratorical form that usually annoyed the British traveller.

Mackay ended the second volume of his travels in New Orleans. There he prepared for a journey up river that was to take the first hundred pages of his third and final volume to describe. The Mississippi, he felt, deserved the deepest respect: "Pursuing its long and snake-like course along the lower level of the valley, it receives on either bank, as it rolls majestically along, tributaries almost as extensive and as lordly as itself. Amongst the chief are the Wabash, the Missouri, the Ohio, the Tennessee, the Red River, the Arkansas, and the White River, all navigable for steamers."[2] And the last practical note did not destroy the Romance – it was the Romance. The Mississippi and the Missouri represented Commerce and Commerce excited Mackay. "The combined navigable channels of the two streams exceed in length three thousand miles," he reported with awe, and that was only the beginning. "Vessels of large draught can, in some instances, ascend into tributaries removed in the fourth degree from the Mississippi." That made for 25,000 miles of inland navigation. In this promising frame of mind,

Alex Mackay prepared to take his boat from New Orleans to St Louis and begin the third volume of his travels.

Before he had booked his passage, he was very pleased to meet in the city an Englishman from Baltimore, an old friend, who had travelled to New Orleans for a single day's business and was now ready to return north. They agreed to travel together along the Mississippi and the Ohio, rivers Mackay was predisposed to like: "The Mississippi! It was with indescribable emotions that I first felt myself upon its waters." How often in his schoolboy dreams he told his readers he had fancied himself beginning this journey. And the childhood imagining may be the surest way of all of guaranteeing a traveller's satisfaction in his adventure and its landscape. Mackay was deeply, if conventionally, moved by the fulfilment of this dream: "The lofty mountain, the illimitable plain, and theseemingly shoreless lake, are all objects which strike the mind with awe. But second to none of them in the sublime emotions which it inspires, is the mighty river."[3]

The basis of this "sublime emotion" was not entirely conventional however. The specimens of the awful that Mackay listed in this passage were all examples taken from the American scene – the endless river was to be compared with shoreless lake, illimitable plain and lofty mountain, but in the excitement of his response there was an element quite uncommon in the Romantic attitude to landscape. The English lake poets enjoyed Nature but a Nature that had been long domesticated – one that struck the American as garden-like. Though they had piped a wood-note wild, they were not celebrating a wilderness. Huge stretches of the landscape that passed by the vantage point on the deck of Mackay's steamer had never been cultivated. But some of it had been developed and what development could be seen showed what the Mississippi Valley was to become. It was this promise as much as anything else that excited Mackay:

> [The Mississippi] was grand, when no sound was heard along its course but the scream of the eagle and the war-whoop of the savage . . . But grander will it be yet, ay far grander, when civilization has tracked it from its mouth to its sources; when industry has converted its sides into a garden, and speckled them with lively towns and glittering cities; and when busy populations line its shores, and teem along the banks of all its tributaries. Then, and then only, will the Mississippi fulfil its destiny.[4]

The European landscape gave token of the past and it received its enriching and Romantic dimension from History; for Mackay the American landscape gave promise of the future and received its enriching and Romantic dimension from Progress.

To look upon the Mississippi Valley like this the traveller had to embrace the Americans' view of themselves as a rising people. It required that the claims of the Declaration of Independence and the promise of the Constitution be taken at face value. Mrs Trollope did not believe that America was rising: "Surely," she said, "this country may be said to spread rather than to rise," and so believing had hated the Mississippi. In her landscape, Fanny Trollope wanted evidence of the past, even the beautiful Ohio had to be improved by ruined castles. Fanny Trollope's imaginative activity here was evidence for Mackay of quite the opposite – it was a failure of imagination: "Viewed in the double light of what it is and what it is to be, it is marvellous how some can look upon the Mississippi as nothing more than a 'muddy ditch.'" This had been Charles Dickens's view but it was no more than coarse to a man like Mackay who saw the mud as a sign of the power of the river and as a promise of its accomplishment. What were for Dickens signs everywhere of promise unfulfilled, proofs of the bad faith of the American people, were for Mackay the indisputable evidence of the creation of new territory and that what these people promised they would perform. The language of the promoter and the land salesman that Dickens had so readily captured in *American Notes* and *Martin Chuzzlewit* was language that Mackay adopted without irony. He believed that the traveller in the Mississippi Valley must be a visionary, and with a vision of the future before him would see as trivial the cheating here and the swindling there in that region "which is rapidly becoming the chief theatre for Anglo-Saxon enterprise, and will yet witness the greatest triumphs of Anglo-Saxon energy and skill."[5]

The term "Eden", which Dickens used so effectively to damn the swamplands sold to the commercially ignorant, was taken by Mackay as a real description of this real estate. As he looked at the west bank of the river on his journey north, he saw, he said, that "there are many 'Edens' on this side of the river; that the general character of the soil upon it, from the delta to its sources, is of the most fertile description." Mud was not pollution; mud was wealth. Though he did not deny that the western bank was "one unbroken,

45. "The Thriving City of Eden as it appeared on paper"

"Dear me! It's really a most important place!" cried Martin, turning round.
"Oh! it's very important," observed the agent.
"But, I am afraid," said Martin, glancing again at the Public Buildings, "that there's nothing left for me to do."
"Well! it ain't all built," replied the agent. "Not quite." (Charles Dickens)

unmitigated and monotonous flat" [6] he could not or would not allow this monotony and this mud to depress him.

Mackay strove for a continental vision in *The Western World.* The endless flat of the Mississippi Valley plain was the product of a Titanic labour. He saw "the vast desert" before the Rockies as a place, despoiled by wind and wave, to produce a land where "in some cases the rich black mould is found as much as a hundred feet deep, and when turned up, is as light and free as the driven snow." The image linked the snows of the Rockies with the soils of the

Valley in a remarkable fashion; but Mackay was excited by the fact of a hundred feet of workable soil in a way that Fanny Trollope and Charles Dickens were not. A hundred feet of soil excited the commercial imagination to an ecstasy; if the novelists found this vulgar, Mackay found the novelists vulgar. The mud was the occasion, not the graveyard of hope, and when Mackay reached Cairo, Illinois, he saw it quite differently from the way Dickens had seen it. It was, he said, a city planned but a city that had so far defeated construction because of marsh ground. It would arise in time. It was not a question either of despair or dishonesty, Mackay implied, merely a matter of problem solving. He had already said of New Orleans that it was "commerce alone that could call forth, and sustain, a vast emporium on the sedgy delta of the Mississippi"[7] and if commerce could plan and construct New Orleans, commerce could do the same at the confluence of the Mississippi and the Ohio.

Just before Mackay had set out on his journey up river from New Orleans, he had invoked the name of de Tocqueville, who had, he said, regarded the Mississippi Valley as "the most magnificent habitation that God ever designed for men." The note that this quotation struck contained that semi-mystical element that men liked to invoke when contemplating the great valley. De Tocqueville, who tried always to seek out the causes of things, had his own word to say on the nature of this rhetorical impulse. He noted that the Americans talked plainly enough in business but that they were given to an inflated oratory. The citizen, he said, either addresses one individual or the large group. He lifts his head and he sees the multitude. And though de Tocqueville was prepared to admit that the American, especially the American Congressman, might often be the most fulsome of orators, he was not prepared to accept that the Americans were merely a nation of braggarts, who spoke loudly because they had nothing to speak about. The American politician had learned his habit early. The debates of the 1770s and the 1780s had held the attention of the whole world. "The proceedings within the Parliament of England for the last hundred years," wrote de Tocqueville in the second part of *Democracy in America*, "have never occasioned any great sensation outside that country."[8]

The Americans liked de Tocqueville's book for all manner of the highest reasons despite the fact that it was a book that made more telling criticisms of American life than those contained in many abused British books. If he appeared to contemporaries to be in "the first class of philosophical thinkers," it was because his lofty tone seemed to raise him above the level of party and national dispute. It was not only the Americans who liked what he had to say; so did the British. Captain Basil Hall himself, no less, praised the book (Part I that is) in the *Quarterly Review* as early as 1836 and paid M. de Tocqueville generous tribute: "We ourselves had examined the subject carefully on the spot . . . Nevertheless, we have to acknowledge that M. de Tocqueville's book has weeded out of us a great many long-cherished fallacies . . . He has opened our eyes to the perception of numberless things which we had either entirely overlooked or entirely misconceived."[9]

The remarkable popularity of *Democracy in America* on both sides of the Atlantic was something that continued to fascinate those who read the book. In 1862, the *North American Review* wrote, in a memorial article on the great Frenchman,

> Englishmen were glad to see a work appear which tended to confirm a constitution sustained by an equipoise between crown and people. Americans venerated the man who, alone of all the foreigners who had crossed the Atlantic, fully understood a system so much reviled in the Old World, and who impartially and accurately discerned the merits and faults of a republican government.[10]

And that last comment was as relevant as any: de Tocqueville was perceived to have understood what republican government was about, therefore his criticisms were not only acceptable but, more to the point, useful.

In de Tocqueville (as in Bryce) the Americans could catch the authentic ring of their own millennial rhetoric and they could and did respond with rapture. De Tocqueville could celebrate the promise of their land with the enthusiasm that for the Americans its size demanded. "The Indians occupied without possessing it," wrote de Tocqueville in his Preface, "those wide and deep rivers; that inexhaustible valley of the Mississippi; the whole continent, in short, seemed prepared to be the abode of a great nation yet unborn." The Americans had been preoccupied with this vision of themselves as a great nation from the first times that they had begun to think of themselves as a people at all. Mr Benjamin Franklin had been encouraged by his friend Mr Benjamin Vaughan to complete his *Autobiography* because Mr Franklin, said Mr Vaughan, was an exemplum of the American people and: "All that has happened to you is also connected with the detail and manners and situation of a *rising* people."[11]

The Americans were rising in number, as Franklin himself had demonstrated so convincingly; they were expanding in their possession of an ever widening territory; they were improving in their development of a progressive civilisation. And de Tocqueville did not deny these claims; his study of Democracy did not seem to carp and to diminish. "The Union," wrote the Frenchman, "is happy and free as a small people, and glorious and strong as a great nation."[12]

De Tocqueville presented the Americans to themselves as in many ways they wished to be presented: a people engaged in Destiny's greatest plan. In discussing the relationship of the individual to his democracy of fifteen millions of individuals, de Tocqueville had pointed out that in such numbers of men all working together it was easy for the one, the single voter, to see himself as a party to Mankind, to believe that though it might be foolish to believe that Providence should call him, the one, to great things, it was readily to be believed that Providence might be calling these Numbers to one great thing. De Tocqueville tended to use the same language himself, in describing the movement of people into the great inhabitable valley of the Mississippi.

This was, de Tocqueville informed his European reader, a double migration, one that removed the European from Europe to the seaboard cities of America and moved the American into the West. "This double emigration is incessant; it begins in the middle of Europe, it crosses the Atlantic Ocean, and it advances over the solitudes of the New World. Millions of men are marching at once towards the same horizon." De Tocqueville was making a special point in this observation – a technical point, it might be called. The West was being populated not by the European immigrant but by the American migrant. But the language caught up something grander than any technicality or demographic detail. The image of those "millions of men marching towards the same horizon" made a point that stirred the blood in some obscure way. Dispassionate though de Tocqueville always appeared to remain, there was an emphasis here that he did not wish underplayed: "No event can be compared with this continuous removal of the human race," he commented, "except perhaps those irruptions which caused the fall of the Roman Empire."[13]

Alexis de Tocqueville marked the contrast here. The barbarians of the third and fourth centuries pressed towards the rich lands of Europe and Italy; now civilised man pressed towards a wilderness. Here again the analysis of one in "the first class of philosophical thinkers" coincided with the highest flight of rhetoric of the stump orator. No politician could have done better for himself than to have declaimed at a 4 July gathering a selection of those generous things that de Tocqueville had to say about the work of the Great Republic:

Millions of civilized Europeans are peaceably spreading over those fertile plains, with whose resources and extent they are not yet themselves accurately acquainted. Three or four thousand soldiers drive before them the wandering races of the aborigines; these are followed by the pioneers, who pierce the woods, scare off the beasts of prey, explore the courses of the inland streams, and make ready the triumphal march of civilization across the desert.[14]

This was the grand fact of the North American continent. It was one to which de Tocqueville constantly reverted in his study of the American people. The growing population, and its expansion into the Mississippi Valley seemed to share in that inevitability which, said de Tocqueville, marked as a providential fact the gradual development of the principle of equality through time. In the Mississippi Valley, the event was shown to be taking place in space: "This gradual and continuous progress of the European race towards the Rocky Mountains has the solemnity of a providential event; it is like a deluge of men rising unabatedly, and *daily* driven onwards by the hand of God."[15]

These were moving words, and other travel writers began to echo de Tocqueville as he echoed the Americans' own fondest image of themselves. Sir Charles Lyell travelling through North America in the early 1840s reiterated this keynote on which de Tocqueville had ended the first part of his study of America:

De Tocqueville calculated that along the borders of the United States, from Lake Superior to the Gulf of Mexico, extending a distance of more than 1,200 miles as the bird flies, the whites advance every year at a mean rate of seventeen miles; and he truly observes that there is a grandeur and solemnity in this gradual and continuous march of the European race towards the Rocky Mountains.

Charles Lyell quoted direct de Tocqueville's reference to the impelling "hand of God." Even those who did not like what the whiteman was doing in his continuous march could not but acknowledge some kind of providential influence in what they saw happening. Anthony Trollope, like many Englishmen, was disgusted by frontier morality. An instance that he quoted in his book, *North America*, was the destruction of the Minnesota Indians but his response here was equivocal. He had already put the moral dilemma to his readers: "Of filibustering, annexation, and polishing savages off the face of creation, there has been a great deal, and who can deny that humanity has been the gainer? It seems to those who look widely back over history, that all such works have been carried on in obedience to God's laws."[16]

There it was: the cutting edge of the frontier was brutal but its movement forwards was majestical. It exactly appealed to those most elevated self-projections of the nineteenth-century Anglo-Saxon just as it disgusted the finer feelings of the Victorian gentleman. It was easier if the traveller did not have finer feelings. Then he could enter into the Romance of the West and the populating of the Mississippi Valley with unqualified enthusiasm. And this did not mean that he need not feel for the vanishing Indian. A spirit robust enough could relish all aspects of frontier story and cast all actors in its drama in the role of hero. Then the traveller could stand atop the Rocky Mountains and look boldly forward: "I predict, that this country will be acknowledged in the coming future as no mean State. Time is flying, the iron horse is upon the plain, impatient to rush through the heart of the mountains towards the Pacific."[17]

These fine words were part of a dispatch written in August 1867 for the Missouri *Democrat*. "Twenty-two months after this letter had been written, that is in May, 1869, the Great Trans-Continental Railway was completed."[18] The author added this footnote to his text to show how true his word had been. The dispatch writer was no ordinary British traveller. He had been born in Wales as John Rowlands and had been brought up in the St Asaph workhouse. In 1859 he had shipped as a cabin boy to New Orleans and had there been adopted by a good citizen named Henry Stanley. John Rowlands became Henry Morton Stanley; eventually he became Sir Henry Morton Stanley, and a renaturalised British citizen. He had been eighteen years of age when he left Wales, old enough to have

46. Henry M. Stanley

developed an Old World sensibility. But he was a flexible man; not only was he able eventually to renaturalise himself with honour, he was able to serve in both the Confederate Army and the Union Navy when Civil War came to his adoptive country.

Stanley was not representative of British travellers to the American west in the nineteenth century, but they were so varied a group that no one of them could be taken as their spokesman. They spoke for themselves and for special interest groups but not for one another. Stanley adopted the tones of the ambitious American newspaperman when he wrote for the *Democrat* but they were not foreign tones. Later, in a preface to *My Early Travels*, he converted with ease the language of Westward Expansion into the language of Imperial Adventure: "The lessons derived from the near extinction of the Indian are very applicable to Africa," he wrote from his address of Richmond Terrace, Whitehall. "Savages have the minds of children and the passions of brutes, and to place breech-loaders in their hands is as cruel an act as to put razors in the hands of infants."

He blamed the Indians for their own destruction and at the same time he exonerated the American people in the language common to imperialist and expansionist alike: "It is useless to blame the white race for moving across the continent in a constantly increasing tide." He thought that they were no more to blame than Columbus or the Pilgrim Fathers for landing in the first place. "The whites have done no more than follow the law of their nature and being. Moreover, they have as much right to the plains as the Indians, and it would not be a difficult task to prove that they had a better right."[19]

Stanley described this process energetically. The townships had long been set up in Kansas and were being staked out all along the great valley of the River Platte through Nebraska and into Wyoming. "As the 'Iron Horse' advances towards the west, settlements spring up as if by magic along the intended route. The locomotive is the true harbinger of civilisation."[20] Henry Stanley celebrated what he believed was the process of History for his readers and saw no reason to regret the forward movement, the westward movement of "empire and civilisation." This railroad was to replace the Great Father of Waters as the main artery of commerce for the continent and its construction made sure that Cairo, Illinois, should never rise from its mud with the grandeur so certainly predicted for it in the 1840s.

The British traveller, by the very fact that he was a traveller, was interested in the American railroad system, but that system (like the Mississippi itself) was for all who used it more than a mere mode of transportation. Thinking of the rivers as a system helped travellers, some travellers at least, to come to terms with the size of the American continent and the boundlessness of its landscapes; thinking of the American railroad system offered the same kind of opportunity to comprehend the incomprehensible. That the railroads would embrace the whole country gave the imagination the handle it needed. Oliphant in St Paul was told of a system that would be extended to the western boundary of Minnesota and ultimately to the Pacific. And at the same time an equally ambitious project was planned that would link St Paul with New Orleans.[21]

Simply conceived such plans placed a North–South/East–West grid upon the continent and contained it in an imaginative whole. The Civil War delayed most of these projects but their completion was long and eagerly awaited by the British. Of the railroad to the

Pacific, Alex Mackay had written in a footnote updating his book in 1850 that the proposals to link San Francisco and the Mississippi had worked a miraculous change: "The Pacific coast of the continent, so long consigned to inertness and torpidity, has been suddenly transformed into a scene of great activity." The magical quality of the locomotive as the machine of civilisation was accepted by the outsider as a token of America's promised greatness. The completion of the railroad to the Pacific, Mackay wrote, would "hasten the time when America will become the great Exchange of Nations, and the emporium of the civilized world." For Henry Latham, an English barrister examining the effects of the Civil War on the country in the winter of 1866, the Union Pacific Railroad would, when completed, "realise the idea with which Columbus set sail to the West. It will be the shortest route from Europe to China."[22] It was not only to bring about the union of a nation but of the world.

The railroad, with a power that was often called magical, was to realise the "Resources and Prospects of America." It was in railroad cars – 5,000 were made ready for the link between New York and St Louis early in 1865 – that the grain of the Mississippi Valley was to flow to the East, to the Atlantic and to the world rather than along the river and waterways that had been America's first great system of communication. The story of the railroads was only a part of the story of the great plains and always the traveller who was alive to the poetry of numbers was the traveller to respond to the appeal of the Mississippi Valley. "My book bristles with figures," Sir Samuel Morton Peto wrote in the preface to *Resources and Prospects of America, Ascertained during a Visit to the States in the Autumn of 1865*.[23] He intended to amaze and excite his readers and he handled his figures in a brisk, workmanlike fashion as might be expected of a man who was an engineer, politician, and statistician. What could be made of them, he made of them.

One of the first questions that he set himself to answer was why had the United States resisted the law that war depletes population and prosperity? Instead of a land slowly pulling itself together, a land stunned and immobilised by the loss of one million of its young men in the bloodiest civil war in history, Morton Peto saw a landscape alive with commercial activity, a land growing all the time: "I saw villages springing into towns, and towns into cities, with

47. American Indians of the West

"It is impossible to destroy men with more respect for the laws of humanity." (Alexis de Tocqueville of the American Indian Policy.)

a rapidity so marvellous, that one's first idea was to attribute it all to the wand of a magician." The statistical answer was no less exhilarating than that of the fairy-tale: "Were I asked to account for this, I could only do so by attributing it to the wonderful elasticity of the RESOURCES OF THE UNITED STATES."[24]

Anthony Trollope shared with Morton Peto a love of numbers. He too wrote about the size, the fertility, the resources, and the population of the Mississippi Valley with a dramatic sense that transcended the common distinction between the man of letters and the man of numbers. The Civil War was barely six months into its first year when Anthony Trollope arrived with his wife in America and it was one of his main purposes to report on the effects of the war upon the American peoples, their country and their future. Like other Europeans, he also believed that going to the United States would provide some hints on the future of his own country: it was, he said in *North America*, "the best means of prophesying, if I may say so, what the world will next be, and what we will next do."[25]

Trollope saw the Civil War largely as a war to decide who should control the Mississippi Valley and who should control the city of New Orleans and the Delta. The West, he said, needed access to the Gulf and it must have it. He compared the position of the great Western States to that of the Austro-Hungarian Empire. Austria depended upon the Danube and all her policy must revolve round control of the river. Anthony Trollope still thought in 1862 in terms of the waterway and not of the railroad. He reported the pride of the citizens of another of the great river cities: "They boast at St. Louis that they command 46,000 miles of navigable river water," and on the next page he reminded his readers: "It must be remembered that these rivers flow through lands that have never been surpassed in natural fertility."[26]

St Louis was not in 1862 defying the laws of war and prosperity. Its trade was blighted and its shores were lined with steamships that could not move South because of the war. But this blockading of the great river and the loss of trade to St Louis and New Orleans was not impeding the development of the West; it was not checking at all the flow of grain from the prairies. Anthony Trollope had already reported on the unimpeded flow of the grain from the prairies: "I saw wheat," he wrote, "running in rivers from one vessel into another, and from the railroad vans up into the huge bins on the top stores of the warehouse . . . I ascertained that the work went on, weekday and Sunday, day and night incessantly; rivers of wheat and rivers of maize ever running . . . And then I believed, understood and brought it home." The river that he had seen flowing so incessantly, so powerfully, a river of grain and not of water, was to be seen in a lake city, not a river city, the City of Chicago. What Anthony Trollope had believed, had understood and had brought home to him was the fertility of America. In a magnificent chapter that he called "Ceres Americana," he described in detail the working of the Chicago grain trade. It was a trade impelled by the simple fact that the price per bushel of Indian corn in Bloomington, Illinois was 10 cents and the price of a bushel of Indian corn in Liverpool, Lancashire was 89 cents. "Ceres Americana" celebrated the joy of commercial victory and was filled with the sweetest music of the poetry of statistics. All over North America, Anthony Trollope resisted the claims of North America to his respect; he disliked its children, its ladies, its society, its cities, its hotels, and its manners. If he did not dislike them as much as his mother had done, he disliked them well enough. But exhilaration at the fact of Chicago overrode other considerations. It was he said, "the most remarkable city among all the remarkable cities," and he was willing to forgive it a great deal. Much that had been undertaken there had failed and a lot did not work but "Chicago was intended as a town of export for corn, and therefore, the corn stores had received the first attention. When I was there, they were in perfect working order."[27]

Though Chicago seemed to Anthony Trollope so remarkable a city, his subsequent remarks about the trade through St Louis and the importance of New Orleans showed that he had not realised that Chicago was never to lose the advantage that the Civil War had given it. With the coming of peace that great market-place did not decline. But Chicago had brought it home to Anthony Trollope that her granaries and her statistics held truths that had to be faced in their own terms. Chicago represented something to which his mother's contempt for democracy would not be a sufficient response. The population of the United States was thirteen million when Mrs Trollope had set up store in Cincinnati. That population had grown steadily in the next three decades and its figures meant something rather different to Fanny Trollope's son:

> The States already boast of thirty millions of inhabitants, – not of unnoticed and unnoticeable beings, requiring little, knowing little, and doing little, such as are the Eastern hordes which may be counted by tens of millions; but of men and women who talk loudly and are ambitious, who eat beef, who read and write, and understand the dignity of manhood. But these thirty millions are as nothing to the crowds which will grow sleek and talk loudly, and become aggressive on these wheat and meat producing levels.[28]

There was little affection for the Americans in this passage – if Anthony Trollope's book on America was liked better than his mother's book that was only because her book had been so impressively hated. There was a great deal of racism in the casual dismissal of Asian populations but there was also an awe and an expectation that Anthony Trollope did not try to hide. He readily acknowledged what the English had been unable to accept in any way at all thirty years before: "With no antecedents of grandeur, the nation, with its Congress, has made itself one of the five great nations of the world."[29] It was a nation to be compared in terms of political realities with England, with France, with Austro-Hungary, and with Russia.

The river flow of wheat through Chicago had made Trollope understand that this had to be the reality. Not everyone in England was prepared to admit this in the 1860s and it was one of the main themes of the travel literature to bring home to the English reader the reality that was in the American West. As Trollope had made the claim at the beginning of the Civil War, so Morton Peto was to make it at the end of the Civil War and he brought all the figures of his book together towards that one end: "Many amongst us," he wrote in its last pages, "are accustomed to smile when we hear the Americans speak of the United States, in their accustomed manner, as 'a great nation.' But there is no mere boast in that description. Emphatically, America is 'a great nation.'"[30]

The appeal to greatness by way of numbers was not calculated to win favour with all travellers. The great statistical claims of America and of Americans excited repulsion as much as they excited attraction and in Matthew Arnold they excited a holy frenzy. His lecture tour of 1882 and 1883 was a kind of crusade against the religion of statistics. The title of his most repeated lecture was "Numbers; or the Majority and the Remnant." He told his audiences in his opening remarks that "your numbers afford a real and important ground for satisfaction." This sentiment was not repeated. His lecture went on "'The majority are bad,' said one of the wise men of Greece; but he was a pagan. Much to the same effect, however, is the famous sentence of the New Testament: 'Many are called, but few chosen.'"[31] His Chicagoan audience had it from Hebrew and Hellene alike. Arnold did not ask that the Americans return to a feudal society – though a failure of "respect" was a mark, and not the least damning, of the failure of the American social order in Arnold's opinion. He asked them to find within themselves that saving remnant of which Isaiah had spoken when calling upon the Israelites to save themselves from the wrath of God. Arnold's denunciation of Democracy advanced as a message of the Hebrew prophet and the Greek philosopher alike sought to replace the rule of "Numbers" with a new elite – a spiritual, a cultivated elite – and he would deny the Americans title to "civilization" until they had so done. The title of Arnold's book was intended as salt in a wound: *Civilization in the United States: First and Last Impressions*. It was however a wound that had been inflicted so often by the British and had healed so thoroughly that the Americans did not mind terribly much.

CONCLUSION

There is no foreign land; it is the traveller only that is foreign, and now and again, by a flash of recollection, lights up the contrasts of the earth.

Robert Louis Stevenson, *The Silverado Squatters*

14

TRANSATLANTIC VIEWS

When Anthony Trollope went to Niagara, he conferred on it not only an American pre-eminence but a global one:

> Of all the sights on this earth of ours which tourists travel to see, – at least of all those which I have seen, – I am inclined to give the palm to the Falls of Niagara . . . I know no other one thing so beautiful, so glorious, and so powerful . . . At Niagara there is that fall of waters alone. But that fall is more graceful than Giotto's tower, more noble than the Apollo. The peaks of the Alps are not so astounding in their solitude.

The inclusiveness of this reference was suggestive. The Falls were yoked not only with other grand natural phenomena, their logical class, but with great works of art. Trollope's statement was comparable to contemporary American expressions of the urge to visit Europe: "it is something to say I have lived and looked upon Alps, cathedrals, and the greatest works of the greatest artists," said Oliver Wendell Holmes to John Lathrop Motley.[1] The great, comprehensive categories at once suggested the significance of both art and nature for these men. At the same time they reduced everything to the condition of things "which tourists travel to see"; important as they were, they were not things that men lived by, or with, or in. They became part of the things that the tourist did, and that was eventually to become the verb to describe the typical activity of the tourist; he did not see Niagara, Giotto's tower in Florence, the Alps, or York Minster – he did all these things, one after another. And he did them faster and faster by aid of improving transport.

The American traveller in England at the beginning of the nineteenth century was eloquent in his descriptions of the English road system and surprised beyond measure at the facility of everything to do with travel. James Fenimore Cooper contrasted his smooth journey at an average speed of eleven miles an hour from Dover to London in 1828 with the footpads, coaches and dangers of Fielding's world. And Cooper was writing towards the end of the

48. A Bark Canoe on the Upper Mississippi

The wooded banks echoed back our lusty French choruses, which we wound up with a British cheer, and shot out upon the broad bosom of the lake as it glittered in the rays of the declining sun. (Laurence Oliphant)

great coaching period (the first railway was already in operation). In 1805, Benjamin Silliman wrote home enthusiastically to New Haven about a newly designed carriage called the *barouche*: "it is a kind of elliptical coach, of which the top falls on springs like a calash, and leaves the inside entirely open for air and prospect. We saw ladies half reclining in such carriages, and reading elegant volumes."[2] The picture is delightful. No wonder Americans thought it the perfection of travel; their own roads were universally declared the worst in the world.

The taste for tourism developed first in a landscape where there was "the connecting touch" in every corner and "an impression in every bush."[3] And the taste developed at a time when travelling in England suddenly became easy – it became something for the lady as well as for the gentleman. Newly macadamed roads ensured that travel need no longer be labour. The root meaning of the word – painful work, like the travail of childbirth – showed how the ancients regarded the activity. But from the end of the eighteenth century, the word *travel* was to denote play not work. The taste for touring was a genteel taste, in keeping with the genteel quality of those who bowled along on smooth roads in easy carriages. Gradually this ease of travel was to spread to the Continent and as it did, it was to make obsolete the notion of the grand tour since the traveller need no longer to be a very wealthy young man, well-armed and ready for hardship.

The English habit of touring England had not waited upon the arrival of the American traveller, whose arrival in numbers might be dated from 1815 with the end of the 1812–15 War. The English had been touring their own country for some time before that. London, the universities, and the spas (especially Bath) were already established touring points at the beginning of the eighteenth century. The Lake District was added to the intineraries towards the end of the century. The addition of the Lake District signified that scenery attracted tourists as well as the haunts of men. This was a crucial development for the whole history of travel literature. But it was itself only one of the manifestations of the great revolution in sensibility that goes by the name of the Romantic movement. The influence of the Reverend William Gilpin should not be underestimated here, and he was aware when he wrote his first book on the picturesque in 1770 that he was proposing something new for the traveller. He began:

> We travel for various purposes; to explore the culture of soils; to view the curiosities of art; to survey the beauties of nature; to search for her productions; and to learn the manners of men; their different politics and modes of life.
>
> The following little work proposes a new object of pursuit; that of not barely examining the face of a country; but of examining it by the rules of picturesque beauty.[4]

In these paragraphs, Gilpin distinguished a number of ways of examining or looking at the countryside, two of which might seem to overlap: surveying the beauties of nature and examining the country by the rules of picturesque beauty. But an important distinction was contained here. It is explained in Sutherland Lyall's introduction to the reprinted *Observations on the River Wye*: "[Gilpin's] entirely convincing argument was that while the scenery of Northern Italy, the Alps, and the Rhine was highly regarded by tourists because of its beauty or grandeur or sublimity, it was the English countryside which possessed in far greater profusion landscape which was equally admirable for a different quality, its picturesqueness." And the picturesque was "landscape that would look good in a picture."[5] Gilpin had trained his eye to appreciate the domesticated English landscape and undertook to train the eye of his reader.

Where the nobleman, like Viscount Cobham at Stowe or his next-door neighbour, the Duke of Grafton at Wakefield, had employed William Kent and Launcelot ("Capability") Brown to pull down mountain, raise up hill, drain fen and dig lake, rase village and plant forest, the middle-class man had to use other means of rearranging nature to suit his pleasure. He had already learned to travel from great home to great home in order to walk about the grounds and view the prospects; now, he was learning to travel about the countryside looking at it, as it were, with the eye of a Kent or a Brown, with the eye, that is, of the landscape gardener. He did not move mountains physically; he moved them imaginatively. And he moved himself about to gain the best vantage point that taste and fancy dictated. To aid in this pursuit, gentlemen carried with them an optical device known as a Claude-glass – "a some-what convex dark or coloured hand mirror," says the dictionary, "used to concentrate the features of a landscape in subdued tones." Edmund Gosse is quoted as telling us that "Gray walked about everywhere with that pretty toy, the Claude-Lorraine glass in his hand." The darkened colouring of the glass was intended to reproduce what was seen to be the golden tone of a Claude, but that, says Kenneth Clark, was as much an effect of the varnish on the surface as it was of the artist's brush work.[6]

Gilpin was not in fact an advocate of the mirror; he was more interested in training his readers to see the picturesque in nature without the aid of an optical device, by means of preselection of localities and imaginative selection of elements. This was why he began by advising his readers to tour the River Wye: "Every view on a river, thus circumstanced, is composed of four grand parts; the *area*, which is the river itself; the *two side-screens* which are the opposite banks and mark the perspective; and the *front-screen*, which points out the winding of the river." The influence of Gilpin's work is evident in the English guidebooks of the late eighteenth century. The earliest guide to the Lake District was published in 1778 by Thomas West. In a history of the subject John Vaughan explains how West went about his task:

Taking Gilpin as his guide, West established the conventions for reacting to the English Lakes and provided a vocabulary in which to describe them. Armed with a landscape mirror or Claude-glass the visitor was directed to a series of stations from which to examine the scenery rather than to explore the area in general. Outlines of ready-made views were composed for the tourist and illustrated the guides.

West, explaining how the tourist should hold the glass, pointed out that the sunshine should be strong and that the "'person using it ought always to turn his back to the object he wishes to view.'"[7]

The technical jargon of William Gilpin, the formulae that were wielded so expertly by the characters, and so wickedly by the author, of *Northanger Abbey*, were a thing of the past by 1815.[8] On the other hand, the picturesque way of looking at landscapes and literature, at the past and poets, may have been said to have become so much a part of the general mode of perception of the age that its triumph was universal; the fashion was dead because it had become the norm. Men and women no longer had any need of carrying Claude-glasses about with them because they had learned instinctively to adjust the composition of any painterly landscape according to the precepts of the picturesque. Gilpin's way of looking at things had become part of the general visual syntax of Romantic sensibility. This was the way that any man or woman looked about him or her for those brief periods when he or she abandoned his or her everyday occupation and took up – no matter that it was prepackaged – an artist's view of things, took, that is, a tour.

In 1886, Oliver Wendell Holmes had felt obliged to spend nearly a week in Stratford so that "the church, its exterior, its interior, the birthplace, the river had time to make themselves permanent images in my mind. To effect this requires a certain amount of exposure, as much as in the case of a photographic negative."[9] The image of the camera was apposite. Only six years before the Eastman Company had begun the mass marketing of the "Kodak", and this device was to give the tourist who was less impressionable than Holmes or Coxe, Dickens or Mackay, some other way of taking an impression.

The Claude-glass was not superseded by the camera; indeed the camera was not invented until some years after people had ceased to use the glass. The heyday of the Anglo-American travel book was in that period, roughly from 1810 to 1880, when the Claude-glass had disappeared and the Kodak camera had not yet appeared. During that time, men and women whose eye was modified to perceive picturesquely prepared their minds with the chemical solution of memory and imagination, legend and literature, etching and picture, by prejudice and predisposition, by careful practice of the art of informed anticipation and by the mysterious process of the cultivated *déjà vu*. They prepared themselves to receive impressions so that, as Holmes put it, the proper conditions and the proper exposure might create permanent images in their minds. It was with this collection of plates that they returned to Boston and New York, to London and Edinburgh to develop them into the impressions of the travel book.

The image of the eighteenth-century gentleman on tour, Claude-glass in hand, prefigured that of the modern, democratic tourist, camera in hand, not making pictures but taking them at prearranged locations; prospect and view gave way to snapshot and postcard. And there may be a deeper link between Claude-glass and camera. Susan Sontag points out in her book *On Photography* that "photography develops in tandem with one of the most characteristic of modern activities: tourism." Sontag sees the camera as a device interposed between the tourist and the landscape, controlling and containing the experience of seeing new phenomena and providing the tourist with a ready-made explanation of what he is doing there in the first place. The tourist's job is to take pictures, and the guides tell him where to do it.

Certainly, before nature had been tamed man's insecurity in the face of what later was to be perceived as "landscape" was so great that self-protection dominated aesthetic reactions. Yet, the picture of Mr Gray turning his back upon nature in order to create a picturesque view in his hand-mirror does not suggest that he expected a wild beast to bound from the side-screens and devour him. Nature captured in the mirror might well be described as space possessed. Mr Gray's insecurities, if he had any, would have been of an aesthetic and not a physical nature. In that respect he was like the modern tourist. However Gray, Gilpin, and the active creators of a new mode of perception had anxieties of a higher order than those of the passive man or woman on tour hoping that he or she had responded to landscape, building, picture, or person according to a pre-ordained fashion. Nonetheless the tourist has inherited some part of the role of hunter; a notion expressed by Sontag's formula: "When we are afraid, we shoot, But when we are nostalgic, we take pictures."[10]

The formula suggests another element in the gentlemanly art of picturesque view-making, a concern with the past. This was not immediately evident in the prescriptions for the compositional elements that Gilpin and others sought for their landscapes, but it was evident in the scenic effects – the Gothic ruin was as essential a part of the English picturesque landscape as the Classical ruin was part of the Claudian ideal landscape. The picturesque landscape was an associative one and history provided the most evocative associations. "In every *historical country*," wrote Gilpin, "there are a set of ideas, which peculiarly belong to it. *Hastings*, and *Tewksbury*; *Runnemede*, and *Clarendon*, have all their associative ideas. The ruins of abbeys, and castles have another set: and it is a soothing amusement in travelling to assimilate the mind to the *ideas of the country*."[11] It was because the United States was not a *historical country* that nineteenth-century English travellers had trouble with it.

So important was the ruin to the English landscape that men had no compunction about building ruins where history had failed to provide them. Gilpin had a special tribute to pay to Oliver Cromwell on this score: "Ragland-castle," he wrote, "owes its present picturesque form to Cromwell; who laid his iron hand upon it; and shattered it into a ruin." A disappointment of Gilpin's tour of the Wye Valley was that its great attraction, namely the ruined Abbey of Tintern, was not ruin enough – "a number of gabel-ends hurt the eye with their regularity; and disgust it by the vulgarity of their shape," he noted sorrowfully. "A mallet judiciously used (but who durst use it?) might be of service in fracturing some of them; particularly those of the cross isles, which are not only disagreeable in themselves, but confound the perspective."[12] The nineteenth century was to lament its own failure of eye and nerve that prevented the construction of Gothic abbeys and cathedrals as noble as those of the past; the eighteenth century lamented the failure of eye and nerve to destroy them.

The erection, or the creation of sham ruins set the note of the early Gothic revival. It was a stage in sensibility beyond which taste has now evolved. The delicious terrors and awful frissons excited in the heroines of Gothic novels are an archaic psychic experience. In his study of the phenomenon in *The Gothic Revival*, Kenneth Clark describes the change of sensibility as one that involves the moral as much as the aesthetic faculties: "We might well be stirred by the sudden prospect of ruins, but once we knew them to be artificial our pleasure would evaporate . . . Somehow, at some period since the eighteenth century, simple Romanticism has changed into a complex ethical position; our critical outfit is no longer complete without the weapons of morality." The desire for authenticity in ruins, buildings, artefacts, kings and queens which was a distinctive feature of the nineteenth-century American traveller's need in response to the English landscape (no less than in the modern aesthetic response to architecture), was not a professional historian's interest; the travellers were not particularly concerned with proofs and evidence; it was simply that he or she had to believe in order to feel. When Harriet Beecher Stowe went to Stoke Poges to meditate on Gray's elegy, she discovered afterwards that she had pondered, mused, and emoted in the wrong churchyard. She was only amused by her experience. Her feelings had been the right ones but they could never be right in that particular churchyard again.[13] The sham ruin, like the mistaken shrine, did not necessarily evoke sham emotions. It is worth noting that two hundred years later the sham ruins do suggest the past, the eighteenth-century past, with as sure a touch as the ruins of Tintern Abbey suggest the Middle Ages. Whatever the ruins may have said to the gentlemen who commissioned them and the landscape artists who designed them, they speak clearly enough now of their builders and admirers. They have passed into their place in the English landscape; the sham ruin is an authentic English effect.

By looking at England from a historical vantage point, the traveller could organise his vision and give depth, reference, association, pattern, and therefore meaning, to what he saw. He knew as it were, what he was doing on top of his hill and why he was there. The American literary traveller, a devout student of English fashion and taste, learnt like the Englishman to appreciate the picturesque past, and understood easily the associative, antiquarian meaning of historical effects in a landscape. The fact that he had travelled three thousand miles combined the historical with a geographical perspective so that both time and space united to intensify his sense of the picturesque. The American had added England to the itinerary of the eighteenth-century English grand tour. England was for the American, as it was not for the Englishman, a classic land, and Americans pointed out that England was to them as Italy and Greece were to the Englishman. The American included in his enjoyment of England elements other than or additional to those enjoyed by the Englishman; elements that surprised and sometimes annoyed the Englishman. Not least among these elements was the Englishman himself. Washington Irving was very conscious of the advantage of the American perspective and he gave it the classic statement in *The Sketch-Book*.

The American writer brought to the English landscape tradition a heightened sense of the past, heightened by an intense sense of loss. It was this sensation that made for the special quality of the American reaction to the English countryside. The American search for the "real thing," the real England, became by the end of the nineteenth and the beginning of the twentieth century however an important theme of English writing about England. "English poets early in this century," says Stephen Spender, "were in search of a true England, which they identified with the countryside and romantic poetry. They were reverting to the idea of a patria." They looked for an England that was "part nature and part dream or haunting." And the strongest image was that of England as "dust, precious dust."[14] This was the image that Oliver Wendell Holmes had used to describe the topsoil of England.

In *The American in England*, Robert E. Spiller presents Washington Irving as a paradoxical figure –

> it was a strange twist of fate which put into the hands of a visitor from the hustling, industrious young country across the water the task of crystallizing a spirit which was mellow because it was breathing its last deep draughts of old English air. Addison and Steele – even Lamb and Dickens – were unable to appreciate it with quite the same kindly detachment.[15]

But it was less a paradox than a process of logic that when the English chose to set a distance between themselves and certain elements within their reality, indeed within themselves, that they should adopt the posture (and with that posture, the rhetoric) of a people and a literature who had experienced that separation and alienation not only through the work of time but through the passage of space and the operation of politics. The English did not require American invention to develop the sentiments expressed in *The Sketch-Book of Geoffrey Crayon* but they had no compunction about adopting so admirable a means of expressing these sentiments.

The nineteenth-century American celebration of the English countryside should be seen as a contribution to a continuing tradition of English letters that had its origin in the eighteenth century at least. But the American emotional vehicle, on the road by 1820, came so well-equipped that it saved subsequent sentimental Englishmen trouble when they went in search of England. In James's tale, Mr Richard Searle, Englishman, of Lockley Park, Worcestershire, expressed the great difference in his attitude to England from that of Mr Clement Searle, American, of New York, in strong terms: "'He pretends to the Lord knows what fantastic passion for my place. Let him respect it, then. Let him, with his tawdry parade of imagination, imagine a tithe of what I feel. I love my estate; it's my passion, my life, myself!'"[16] But the English were nonetheless quite as capable as Mr Clement Searle, when in their sentimental, romantic, holiday, or historical mood, of conceiving their country in much the same terms (at least rhetorically) as those described by Mr Richard Searle as the "tawdry parade of imagination."

Henry James sympathised with both Searles, English and American, and Henry James eventually achieved a transatlantic view of both England and America. When James landed at New York in August 1904 after twenty uninterrupted years in Europe, he found himself as overwhelmed by impressions as he had been in February 1869 when he had landed at Liverpool. Impressions in New York came at him like a wave: "It floated me, my wave, all that day and the next . . . The subject was everywhere – that was the beauty, that the advantage."[17] The repetition of this experience measured the distance that James had travelled between his arrival at the great gate of the Old World in 1869 and his arrival at the great gate of the New in 1904.

Some days after landing in America, James took the Wall Street Ferry to the Hoboken shore of the Hudson. He was not exhilarated; now he was disgusted with the dilapidated appearance of New York's water front. And he asked himself "why antique shabbiness shouldn't plead on this particular waterside the cause it more or less successfully pleads on so many others."[18] For James, New York's ugliness was merely ugly. It had no redeeming vibration. America had to be new or it was nothing. James was as disappointed as any Englishman with New York's appearance and for similar reasons. Americans coming to Liverpool at the beginning of the nineteenth century had disliked it because it was too new; at the beginning of the twentieth century James disliked New York's waterfront because it was too old.

But some days later still, when he walked up Fifth Avenue from Washington Square to 14th Street, impressions rushed upon him again. "The assault of suggestion," he wrote in *The American Scene*, "is too great; too large, I mean, the number of hares started before the pursuing imagination." He was in the streets of his childhood and when the impressions excited by memory were most intense, he found himself haunted by a "sense of dispossession." There was a strange link here with the sense of dispossession experienced by the American landing on the English shore. James had become an alien in a city that had, on "the terrible little Ellis Island," made a scientific practice of assimilating aliens.[19]

In an odd fashion, the American scene lacked association for James. He had very personal memories, and these were, as Percy Lubbock says, of New York, Newport, and Boston; "to the country beyond he came for the most part as a complete stranger." "Dispossession" robbed James of the value of the personal memories; beyond that there seemed to be nothing. The intensity of the excitement generated by his return, the strength of both his attraction to and his repulsion from what America had become and was becoming did not conceal the fact that America was as "uninteresting" a country for James as it had been for his friend Matthew Arnold. James was not fired by American history, nor Indian legend; he was not excited by statistical visions of the Mississippi Valley, nor by the huntsman's keenness in the Prairie. His book on America died within him when he came to cross the Father of Waters and he could not carry on to complete the second volume of his travels. He had discharged the excitations of New York and New England; he had recorded his awe at the illimitable train journey from Massachusetts to Florida; and having got so far, his impressions ceased to be alive within him. He could not put himself to the labour of writing without inspiration.[20]

But when James was excited by the "hares" of suggestion, he

produced his most intense travel writing; in this there was a sense of predatory panic. The recipient of so much sensory and suggestive material must pay the price of letting some of it escape. "A small sharp anguish attends the act of selection and the necessity of omission." James had called his anxiety of 1869 "an absurd special stress" because it went beyond the fear in New York that he would not be able to get down on paper everything he felt. In Liverpool and London, it had not been expression but perception itself that had been strained. The solution to his perceptual problems he found difficult to describe for he had had "as who should say, to improvise a local medium and to arrange a local consciousness."[21] No traveller in a hundred and more volumes came any closer to identifying this peculiar perceptual experience of the alien. Few travellers indeed even began to perceive their perception undergoing this process of adjustment – though there were many who wrote of dreamlike states, disorientations or of great brightness and great sharpness in the scene around them. As James later realised, the "local medium" and "local consciousness" created by the needs of extraordinary-sense perception made for distortions of common-sense perception that put the traveller at a distance from the very thing that he saw so clearly and which he would, were he able, contact so closely.

One effect of the traveller's creating his "local consciousness" was that it made people subordinate to places. The young James found that he "really conversed with [places], at happy moments, more than the figures that moved in them." The people of London became "submissive articles of furniture."[22] People became things. This reification of humanity affected all travellers to some degree. It was more obvious in the attitudes of the American in Britain; he had gone as much to see things as people in the first place. It was less obvious in the attitudes of the Briton in America; he had gone to see "people rather than things." It was invidious for all that. Few Britons ever realised that they were making those very people into things; some Americans on the other hand were able to discard their initially naive consciousness and restore humanity to some of the people they were looking at.

Basil and Margaret Hall were Britons who made little attempt to empathise with the Americans; nonetheless, the Halls were imaginative people and both were strongly affected by the disorientation that travelling to foreign lands induced. Basil Hall was, in fact, more conscious of this experience than most travellers, and he wrote more directly of it. His New York City of 1827 "seemed at times, more like a dream than a sober reality"; and in the Hudson Valley everything "continued to look new to our eyes; and the dreaming sort of feeling I have before tried to describe, was more or less present to our thoughts still." It was significant that Hall referred to the shared thoughts, "our thoughts," of himself and his wife. It might have been the intimacy of their relationship that permitted them to become aware of a subjective experience that other travellers may have believed was less than common. "[I] have frequently," he wrote, "caught myself, in distant countries, looking with surprise at the people bustling about."[23] His own surprise, he observed, was partially induced by the lack of surprise in the native peoples – they did not show any awareness of how remarkable it was that they were as they were.

The Halls' "dreaming sort of feeling" had something in common with the "rare emotion" that Henry James spoke of as the object of the romantic tourist's, the "passionate pilgrim's" quest. The "rare emotion" was the sign for the American in England that he had come upon the "real thing" – the real England that had been anticipated by the traveller from the moment his ship left the American shore. The Halls identified their hypersensitivity to the surrounding scene as a dream state but they did not link it with some kind of higher "reality." They did not value the sensation quite so much as a result and seemed, in fact, to have felt that they had accomplished something worthwhile by ridding themselves of its effects, agreeable as these were. When at the end of October 1827 the Halls returned to New York from the tour of New York State and New England, Mrs Hall wrote home to her sister again, "We feel as if we had returned home in coming to New York, and all the strange dreamy feeling that we had so strongly during our first visit has given way to the most perfect familiarity with all the objects that surround us."[24] This was something like a reversal of the American experience of England. Margaret Hall had begun to appreciate New York because it was becoming like the place she had left behind. And if ever she and her husband really liked anything in America, it was because it reminded them of something similar at home. To the extent that America became English, they could enjoy America.

The search for an English appearance in the American scene

dominated the response of the English traveller to America until well after the Civil War, first searching out "English" effects and only then gradually broadening to include the "American" within the compass of what was to be enjoyed. The case, as it were, for the English landscape, was put by Anthony Trollope in 1862. "Landscape beauty, as I take it," he wrote in *North America*, "consists mainly in four attributes: in water, in broken land, in scattered timber, – timber scattered as opposed to continuous forest timber, – and accident of colour." One of the distinguishing features of the American natural landscape was size, but, said Trollope, "size has but little to do with it . . . A landscape should always be partly veiled and display only half its charms." Trollope called this kind of landscape the good landscape, not the English landscape, but he frankly admits that he had in mind the English park surrounding the country house. Along the upper reaches of the Mississippi, he found his good landscape and it was to be found at certain points along the Hudson, particularly at West Point, "the glory" of the river; but these landscapes were typically English, as it were, and for this reason admired by the novelist.[25] At the same time, Trollope sounded very like the Reverend William Gilpin.

Gilpin had had this to say about the problem of rock in the natural scene: "Connect it with wood, and water, and broken ground; and you make it in the highest degree interesting." The rock provided just that "accident of colour" (and of shape) that was needed to complement the attributes found "in water, in broken land, in scattered timber." And the picturesque rock was a feature then of the Hudson and Upper Mississippi landscapes. "Size has but little to do with it" said Trollope; Gilpin before him had written: "The case is, the immensity of nature is beyond human comprehension. She works on a *vast scale*; and no doubt, harmoniously, if her schemes could be comprehended." It was a failure of comprehension that rendered the "continuous forest timber" so unattractive to the English eye; the vast scale of forest, prairie, and river valley in the case of the Lower Mississippi, rebuffed the traveller who was looking for the picturesque. He was like Gilpin's artist "confined to a *span*. He lays down his little rules therefore, which he calls the *principles of picturesque beauty*, merely to adapt such diminutive parts of nature's surfaces to his own eye, as come within its scope."Gilpin diminished his own principles and his own practice by this presentation but only by contrast with the great All-Seeing Eye of God. Divine vision could comprehend Nature's whole scheme; human vision had to be content with a part. This was why Gilpin argued for the rearrangement of the compositions of the patterns of Nature and could at the same time hold Nature to be the ultimate source of beauty and judgement: "Nature," he wrote, "is always great in design; but unequal in composition. She is an admirable colourist; and can harmonize her tints with infinite variety, and inimitable beauty: but is seldom so correct in composition, as to produce an harmonious whole. Either the foreground, or the background, is disproportioned: or some awkward line runs across the piece: or a tree is ill-placed." If this seemed to fault Nature, Gilpin restored the proper balance between artist and Nature on the next page: "His picture must contain a *whole*: his archetype is but a *part*."[26]

On the small scale to which the picturesque artist confined himself, the appearance of Nature was necessarily uneven, unharmonious, even grotesque. The picturesque artist necessarily concerned himself with what was by comparison the trivial, the petty. The components appropriate for the picturesque painting were necessarily small in scale and limited in number; necessarily, they limited response to landscape even while they provided the starting point for appreciating landscape at all. In the same way picturesque principles brought the traveller to look at a landscape aesthetically in the first place but then confined him in terms of the what and the how of appreciation. Picturesque principles were simultaneously opportunity and obstruction.

The English who looked out for the picturesque in the American landscape believed themselves looking for the best in that landscape and believed that the Americans had turned their backs upon beauty. The American's fault in this seemed the more egregious because the land itself could appear so beautiful. In the Hudson Valley Fanny Kemble wrote: "Oh, surely, surely, there will come a time when this lovely land will be vocal with the sound of song, when every close-locked valley and waving wood, rifted rock and flowing stream, shall have their praise. Yet 'tis strange how marvellously unpoetical these people are! How swallowed up in life and its daily realities, wants and cares!"[27]

Kemble's lament made curious parallels with the American

49. Thomas Colley Grattan

response to the English landscape. Benjamin Silliman of Yale noted in his *Journal* of 1805 that on a barge trip from Westminster to Richmond the Englishmen in his company neither cared for the things they were seeing nor could they tell him anything about them. This was a constant nineteenth-century American complaint about the English. "I wonder," wrote Charles Eliot Norton in the middle of the century to his friend Arthur Hugh Clough, "if the English are quite worthy of the good things they have got, worthy in the mere lowest way of appreciation." There seemed so much that was so rich that the American found it hard to credit the apparent indifference of the English population. On the other hand, Silliman himself, a volume after he had complained about the English refusal to respond to Richmond Hill, defended his own enthusiasm for castles by asking his readers: "How can it be otherwise with an American in whose country there are no such monuments?"[28]

The English landscape was enriched by its historical monuments, by its ancient, evocative place names, by its ancient relationship

50. Horace Greeley

with its ancient literature so that landscape suggested literature and literature landscape. English place names were more immediately potent in their effect upon the American than upon the Englishman because the places had always been part of the Englishman's life; his landscape had always been filled with castles and cathedrals. The American could presume that this difference in reaction between Englishman and American represented a higher spiritual life in the American, "a richer use of his" than the Englishman's own. And in feeling this sense of superiority, the Reverend A. Cleveland Coxe felt exactly as Fanny Kemble felt in the Hudson Valley.

The tourist instinctively regarded himself as one who appreciated what inhabitants overlooked. The ancient village of Whitmarsh in Warwickshire, bypassed by the world, by the railway and even by the stagecoach, buried among elms and yews of incalculable age, was a Saxon place under the influence of hoar antiquity but, said Nathaniel Hawthorne, "it is only an American who can feel it." Hawthorne looked about him and about Warwickshire and concluded that the English population should be moved "to some convenient wilderness in the Great West and England be re-

51. William Howard Russell

populated with half the number of appreciating Americans. It would, he thought, do both nations good. Even before Hawthorne had left Whitmarsh he had provided himself with two good reasons why that should not be an answer. First, the American lost his sense of hoar antiquity if he remained too long in England; second, life in Whitmarsh was fossilised – "Better than this is the lot of our restless countrymen." The vitality and change of the United States were much to be preferred to "such monotony of sluggish ages."[29] This sudden repulsion from all that was old, unchanged and unchanging, was the reaction to the intense attraction that the past had first exercised.

The Briton in America experienced similar intense moments of repulsion, but they had to do with rawness and size not with hoarness and age. But although regret at leaving was almost always tempered by relief, the sense that there was a special relationship between England and America was evident everywhere in the commentary of these writers. Contemplation of the great shared heritage, contemplation delayed to a last chapter or even a last page, invariably raised the traveller above the pettiness of timetable and damp linen, mellowing him for the pieties of racial and cultural myth. Only a few left for home like Captain and Mrs Basil Hall of the Royal Navy or Horace Greeley of the New York *Tribune* without a tear and even they did not deny a family resemblance in the rebellious daughter or the indifferent mother. The racial identity, the blood tie, was the most recurrent of the pieties and it was seldom far from the consciousness of the traveller. Many believed that the transplanted English stock in America remained true to itself and that the blood, the language, the spirit of an older, and even of a better, England were alive in the ex-colony. New England at least could be represented as an older England. Here was a reversal of the symbolic patterns devised for reaction to the two landscapes. And this led to a further paradoxical reversal of patterns at the end of the nineteenth century. As New England became progressively occupied by the Irish and the Italians, some travellers saw a day when the Americans would be crossing the Atlantic eastwards to rediscover America. Only in England, they believed, would the New Englander find his old customs, his stern values, and his own language alive.[30]

It was not within the ability of the majority of men and women to create a new combination of language. It was not within most of these transatlantic travel writers to create an original poetry – either in prose or verse – even out of the experience of the most sublime wilderness or the most exquisite countryside. The capacity for original use of language adhered in the writer and not in the subject. The scene could not provide the viewer with both words and emotions; inspiration would only go so far – that did not include the gift of tongues even if the subject were a manifestation of the divinity. And this was a conclusion to be drawn from reading the landscape descriptions written by the nineteenth-century tourist. But in his struggle towards communicating what he wanted his readers to feel so profoundly, it would be a mistake to conclude that the tourist was not in fact experiencing those feelings that he so often failed to express; it would also be a mistake to conclude that his reader did not catch from this prose the excitement of the rare emotion.

NOTES

In these notes references are made by way of author's name or author's name and short title; full titles may be found in the bibliography. Note numbers are attached to the last citation in a given paragraph and references are given in the order in which they appear in the paragraph.

1 TRANSATLANTIC EYES

1 Taylor, *Views*, vi.
2 Dickens, *Letters* (Pilgrim), 47; Arnold, *Civilization*, 86.
3 *Dictionary of American Biography*, 4: 484.
4 Coxe, 1; James, H., *Hours*, 2; Dickens, *Notes*, 23; Trollope, F., 93.
5 Bercovitch, 152, 186
6 Coxe, 4.
7 Burton, ix; Wortley, 1: v; Bird, 4; Maury, *Statesmen*, 128; Hamilton, 1: iii.
8 Silliman, *Journal*, 1: 3–4; Irving, *Sketch-Book*, 5; Clarke, vii–viii; Locke, v.
9 Austin, 150; Bird, 321.
10 Burton, 73; Kipling, *Sea to Sea*, 180.
11 James, H., *Hours*, 83–4; Harte, 158, 208; Nadal, *Impressions*, 209–16.
12 Bryce, 1: 2.
13 Trollope, A., 537; Hawthorne, *Notebooks*, 92.

2 LANDFALL AND LANDING

1 Irving, *Sketch-Book*, 27.
2 Stewart, 1: 8; Emerson, *Traits*, 39; Brown, 38.
3 Emerson, *Traits*, 38–9.
4 Clarke, 3; Coxe, 1.
5 Stowe, 1 : 14, 18.
6 See Motley, 2 : 403; Holmes, *Days*, 10, 187.
7 James, H., *Hours*, 2.
8 Emerson, *Traits*, 9.
9 Cooper, *England*, 4, 394; *Journal*, 254.
10 Austin, 1.
11 Ticknor, 1 : 408–9.
12 Nadal, *Impressions*, 188; Cooper, *England*, 273.
13 Rahv, xi, 94; Ticknor, 1: 251.
14 Irving, *Sketch-Book*, 28.
15 Fisk, 485–6; Coxe, 313.

16 Stowe, 1: 17; Greeley, 38; Hawthorne, *Notebooks*, 265.
17 Silliman, *Journal*, 1: 70, 75–6, 57, 75.
18 Silliman, *Journal*, 1: 69.
19 Stewart, 1: 20, 13, 20; Clarke, 29.
20 Hawthorne, *Notebooks*, 384; James, H., *Hours*, 2–3.

3 CHESTER: THE REAL ENGLAND

1 Adams, *Education*, 72.
2 Stewart, 1: 25.
3 Fuller, 125; James, H., *Hours*, 61–3, *Letters* (Belknap), 1: 281, 287.
4 Olmsted, 1: 133.
5 Olmsted, 1: 77, 81; Roper, 71.
6 Olmsted, 1: 87–8, 90.
7 Olmsted, 1: 90–1.
8 Olmsted, 1: 99.
9 Hawthorne, *Notebooks*, 433; Olmsted, 1: 117.
10 Olmsted, 1: 121, 123.
11 Olmsted, 1: 125; Irving, *Sketch-Book*, 20; Olmsted, 1: 127.
12 Olmsted, 1: 135; Gilpin, 1.
13 Roper, 21, 33, 137; Fein, 5; Roper, 129; Fein, 29.
14 Fein, caption to figure 75, 8; Roper, 124, 137.
15 Fein, caption to figure 4; Roper, 137, 71.
16 Cobden, 169–70; Burn, 129.
17 Olmsted, 1: 151.
18 James, H., *Hours*, 248, 72–6.
19 Olmsted, 1: 158.
20 Olmsted, 1: 125–6.
21 Olmsted, 1: 158.

4 THE SENTIMENT AND POETRY OF ENGLAND

1 Coxe, 42.
2 Coxe, 4.
3 Coxe, viii–ix, 43, 64.
4 Greeley, 21–2; Coxe, 149–50.
5 Coxe, 89–99.
6 *Dictionary of American Biography*, 4: 481.
7 Coxe, 23–7.
8 *Dictionary of American Biography*, 4: 481–4; Coxe, 292.
9 Bryce, 1: 133.
10 Coxe, 101.
11 Holmes, *Letters*, 1: 135; Stewart, 1: 114, 107–26; Austin, 93; Rush, *Memoranda*, 245.
12 Silliman, *Visit*, 2: 396; Greeley, 20–1.
13 Coxe, 234.

14 Coxe, 103, 269.
15 Coxe, 269, 104.
16 Coxe, 171.
17 Coxe, 277, 278, 42.
18 Hawthorne, *Notebooks*, 351; Holmes, *Days*, 34–5.
19 Coxe, 138, 314.

5 STRATFORD-UPON-AVON: BLESSED BEYOND ALL OTHER VILLAGES

1 Hawthorne, *Notebooks*, 134; Taylor, *Abroad*, 60; Coxe, 180–1, 185, 188; Irving, *Sketch-Book*, 362; Coxe, 183.
2 Lowell, *Letters*, 124–5; James, H., *Essays*, 62, 70; Lowell, *Letters*, 107–8; James, H., *Hours*, 14; *Speech*, 41, 16; *Scene*, 139.
3 Irving, *Sketch-Book*, 364.
4 Coxe, 181–2, 184; Taylor, *Abroad*, 60; Fuller, 166.
5 James, H., *Hours*, 199; Taylor, *Abroad*, 63–4.
6 Browne, 36, 42; Kean, E., 205.
7 Browne, 40, 43; James, W., 2: 166.
8 Parrington, 2: 371; Holmes, *Days*, 91; Stowe, 1: 219.
9 Stowe, 1: 203–4; Beecher, 38–9; Stowe, 204.
10 Stowe, 1: 214; *Britannica* (eleventh edition), 17: 7.
11 *Dictionary of American Biography*, 2: 134–5.
12 Beecher, 25.
13 Beecher, 13–15.
14 Beecher, 18–19.
15 Beecher, 18–20.
16 Campbell, 920–2.
17 Beecher, 28–31.
18 Beecher, 31, 39–40.
19 Beecher, 42.

6 WESTMINSTER ABBEY: THE GREAT VALHALLA BY THE THAMES

1 James, H., *Pilgrim*, 39.
2 Dow, 185–6; Silliman, *Journal*, 1: 173–5.
3 Rush, *Residence*, 51.
4 Fisk, 511–12.
5 James, H., *Golden Bowl*, 39.
6 Irving, *Bracebridge*, 11.
7 Brown, 132–3.
8 Locke, 196.
9 Hawthorne, *Notebooks*, 213.
10 Motley, 2: 399–400.
11 See Motley, 2: 402.
12 Holmes, *Letters*, 1: 134; *Days*, 60.
13 Holmes, *Days*, 59.

14 Coxe, 271; Taylor, *Views*, 41–2.
15 Cooper, *England*, 35–6; Locke, 197–8.
16 Hawthorne, *Notebooks*, 389, 218–19, 619.
17 Hawthorne, *Notebooks*, 247.
18 Hawthorne, *Home*, 218–24; *Notebooks*, 253.
19 Twain, *Europe*, 2–5.
20 James, H., *Hours*, 57.
21 Coxe, 271; Fisk, 528–9; Twain, *Europe*, 8.
22 Twain, *Europe*, 3, 9–10.
23 Twain, *Europe*, 10.
24 Hawthorne, *Notebooks*, 294.

7 ENGLAND: THE AESTHETIC LANDSCAPE

1 James, H., *Letters* (Belknap), 1: 102.
2 James, H., *Years*, 550.
3 James, H., *Pilgrim*, 26–7.
4 James, H., *Letters* (Belknap), 1: 160; *Years*, 549.
5 Edel, *James*, 1: 313; James, H., *Pilgrim*, 41; *Letters* (Belknap), 1: 215.
6 James, H., *Hours*, 197.
7 James, H., *Hours*, 213, 216, 88.
8 James, H., *Letters* (Belknap), 1: 109–10; *Hours*, 88, 216.
9 Lowenthal, 200.
10 James, H., *Hours*, 91; Edel, *James*, 1: 304; Strout, 109–10; James, H., *Ambassadors*, 58.
11 Dulles, 176; Mead, 40.
12 Willis, *Letters*, 44; Wegelin, 37; Rahv, xv; Hawthorne, *Home*, 16–17.
13 Hawthorne, *Home*, 33; *Notebooks*, 495.
14 Hawthorne, *Notebooks*, 565–6; *Home*, 38, 36, 42, 52–3.
15 James, H., *Pilgrim*, 38, 8.
16 James, H., *Years*, 556.
17 James, H., *Hours*, 194; James, W., 2: 307.
18 James, H., *Hours*, 111.
19 James, *Hours*, 31; Wilde, "Impressions," 262; James, H., *Letters* (Belknap), 2: 209; *Letters* (Macmillan) 1: 124.
20 James, H., *Letters* (Macmillan), 1: 310.
21 James, H., *Years*, 549, 565–7.
22 James, H., *Hours*, 315 and see Wharton, 242–3; Norton, 1: 306.
23 Emerson, *Traits*, 43–4; Silliman, *Journal*, 2: 87; Stowe, 1: 48.
24 Nadal, *Village*, 51; *Impressions*, 169, 40; Holmes, *Days*, 189.
25 Rush, *Residence*, 12.
26 Rush, *Memoranda*, 122–6.
27 Rush, *Residence*, 109–10; *Memoranda*, 139–40.
28 James, H., *Hours*, 320; Irving, *Bracebridge*, 10; Norton, 1: 306.
29 Silliman, *Journal*, 2: 88; Motley, 1: 271; Stowe, 2: 56; Motley, 1: 275; Locke, 219.

30 Stewart, 2: 65; James, H., *Hours*, 234; Nadal, *Impressions*, 172.
31 Irving, *Sketch-Book*, 98.
32 Hawthorne, *Notebooks*, 85; Holmes, *Days*, 122; Austin, 253; Coxe, 63; Hawthorne, *Notebooks*, 420; James, H., *Letters* (Belknap), 1: 113.
33 Irving, *Sketch-Book*, 97; *Bracebridge*, 15.
34 Emerson, *Traits*, 102.
35 Austin, 29–30; Adams, *Letters*, 531; James, H., *Letters* (Macmillan), 1: 125; Hawthorne, *Home*, 160.
36 Motley, 2: 280.
37 James, H., *Hours*, 273; *Hawthorne*, 3.
38 Adams, *Education*, 285.
39 Nuhn, 166.
40 Adams, *Education*, 236, 286, 359–60.

8 LANDFALL AND LANDING

1 Combe (Edinburgh), 1: 16; Grattan, 1: 1–2.
2 Grattan, 1: 14; Cobden, 87–8.
3 Dickens, *Notes*, 23; Bird, 12.
4 Maury, *Englishwoman*, 58–9; *Statesmen*, 138.
5 Lambert, 1: 3.
6 Kemble, *Journal*, 1: 1.
7 Kemble, *Journal*, 1: 42, 49.
8 Kemble, *Journal*, 1: 89, 275.
9 Grattan, 2: 76–8.
10 Mackay, 2: 206.
11 Thackeray, 108; Cobbett, *Life*, 35.
12 Marryat, 261.
13 Trollope, F., 25–7.
14 Mackay, 2: 290; Hall, M., 253; Trollope, F., 28.
15 Gleig, 83.
16 Gleig, 89, 91.
17 Hall, M., 257; Hamilton, 1: 327.
18 Russell, 243.
19 Hall, B., 3: 63; Gleig, 353.
20 Gleig, 347.
21 Thackeray, 132, 154–5.

9 THE SEABOARD CITIES

1 Cobbett, *Residence*, 230–1.
2 Nevins, 20; Trollope, F., 268–70.
3 Hall, B., 1: 7.
4 Hall, M., 296–9.
5 Hall, B., 1: 6–7; Mackay, 1: 18.
6 Lambert, 2: 50; Cobbett, *Residence*, 231, 194.
7 Hamilton, 1: 12; Combe (Edinburgh), 1: 27; Marryat, 36.
8 Grattan, 1: 17, 97.

9 Kemble, *Journal*, 1: 50; Hawthorne, *Notebooks*, 204; Maury, *Englishwoman*, 163; Bird, 336; Lyell, 1: 83–91; Combe (Edinburgh), 1: 19–20.
10 Wortley, 1: 1, 65; Dickens, *Notes*, 26.
11 Dickens, *Notes*, 26; James, H., *Scene*, 87.
12 Dickens, *Notes*, 26.
13 Dickens, *Notes*, 78, 80; *Letters* (Nonesuch), 585–6.
14 James, H., *Wings*, 152.
15 Hall, M., 165; Gleig, 132; de Tocqueville, *Democracy*, 2: 56; Russell, 392; Bryce, 1: 75.
16 Crowe, 152; Hall, B., 3: 77; Hall, M., 279.
17 Marryat, 74; Selkirk, 68; Hamilton, 1: 159, 155; Brown, 40–1; Kemble, *Journal*, 1: 178.
18 Kemble, *Journal*, 1: 76.
19 Wortley, 1: 61–2, 275–6, 302, 71.
20 Hall, M., 122; Martineau, 2: 265–7.
21 Selkirk, 68.
22 Hall, B., 1: 23–4; Kemble, *Journal*, 2: 206; Grattan, 1: 30–1; Clough, 190; Lyell, 1: 4, 123.
23 Hamilton, 1: 337; Combe (Edinburgh), 294; Kemble, *Journal*, 1: 195; Trollope, F., 223, 218; Hamilton, 1: 388.
24 Kemble, *Journal*, 2: 269; Martineau, 3: 34; de Tocqueville, *Democracy*, 2: 226–7.
25 Thackeray, 182, 179; Kemble, *Journal*, 1: 241.

10 PICTURESQUE LANDSCAPES: NEW ENGLAND AND THE HUDSON

1 Trollope, F., 315; Mackay, 3: 106; Lambert, 2: 316; Hall, M., 28–9.
2 Lambert, 2: 306–7; Dickens, *Notes*, 71; Hall, B., 1: 143; Hamilton, 2: 307; Cobden, 109; Mackay, 3: 167–70.
3 Hall, B. 1: 160–5, 150; Hamilton, 2: 308.
4 Hall, B., 1: 130.
5 Dickens, *Notes*, 153; Combe (Edinburgh) 1: 33; Hall, B., 1: 129; Cobbett, *Residence*, 23.
6 Cobbett, *Residence*, 23.
7 Cobbett, *Residence*, 17; Martineau, 2: 93–4.
8 Kemble, *Journal*, 1: 167–8.
9 Kemble, *Journal*, 2: 256.
10 Kemble, *Journal*, 2: 270.
11 Kemble, *Journal*, 2:, 256.
12 Kemble, *Journal*, 1: 279.
13 Kemble, *Journal*, 1: 271, 270.
14 Kemble, *Journal*, 1: 260, 263.
15 Kemble, *Journal*, 1: 267–8.
16 Marryat, 70; Emerson, *Traits*, 225; Lambert, 2: 43.
17 Hamilton, 2: 287–8.
18 Grattan, 2: 216, 221, 216–17.
19 Stewart, 2: 145.

11 THE FALLS OF NIAGARA: A DANGEROUS SUBJECT

1 Moore, 94–5.
2 Cobden, 149.
3 Trollope, A., 145; Gilpin, *Wye*, 18.
4 Combe (Edinburgh) 1: 13; Dickens, *Notes*, 16; Mackay, 1: 2.
5 Nadal, *Impressions*, 163; Lowell, *Letters*, 239.
6 Kemble, *Journal*, 2: 253; Marryat, 103.
7 Hamilton, 2: 307, 370–1.
8 Kemble, *Journal*, 2: 286–7.
9 Marryat, 110–13.
10 Domett, 27–30.
11 Dickens, *Notes*, 202–3; Cobden, 106.
12 Dickens, *Letters* (Pilgrim), 231.
13 Kemble, *Journal*, 2: 256.
14 Dickens, *Letters* (Pilgrim), 210–11; *Notes*, 200.
15 Dickens, *Letters* (Nonesuch), 633.
16 Fuller, 164; Coxe, 287; Brown, 138; Stowe, 425.
17 Dickens, *Letters* (Nonesuch), 633; Trollope, F., 309.
18 Trollope, F., 306, 303; Martineau, 3: 81.
19 Trollope, F., 302–3.
20 *Dictionary of National Biography*, 24: 213.
21 Hamilton, 2: 315–19, 225.
22 Hamilton, 2: 322–3.
23 Hamilton, 2: 327–8.
24 Hamilton, 2: 329–30; Bird, 224; Mackay, 3: 131.
25 Mackay, 3: 125.
26 Mackay, 3: 125.
27 Bird, 216–17, 228.
28 Mackay, 3: 128–9; Wortley, 1: 19; Mackay, 3: 128.
29 Mackay, 3: 126; Domett, 28; Bird, 227; Russell, 363.
30 Wortley, 1: 26; Bird, 235; Trollope, A., 99.
31 Cobden, 160.
32 Wortley, 1: 30.
33 Bird, 221.
34 Mackay, 3: 127.
35 Lyell, 1: 53.

12 THE MISSISSIPPI: THE NIGHTMARE LANDSCAPE

1 Flack, 35.
2 Burton, 8, 21, 15.
3 Gleig, 249; Russell, 263.
4 De Tocqueville, 1: 19; Thackeray, 572.
5 Thackeray, 552, 589.
6 Lambert, 2: 122.
7 Mackay, 2: 213, 235–6.

8 Hall, B., 3: 310.
9 Hamilton, 2: 232; Hall, B., 3: 339; Martineau, 1: 211.
10 Featherstonhaugh, 131; Hall, B., 3: 363; Stanley, 102. Hall, B., 3: 326–30.
11 Hall, B., 3: 351–2.
12 Hall, B., 3: 377; Mackay, 3: 298–9; Hamilton, 2: 194–200; Wortley, 1: 237.
13 Hamilton, 2: 191.
14 Hamilton, 2: 192–4.
15 Hamilton, 2: 194, 232.
16 Wortley, 1: 209–10.
17 Wortley, 1: 213–14.
18 Wortley, 1: 215–17.
19 Wortley, 1: 211–12.
20 Marryat, 258; Dickens, *Notes*, 171; Russell, 255, 294.
21 Burton, 15.
22 Hall, B., 3: 380; Burton, 16.
23 Trollope, A., 143.
24 Griffin, 28.
25 Trollope, F., 46–7.
26 Hamilton, 2: 168.
27 Martineau, 1: 236–7; Dickens, *Notes*, 171.
28 Thackeray, 591; Trollope, A., 402–5, 410.
29 Dickens, *Chuzzlewit*, 268, 284.
30 Dickens, *Notes*, 171–2, 187.

13 AMERICA: THE STATISTICAL LANDSCAPE

1 Wortley, 1: 234–5.
2 Mackay, 2: 311–12.
3 Mackay, 3: 3–4.
4 Mackay, 3: 4–5.
5 Trollope, F., 310; Mackay, 3: 5–6.
6 Mackay, 3: 41–2.
7 Mackay, 3: 63, 73; 2: 288.
8 De Tocqueville, 2: 77–9, 92.
9 Combe (Philadelphia) 2: 103; Hall, B., "Tocqueville," 134.
10 *North American Review* 95: 146.
11 De Tocqueville, *Democracy*, 1: 26; Franklin, 110.
12 De Tocqueville, *Democracy*, 1: 171.
13 De Tocqueville, *Democracy*, 1: 303.
14 De Tocqueville, *Democracy*, 1: 302.
15 De Tocqueville, *Democracy*, 1: 414.
16 Lyell, 2: 76; Trollope, A., 131–2.
17 Stanley, 190.
18 Stanley, 190.
19 Stanley, x–xi, viii.
20 Stanley, 88.

21 Oliphant, 259–60.
22 Mackay, 2: 259; Latham, 287.
23 Burn, 137; Peto, ix.
24 Peto, 3, 27–29.
25 Trollope, A., 146–7, 537.
26 Trollope, A., 386–7.
27 Trollope, A., 157–8, 163–6.
28 Trollope, A., 123.
29 Trollope, A., 342.
30 Peto, 389.
31 Arnold, *Discourses*, 5–6.

14 TRANSATLANTIC VIEWS

1 Trollope, A., 95; see Motley, 2: 403.
2 Cooper, *England*, 18; Silliman, *Journal*, 1: 165.
3 James, H., *Hours*, 319.
4 Vaughan, 51–2; Gilpin, 1–2.
5 See Gilpin, iii–iv.
6 Stroud, 50–4: Clark, *Landscape*, 95.
7 Gilpin, 8; Vaughan, 58.
8 Clark, *Revival*, 68.
9 Holmes, *Days*, 101.
10 Sontag, 15.
11 Sontag, 9; Gilpin, 98.
12 Gilpin, 49, 32–3.
13 Clark, *Revival*, 57; Stowe, 2: 48–9.
14 Spender, 205, 181.
15 Spiller, *England*, 296.
16 James, H., *Pilgrim*, 86.
17 James, H., *Scene*, 3.
18 James, H., *Scene*, 2.
19 James, H., *Scene*, 87, 84.
20 See James, *Letters* (Macmillan): "Preface," 1–3.
21 James, H., *Scene*, 422; *Years*, 565.
22 James, H., *Years*, 564.
23 Hall, B., 1: 6, 48.
24 Hall, M., 117.
25 Trollope, A., 144–5, 173–4.
26 Gilpin, 13, 18–19.
27 Kemble, *Journal*, 1: 271.
28 Silliman, *Journal*, 2: 87; Norton, 1: 149; Silliman, *Journal*, 3: 184.
29 Hawthorne, *Home*, 47–9, 53.
30 Holmes, *Days*, 205.

BIBLIOGRAPHY

PRIMARY SOURCES

This bibliography contains the travel books, journals, letters, lectures and essays on which my study is based. I have included some titles to which no direct reference has been made because they were instrumental in the process of selection of material. I also list other books written by the travellers to which I made reference.

Adams, Henry. *The Education of Henry Adams: An Autobiography*. Boston: Houghton Mifflin, 1918.

Letters of Henry Adams (1858–1891). Edited by Worthington Chauncey Ford. Boston: Houghton Mifflin, 1930.

Alcott, Louisa May. *Her Life, Letters, and Journals*. Edited by Ednah D. Cheney. Reprint. Pasadena: Abbotsford, 1966.

Arnold, Matthew. *Civilization in the United States: First and Last Impressions of America*. Boston: Cupples & Hurd, 1889.

Discourses in America. London: Macmillan, 1885.

Austin, William. *Letters from London: Written During the Years 1802 and 1803*. Boston: Pelham, 1804.

Beecher, Henry Ward. *Star Papers; or Experiences of Art and Nature*. New York: Derby, 1855.

Bird, Isabella. *The Englishwoman in America*. Foreword and Introduction by Andrew Hill Clark. Milwaukee: Wisconsin, 1966.

Brown, William Wells. *The American Fugitive in Europe: Sketches of Places and People Abroad. With a Memoir of the Author*. Reprint. New York: Negro Universities, 1969.

Browne, Charles. *Artemus Ward in London and Other Papers*. New York: Carleton, 1867.

Bryant, William Cullen. *Letters of a Traveller; or, Notes of Things Seen in Europe and America*. London: Bentley, 1851.

Bryce, James. *The American Commonwealth*. New York: Macmillan, 1914, 1921. 2 vols.

[Burn, James Dawson]. *Three Years Among the Working-Classes in the United States during the War*. London: Smith, Elder, 1865.

Burritt, Elihu. *Thoughts and Things at Home and Abroad*. Boston: Phillips, Sampson, 1854.

Burton, Richard Francis. *The City of the Saints, and Across the Rocky Mountains to California*. New York: Harper, 1862.

Catlin, George. *Catlin's Notes of Eight Years' Travels and Residence in Europe with his North American Indian Collection.* London: by the author, 1848. 2 vols.

Clarke, James Freeman. *Eleven Weeks in Europe, and What May Be Seen in that Time.* Boston: Ticknor, Reed, 1852.

Clough, Arthur Hugh. *Prose Remains of Arthur Hugh Clough. With a selection from his Letters and a Memoir.* Edited by his wife. London: Macmillan, 1888.

Cobbett, William. *Life and Adventures of Peter Porcupine.* Edited by G. D. H. Cole. London: Nonesuch, 1927.

A Year's Residence in the United States of America. Edited by J. Morpurgo. Fontwell, Sussex: Centaur, 1964.

Cobden, Richard. *The American Diaries of Richard Cobden.* Edited with an Introduction and Notes by Elizabeth Moon Cawley. Princeton: Princeton, 1952.

Combe, George. *Notes on the United States of North America during a Phrenological Visit in 1838–39–40.* Edinburgh: Maclachlan, Stewart, 1841. 3 vols.

Notes on the United States of North America during a Phrenological Visit in 1838–39–40. Philadelphia: Carey & Hart, 1841. 2 vols.

Cooper, James Fenimore. *Gleanings in Europe: England.* Edited by Robert E. Spiller. New York: Oxford University Press, 1930.

The Letters and Journals of James Fenimore Cooper. The Belknap Edition, vol. 1. Edited by James Franklin Beard. Cambridge, Mass: Harvard University Press, 1960.

[Cooper, James Fenimore]. *Notions of the Americans: Picked up By a Travelling Bachelor.* Philadelphia: Carey, Lea & Carey, 1828. 2 vols.

Cornwallis, Kinahan. *Royalty in the New World; or, The Prince of Wales in America.* New York: Doolady, 1860.

Coxe, Arthur Cleveland. *Impressions of England; or Sketches of English Scenery and Society.* Philadelphia: Lippincott, 1863.

Crane, Stephen. *Stephen Crane: Letters.* Edited by R. W. Stallman and Lillian Gilkes. With an introduction by R. W. Stallman. New York: George Braziller, 1960.

Crowe, Eyre. *With Thackeray in America.* New York: Scribner, 1893.

Crowninshield, Clara. *The Diary of Clara Crowninshield: A European Tour with Longfellow, 1835–1836.* Edited by Andrew Hilen. Seattle: Washington University Press, 1956.

Dickens, Charles. *American Notes and Pictures from Italy.* Introduction by Sacheverell Sitwell. London: Oxford University Press, 1957.

The Letters of Charles Dickens. The Nonesuch Edition. Edited by Walter Dexter. Volume III: *1858–1870.* London: Nonesuch, 1938.

The Letters of Charles Dickens. The Pilgrim Edition. Edited by Madeline House, Graham Storey, and Kathleen Tillotson. Vol. 3: *1842–1843.* Oxford: Clarendon, 1974.

The Life and Adventures of Martin Chuzzlewit. London: Chapman & Hall, 1844.

Dilke, Charles Wentworth. *Greater Britain.* London: Macmillan, 1868. 2 vols.

Domett, Alfred. *The Canadian Journal of Alfred Domett.* Edited by E. A. Horsman and Lillian Rea Benson. London, Ontario: Western Ontario University Press, 1955.

Douglass, Frederick. *My Bondage and My Freedom.* Reprint. New York: Arno and the New York Times, 1968.

Life and Times of Frederick Douglass. Written by Himself: His Early Life as a Slave, His Escape from Bondage and his Complete History. With a new Introduction by Rayford W. Logan. Reprint. London: Collier, 1969.

Dow, Lorenzo. *The Life, Travels, Labors, and Writings of Lorenzo Dow. Supplementary Reflections by Peggy Dow.* New York: Miller, Orton, and Mulligan, 1857.

Emerson, Ralph Waldo. *English Traits.* Boston: Phillips, Sampson, 1856.

The Heart of Emerson's Journals. Edited by Bliss Perry. Boston: Houghton Mifflin, 1926.

Featherstonhaugh, George W. *Excursion through the Slave States, from Washington on the Potomac to the Frontier of Mexico.* London, 1844. 2 vols.

Fisk, Wilbur. *Travels on the Continent of Europe.* New York: Harper, 1838.

Flack, "Captain." *A Hunter's Experiences in the Southern States of America.* London: Longmans, Green, 1866.

[Fuller], Margaret Fuller Ossoli. *At Home and Abroad; or, Things and Thoughts in America and Europe.* Edited by her brother, Arthur B. Fuller. Boston: Roberts, 1874.

Gleig, George Robert. *The Campaigns of the British Army at Washington and New Orleans.* London: Murray, 1836.

Gosse, Edmund. *The Life and Letters.* By Evan Charteris. London: Heinemann, 1931.

Critical Kit-Kats. London: Heinemann, 1896.

Grattan, Thomas Colley. *Civilized America.* With a new Introduction by Marvin Fisher. Reprint. New York: Johnson, 1969. 2 vols.

Greeley, Horace. *Glances at Europe.* New York: Dewitt & Davenport, 1851.

Griffin, Lepel Henry. *The Great Republic.* London: Chapman & Hall, 1884.

[Hall, Basil]. "Tocqueville on the State of America," *Quarterly Review* 57 (1836), 132–62.

Hall, Basil. *Travels in North America, in the Years 1827 and 1828.* Edinburgh: Cadell, 1830. 3 vols.

Hall, Margaret Hunter. *The Aristocratic Journey: Being Outspoken Letters Written During a Fourteen Months Sojourn in America, 1827–8.* Edited by Una Pope Hennessey: London; 1931.

[Hamilton, Thomas]. *Men and Manners in America.* By the author of *Cyril Thornton, etc.* Edinburgh: Blackwood, 1833. 3 vols.

Harte, Bret. *The Letters of Bret Harte.* Assembled and edited by Geoffrey Bret Harte. Boston: Houghton Mifflin, 1926.

Hawthorne, Nathaniel. *The English Notebooks.* Edited by Randall Stewart. New York: Modern Language Association, 1941.

Our Old Home: A Series of English Sketches. Edinburgh: Paterson, 1884.

Passages from the English Notebooks of Nathaniel Hawthorne. Edited by Sophia Hawthorne. London: Strahan, 1870.

Holmes, Oliver Wendell. *Life and Letters.* By John T. Morse. Cambridge, Mass: Riverside, 1896.

Our Hundred Days in Europe. Riverside Edition. Vol. 10. Boston: Houghton Mifflin, 1893.

Howe, Julia Ward. *Julia Ward Howe, A Life and Letters: 1819–1910.* By Laura E. Richards and Maud Howe Elliott. Assisted by Florence Howe Hall. Boston: Houghton Mifflin, 1916. 2 vols.

Howells, William Dean. *Life in Letters.* Edited by Mildred Howells. New York: Doubleday, Doran, 1928. 2 vols.

Irving, Washington. *Bracebridge Hall, or The Humorists: A Medley. By Geoffrey Crayon, Gent.* Philadelphia: Lippincott, 1873.

Oliver Goldsmith. Abbotsford. Newstead Abbey. The Knickerbocker Press Standard Library Edition. Vol. 4. New York: Putnam, no date.

The Sketch-Book of Geoffrey Crayon, Gent. The Knickerbocker Press Standard Library Edition. Vol. 3. New York: Putnam, no date.

Tour in Scotland 1817 and Other Manuscript Notes. Edited with a Critical Introduction by Stanley T. Williams. New Haven: Yale University Press, 1927.

James, Alice. *The Diary of Alice James.* Edited with an Introduction by Leon Edel. New York: Dodd, Mead, 1964.

James, Henry. *The Ambassadors. The Bodley Head Henry James.* Vol. 8. Introduction by Leon Edel. London: Bodley Head, 1970.

The American Scene. Introduction by Irving Howe. New York: Horizon, 1967.

Autobiography: A Small Boy and Others. Notes of a Son and Brother. The Middle Years. Edited with an Introduction by Frederick W. Dupee. New York: Criterion, 1956.

English Hours. Illustrated by Joseph Pennell. Boston: Houghton Mifflin, 1905.

Essays in London and Elsewhere. New York: Harper, 1893.

The Golden Bowl. The Bodley Head Henry James. Vol. 9. Introduction by Leon Edel. London: Bodley Head: 1971.

Hawthorne. New York: Harper, 1879.

Henry James: Letters. The Belknap Edition. Edited by Leon Edel. Cambridge, Mass.: Harvard University Press, 1974–.

The Letters of Henry James. Selected and edited by Percy Lubbock. London: Macmillan, 1920. 2 vols.

A Passionate Pilgrim and Other Tales. Boston: Houghton Mifflin, 1917.

Portraits of Places. Boston: Osgood, 1884.

The Question of Our Speech, The Lesson of Balzac: Two Lectures. Boston: Houghton Mifflin, 1905.

The Wings of the Dove. The Bodley Head Henry James. Vol. 7. Introduction by Leon Edel. London: Bodley Head, 1969.

James, William. *The Letters of William James.* Edited by his son, Henry James. London: Longmans, Green, 1920.

Kean, Charles and Ellen. *Emigrant in Motley*. Edited by J. M. D. Hardwick with a Foreword by Anthony Quayle. London: Rockliff, 1954.

Kemble, Frances Anne Butler. *Journal*. London: Murray, 1835. 2 vols.

A Journal of a Residence on a Georgian Plantation in 1838–1839. Edited with an Introduction by John A. Scott. New York: Knopf, 1961.

Further Records. London: Bentley, 1890. 2 vols.

Kingsley, Charles. *Charles Kingsley's American Notes: Letters From a Lecture Tour*. Edited by Robert Martin. Princeton: Princeton University Press, 1958.

Kipling, Rudyard. *From Sea to Sea: Letters of Travel Part II. The Writings in Prose and Verse of Rudyard Kipling*. Vol. 16. New York: Scribner, 1899.

Letters of Travel, 1892–1913. Garden City, New York: Doubleday, Page, 1920.

Lambert, John. *Travels through Canada and the United States of North America in the years 1806, 1807, and 1808*. London: Baldwin, Cradock & Joy, 1816. 2 vols.

Latham, Henry. *Black and White: A Journal of a Three Months' Tour in the United States*. Reprint. New York: Negro Universities Press, 1969.

Lawrence, George Alfred. *Border and Bastille*. By the author of *Guy Livingstone*. London: Tinsley, 1863.

Locke, David R. *Nasby in Exile; or Six Months of Travel*. By David R. Locke (Petroleum V. Nasby). Toledo: Locke, 1882.

Longfellow, Henry Wadsworth. *The Letters*. The Belknap Edition. Edited by Andrew Hilen. Vol. 1: *1814–1836*. Cambridge, Mass.: Harvard University Press, 1966.

Lowell, James Russell. *Fireside Travels*. The Elmwood Edition. Edited by Charles Eliot Norton. Vol. 1. Boston: Houghton Mifflin, 1904.

Letters of James Russell Lowell. The Elmwood Edition. Edited by Charles Eliot Norton. Vol. 16. Boston: Houghton Mifflin, 1904.

Lyell, Charles. *Travels in North America; With Geological Observations on the United States, Canada, and Nova Scotia*. London: Murray, 1845. 2 vols.

Mackay, Alexander. *The Western World; or Travels in the United States in 1846–47*. London: Bentley, 1850. 3 vols.

Marryat, Frederick. *Diary in America*. Edited with a Foreword by Jules Zanger. Bloomington: Indiana University Press, 1960.

Martineau, Harriet. *Society in America*. London: Saunders & Otley, 1837. 3 vols.

Maury, Sarah Mytton. *An Englishwoman in America*. London: no publisher and no date.

The Statesmen of America in 1846. Philadelphia. Carey & Hart, 1847.

Melville, Herman. *Journal of a Visit to London and the Continent*. Edited by Eleanor Melville Metcalf. Cambridge, Mass.: Harvard University Press, 1948.

Moore, Thomas. *The Letters of Thomas Moore*. Edited by Wilfred S. Dowden. Vol. 1: *1793–1818*. Oxford: Clarendon, 1964.

Motley, John Lathrop. *The Correspondence*. Edited by George William Curtis. New York: Harper, 1889. 2 vols.

Nadal, Ehrman Syme. *Impressions of London Social Life with Other Papers Suggested by an English Residence*. New York: Scribner, Armstrong, 1875.

A Virginian Village and Other Papers together with Some Autobiographical Notes. New York: Macmillan, 1917.

Norton, Charles Eliot. *Letters*. With Biographical comment by his daughter Sara Norton and M. A. DeWolfe Howe. Boston: Houghton Mifflin, 1913. 2 vols.

Nuttall, Thomas. *A Journal of Travel into Arkansa* [*sic*] *Territory*. Philadelphia, no publisher, 1821.

Travels in the Old North-West in 1810. *Chronica Botanica* 14 (1951), 1–88.

Oliphant, Laurence. *Minnesota and the Far West*. Edinburgh: Blackwood, 1855.

Olmsted, Frederick Law. *Walks and Talks of an American Farmer in England*. New York: Putnam, 1852. 2 parts.

Peto, Samuel Morton. *Resources and Prospects of America, Ascertained During a Visit to the States in the Autumn of 1865*. New York: Strahan, 1866.

Rush, Richard. *A Residence at the Court of London*. London: Bentley, 1833.

Memoranda of a Residence at the Court of London: Comprising Incidents Official and Personal from 1819 to 1825. Philadelphia: Lea & Blanchard, 1845.

Russell, William Howard. *My Diary North and South*. Boston: Burnham, 1863.

[Selkirk], Thomas Douglas. *Lord Selkirk's Diary, 1803–1804. A Journal of his Travels in British North America and the United States*. Edited with an Introduction by Patrick White. *The Publications of the Champlain Society* 35 (1958).

Silliman, Benjamin. *A Journal of Travels in England, Holland, and Scotland*. New Haven: Converse, 1820. 3 vols.

A Visit to Europe in 1851. New York: Putnam, 1853. 2 vols.

Stanley, Henry M. *My Early Travels and Adventures in America and Asia*. Vol 1. London: Sampson Low, Marston, 1895.

Stephen, Leslie. *The Life and Letters*. By Frederic William Maitland. London: Duckworth, 1910.

Stevenson, Robert Louis. *From Scotland to Silverado, comprising "The Amateur Emigrant" and "The Silverado Squatters" and four Essays on California*. The Belknap Edition. Edited by James D. Hart. Cambridge, Mass.: Harvard University Press, 1966.

Stewart, Charles. *Sketches of Society in Great Britain and Ireland*. Philadelphia: Carey, Lea, & Blanchard, 1835. 2 vols.

Stowe, Harriet Beecher. *Sunny Memories of Foreign Lands*. Boston: Phillips, Sampson, 1854. 2 vols.

Sturge, Joseph. *A Visit to the United States in 1841*. Boston: King, 1842.

Taylor, J. Bayard. *At Home and Abroad: A Sketch-Book of Life, Scenery, and Men*. New York: Putnam, 1886.

Views A-Foot; or Europe Seen with a Knapsack and Staff. With a Preface by N. P. Willis. New York: Wiley & Putnam, 1847.

Thackeray, William Makepeace. *The Letters and Private Papers of William Makepeace Thackeray*. Collected and Edited by Gordon N. Ray. Vol. 3: *1852–1856*. Cambridge, Mass.: Harvard University Press, 1946.

Ticknor, George. *Life, Letters, and Journals of George Ticknor*. Originally edited by George S. Hillard, Mrs Ticknor and Anna Eliot Ticknor. New Edition edited by Ferris Greenslet. Boston: Houghton Mifflin, 1909. 2 vols.

Tocqueville, Alexis de. *Democracy in America*. The Henry Reeve Text as revised by Francis Bowen. Now further corrected and edited with a Historical Essay, Editorial Notes and Bibliographies by Phillips Bradley. New York: Vintage, 1945. 2 vols.

Journeys to England and Ireland. Translated by George Lawrence and K. P. Mayer. Edited by J. P. Mayer. London: Faber, 1958.

Trollope, Anthony. *North America*. Edited with an Introduction, Notes and new materials by Donald Smalley and Bradford Allen Booth. New York: Knopf, 1951.

Trollope, Frances. *Domestic Manners of the Americans*. London: Whittaker, Treacher; New York: reprinted for the Booksellers, 1832.

Twain, Mark. *The Autobiography of Mark Twain*. As Arranged and Edited, with an Introduction and Notes by Charles Neider. New York: Harper & Brothers, 1959.

Europe and Elsewhere. The Stormfield Edition. Vol. 29. New York: Harper & Brothers, 1929.

Letters of Mark Twain. With a Bibliographical Sketch and Commentary by Albert Bigelow Paine. London: Chatto & Windus, 1920.

Wharton, Edith. *A Backward Glance*. New York: Appleton-Century, 1934.

Wilde, Oscar. "American Women," *The Works of Oscar Wilde*. The Sunflower Edition. Vol. 14: 3–34. New York: Lamb, 1909.

"Impressions of America," *The Works of Oscar Wilde*. The Sunflower Edition. Vol. 9: 239–50. New York: Lamb, 1909.

Willis, Nathaniel Parker. *Letters from Under a Bridge and Poems*. London: Virtue, 1840.

Pencillings By the Way. London: Macrone, 1835. 3 vols.

Wortley, The Lady Emmeline Stuart. *Travels in the United States, etc. During 1849 and 1850*. London: Bentley, 1851. 3 vols.

SECONDARY SOURCES

This bibliography contains material other than travel and related literature that is referred to in my study. In addition I have included works on the subject to which direct reference has not been made but which constitute part of my background reading. Major works of reference have not been listed.

Beard, Charles A. and Mary R. *The Rise of American Civilization*. New York: Macmillan, 1946.

Bercovitch, Sacvan. *The Puritan Origins of the American Self*. New Haven: Yale, 1976.

Berger, Max. *The British Traveller in America, 1836–1860*. New York: Columbia, 1943.

Bewley, Marius. *The Complex Fate: Hawthorne, Henry James and Some Other American Writers*. With an Introduction and Two Interpolations by F.R.Leavis. London: Chatto & Windus, 1952.

Bowen, Frank C. *A Century of Atlantic Travel: 1830–1930*. London: Sampson Low, Marston, no date.

Brodie, Fawn M. *The Devil Drives: A Life of Sir Richard Burton*. London: Eyre & Spottiswoode, 1967.

Brogan, Dennis W. *The American Character*. New York: Knopf, 1950.

Brooks, J. G. *As Others See Us: A Study of Progress in the United States*. New York: Macmillan, 1910.

Brooks, Van Wyck. *The Pilgrimage of Henry James*. London: Cape, 1928.

The World of Washington Irving. London: Dent, 1945.

Campbell, Oscar and Quinn, Edward. *A Shakespeare Encyclopaedia*. London: Methuen, 1966.

Clark, Kenneth. *The Gothic Revival: An Essay in the History of Taste*. London: Murray, 1962.

Landscape into Art. London: Murray, 1949.

Commager, Henry S. *America in Perspective: The United States Through Foreign Eyes*. Edited, with an Introduction and Notes. New York: Random House, 1947.

The American Mind: An Interpretation of American Thought and Character Since the 1880's. London: Oxford University Press, 1950.

Britain through American Eyes. Edited, with an Introduction and Commentaries. London: Bodley Head, 1974.

Collins, P.A.W. *Dickens: The Critical Heritage*. London: Routledge & Kegan Paul, 1971.

Conrad, Peter. *Imagining America*. London: Routledge & Kegan Paul, 1980.

Dulles, F. R. *Americans Abroad: Two Centuries of European Travel*. Ann Arbor: Michigan, 1964.

Edel, Leon. *Henry James*. London: Hart-Davis, 1953– . 5 vols. to date.

Fein, Albert. *Frederick Law Olmsted and the American Environmental Tradition*. New York: George Braziller, 1972.

Franklin, Benjamin. *The Autobiography of Benjamin Franklin*. Edited with Introduction by Gordon S. Haight. New York: Black, 1941.

Gilpin, William. *Observations on the River Wye and Several Parts of South Wales, & Relative Chiefly to Picturesque Beauty; Made in the Summer of the Year 1770*. New Introduction by Sutherland Lyall. Richmond, Surrey: Richmond, 1973. Reprint.

Hunter, Louis C. *Steamboats on the Western Rivers: An Economic and Technological History*. Cambridge: Harvard University Press, 1949.

Hussey, Christopher. *The Picturesque: Studies in a Point of View*. London: Cass, 1967.

Johnson, Edgar. *Charles Dickens: His Tragedy and Triumph*. Boston: Little, Brown, 1951. 2 vols.

Krapp, George Philip. *The English Language in America*. New York: Ungar, 1960. 2 vols.

Lawrence, D. H. *Studies in Classic American Literature*. London: Secker, 1924.

Le Clair, Robert C. *Three American Travellers in England: James Russell Lowell, Henry Adams, Henry James*. Philadelphia: Pennsylvania, 1945.

Long, Orie W. *Literary Pioneers: Early American Explorers of European Culture*. Cambridge: Harvard University Press, 1935.

Lowenthal, D. and Prince, H. C. "English Landscape Tastes," *Geographical Review* 55 (1965), 186–222.

Mead, Margaret. *And Keep Your Powder Dry: An Anthropologist Looks at America.* New York: Morrow, 1943.

Mencken, H. L. *The American Language: An Inquiry into the Development of English in the United States.* The fourth edition and the two supplementary editions, abridged, with annotations and new material by Raven I. McDavid, Jr, with the assistance of David W. Maurer. London: Routledge & Kegan Paul, 1963.

Mesick, Jane Louise. *The English Traveller in America: 1785–1835.* New York: Columbia, 1922.

Morton, H. V. *In Search of England.* London: Methuen, 1938.

Mowat, Robert B. *Americans in England.* London: Harrap, 1935.

Nevins, Allan. *American Social History as Recorded by British Travellers.* Compiled and Edited. New York: Holt, 1923.

North American Review. "Alexis de Tocqueville," 95 (1862), 138–63.

Nuhn, Ferner. *The Wind Blew from the East: A Study in the Orientation of American Culture.* With a new Foreword by the author and with a new Introduction by Ellis Allen Johnson. Port Washington: Kennikat, 1967.

Parrington, Vernon Louis. *Main Currents in American Thought: An Interpretation of American Literature from the Beginnings to 1920.* New York: Harcourt, Brace, 1930.

Pope-Hennessy, Una. *Three English Women in America.* London: Benn, 1929.

Rahv, P. *The Discovery of Europe: The Story of American Experience in the Old World.* Edited with an Introduction and Comments. Boston: Houghton Mifflin, 1947.

Rapson, Richard L. *Britons View America: Travel Commentary, 1860–1935.* Seattle: Washington, 1971.

Roper, Laura Wood. *FLO: A Biography of Frederick Law Olmsted.* Baltimore: Johns Hopkins University Press, 1973.

Rowe, John Carlos. *Henry Adams and Henry James: The Emergence of a Modern Consciousness.* Ithaca: Cornell University Press, 1976.

Shepperson, Wilbur S. *Emigration and Disenchantment: Portraits of Englishmen Repatriated from the United States.* Norman: Oklahoma, 1965.

Sontag, Susan. *On Photography.* New York: Farrar, Straus & Giroux, 1978.

Spender, Stephen. *Love-Hate Relationships: English and American Sensibilities.* New York: Random House, 1974.

Spiller, Robert E. *The American in England During the First Half Century of Independence.* New York: Holt, 1926.

The American Literary Revolution: 1783–1837. Edited with a Preface and Explanatory Notes. New York: New York University Press, 1967.

Stewart, Randall. *Nathaniel Hawthorne: A Biography.* New Haven: Yale, 1948.

Stroud, Dorothy. *Capability Brown.* With an Introduction by Christopher Hussey. London: Country Life, 1950.

Strout, Cushing. *The American Image of the Old World.* New York: Harper & Row, 1963.

Trilling, Lionel. *Matthew Arnold.* London: Unwin, 1963.

Tuckermann, Henry T. *America and Her Commentators: With a Critical Sketch of Travel in the United States.* New York: Kelley, 1970. Reprint.

Turner, Frederick Jackson. "The Significance of the Frontier in American History," in *The Turner Thesis Concerning the Role of the Frontier in American History*, pp. 1–18. Edited with an Introduction by George Rogers Taylor. Boston: Heath, 1967.

Vaughan, John. *The English Guide Book, c. 1780–1870: An Illustrated History.* Newton Abbot: David & Charles, 1974.

Wagenknecht, Edward. *Washington Irving: Moderation Displayed.* New York: Oxford University Press, 1962.

Wecter, Dixon. *The Saga of American Society: A Record of Social Aspiration, 1607–1937.* London: Scribner, 1937.

Wegelin, Christof. *The Image of Europe in Henry James.* Dallas: Southern Methodist, 1958.

Weintraub, Stanley. *The London Yankees: Portraits of American Writers and Artists in England, 1894–1914.* London: Allen, 1979.

INDEX